THE STEP-BY-STEP GUIDE TO ENGINE BLUEPRINTING

PRACTICAL METHODS FOR RACING AND REBUILDING

RICK VOEGELIN

S-A DESIGN

CarTech
Auto Books & Manuals

Drawings By Jim Dennewell

1997 Revisions by Ed Staffel

Layout By Bruce Leckie

ISBN-13 978-1-884089-26-8
ISBN-10 1-884089-26-7

Order No. SA21

Printed in China

CarTech®, Inc.,
39966 Grand Avenue
North Branch, MN 55056
Telephone (651) 277-1200 • (800) 551-4754 • Fax: (651) 277-1203
www.cartechbooks.com

OVERSEAS DISTRIBUTION BY:

Brooklands Books Ltd.
P.O. Box 146, Cobham, Surrey, KT11 1LG, England
Telephone 01932 865051 • Fax 01932 868803
www.brooklands-books.com

Brooklands Books Aus.
3/37-39 Green Street, Banksmeadow, NSW 2109, Australia
Telephone 2 9695 7055 • Fax 2 9695 7355

Front Cover: *Photo by Ed Taylor.*

Title Page: *Learning how to use precision tools is an essential part of engine blueprinting. Every component should be checked and re-checked before final assembly.*

Back Cover, Upper Left: *Proper piston-to-wall clearance is essential to protect the skirts from scuffing. Measure the piston diameter at the point specified by the manufacturer.*

Back Cover, Upper Right: *The spring seats on many cylinder heads must be machined to accommodate large diameter valve springs. Many cam companies rent or sell cutters to enlarge the seats.*

Back Cover, Lower: *If you assemble cylinder heads frequently, then you might consider a tool designed specifically for the job. The BHJ Products special dial caliper is designed to measure valve spring installed height quickly and accurately.*

TABLE OF CONTENTS

ACKNOWLEDGMENTS/ INTRODUCTION

ACKNOWLEDGMENTS

The author expresses his gratitude to the following individuals and organizations for enduring constant interruptions to their schedules and for patiently answering his countless questions. This book wouldn't have been possible without their kind cooperation and extensive technical knowledge.

INTRODUCTION

Blueprinting is without question the most used—and most abused—term in engine building. Ask any enthusiast about his motor, and chances are he'll proudly describe it as having been blueprinted all the way from the air cleaner to the oil pan plug.

Press him for further details and you may discover that this entire procedure consisted of rebuilding the carburetor, installing a distributor curve kit, and changing the oil filter. And, yes, a friend of his uncle once adjusted the valves. That may be what "blueprinting" means to some people—but not to the beginning engine builders who have read this book.

In a very strict sense, every engine is blueprinted. By that we simply mean that before an automaker introduces a new powerplant, the design engineers must first transfer their ideas into elaborate drawings that will guide the pat-

tern makers and tooling specialists. But this is an imperfect world, and not every component that falls off the end of the assembly line meets the engineers' exact specifications. Drill bits and machine tools become dull. Grinding stones wear out. Gauges don't always read

properly. Lathes run untrue, and mills flex. In any piece of machinery as complex and complicated as an internal combustion engine, all these inaccuracies add up. Sometimes the mistakes cancel each other out, and the finished part is just what the original blueprints

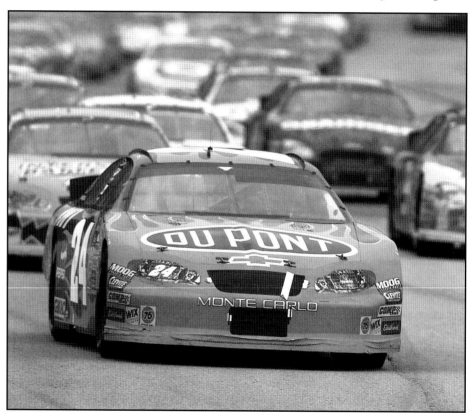

In circle track and road-racing competition, engine durability is vital. A motor assembled with the correct clearances will outlast the competition.

called for. More often, though, they combine to produce a component that is often somewhat less than ideal.

An assembly line is no place for a perfectionist. If engines were built to exact dimensions, even Arab sheiks couldn't afford Chevettes. The car manufacturers are willing to accept parts that are "almost right" or "pretty close"—so long as their deviations aren't so great that they will cause the engine to disassemble itself the instant its new owner takes delivery. Of course, there has to be a reliable means of determining whether a part is "close enough." And that's what a tolerance figure does.

Which brings us back to the blueprints. All of the critical dimensions are assigned a tolerance. For example, a hole that is required to be 0.50-inch in diameter may have a range of +/-0.005-inch. This "plus or minus" figure gives the range of acceptable or "tolerable" variation from the stated dimension. Thus the actual hole could measure between 0.495- and 0.505-inch and still be considered within tolerance. In theory, a hole that is larger or smaller than this range would be reason to scrap the part—or at least to set it aside for repair.

Some tolerances are more critical than others. A hole that simply functions as an oil drain might be one-tenth of an inch (0.10) larger or smaller than the blueprints called for, and yet it could still perform its function perfectly. The hole in the small end of a connecting rod, though, has to be within one ten-thousandth of an inch (0.0001) of the specified diameter if it is to do the job properly. In short, boring the hole in the small end of a connecting rod calls for a thousand times more accuracy than drilling an oil drain hole.

Machine tools and their operators occasionally have bad days. When this happens, the problem of "tolerance stack-up" sometimes arises. It's possible for all of the individual machine operations to be within tolerance, yet the final part may be far out of spec. For example, if a series of holes are all drilled on the "high side" (larger) of the specified tolerance, and the size of these holes is later used as a reference point

Meeting Emissions Standards

If you intend to run a performance engine on the streets , you have a real challenge. Most states have some sort of emissions testing requirements that must be satisfied. Not only must the vehicle meet tailpipe emissions levels, but it must also pass visual equipment inspections. Current laws make tampering with or removing emissions equipment on non-exempt vehicles an offense subject to heavy fines. If your vehicle is not exempt from testing, you will have to make your engine plans and component selection with emissions requirements in mind.

Problems and controversy continue to surround the Federal OBD-II and OBD-III regulations and their inherent limitations on engine modifications to street operated vehicles. The On-Board Diagnostics (OBD) systems use engine malfunction monitors to detect engine problems and then store the "fault" information for later retrieval.

The problem is that sometimes when you add performance equipment like exhaust headers, different cams, larger throttle bodies, and other engine performance parts, the new OBD systems may register these as "malfunctions," even though the performance parts may not result in an increase in tailpipe emissions. When you have the vehicle smog tested, the "fault codes" and "malfunctions" detected may prevent your vehicle from passing, and vehicle operation will be prohibited until the problem is corrected by removing the aftermarket parts. In addition, encrypted computer controls make it more difficult to reprogram or tamper with computerized engine controls.

Many aftermarket performance parts companies have done the research and testing required to meet Federal and State emissions standards for replacement performance parts used in late model street engines. A number of street performance "crate motors" are available from the "Big Three" automakers that satisfy environmental concerns and are street legal engine swaps for certain vehicle and model year applications.

A little research on your part, before you start buying parts and getting machine work done, will enable you to reach the performance levels you want and still keep the air clean.

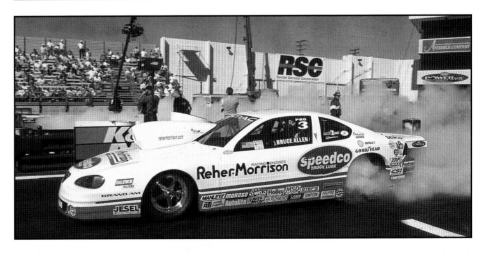

Drag racing demands a powerplant that can produce horsepower at extremely high rpm levels. Careful blueprinting will help an engine survive quarter-mile sprints at 10,000 rpm.

for a series of machining operations, that may also happen to favor the high side of the specifications, the final result could be a component of very bad quality. And a component that is the victim of this tolerance stack-up can be difficult to spot, since it can meet the blueprint specs at each point during the manufacturing process. So an engine piece like this is a mechanical time bomb that's almost certain to cause trouble at some time in the future.

Thus, in a sense, even the engine in your grandmother's Malibu is blueprinted—that is, its components fall within the manufacturer's design specifications (assuming they were at least inspected sometime during their creation). But that's little comfort for racers and performance enthusiasts. In many instances, the acceptable tolerances cover such a wide range, it's a wonder that any production engine is able to live a long and productive life—and yet millions do. The range of permissible main bearing clearances for a Chevrolet V-8, for example, runs from 0.0007- to 0.0035-inch—a spread of almost 0.003-inch. Such a wide variation may be all right for a commuter motor that never sees the far side of 4,000 rpm, but it's hardly suitable for a 600-horsepower big-block!

Engines have an amazing tolerance for abuse. On a fast-moving assembly line, banks of pistons are slammed into cylinder blocks with hydraulic rams. Pneumatic gang wrenches torque down cylinder heads in a matter of seconds. For a conscientious engine builder who devotes an entire weekend assembling a short block such quick-and-dirty techniques may be shocking. But economics are on the side of the assembly line.

The most basic form of blueprinting, then, is simply making sure that all of the tolerances fall within factory specifications. High-volume engine rebuilders generally adopt this approach, which can be characterized by the statement, "if the crank turns, it's good enough." During a straightfor-

ward rebuild, as on the factory production line, there is no attempt to optimize clearances between components. At this level, the performance of the engine is simply a matter of luck—the result of the random selection of parts from a bin. Although you might be technically correct in describing a low-buck rebuilt engine as "blueprinted," it is no more deserving of the title than a lawn mower motor.

In the eyes of most knowledgeable enthusiasts, blueprinting an engine means not only checking clearances but correcting them as well. Careful blueprinting demands that the engine builder pay attention to how the hundreds of parts in an engine all work together. The engine builder must then recognize that changing one component has an effect on many other pieces. In many instances, shop manuals offer no guidelines; the factories never anticipated the high-lift camshafts, high-compression pistons, and high-tech cylinder heads that have become a part of the high-performance scene. Today's performance engine builder must be a part-time automotive engineer, since he has to make sure that the components he has selected will work together. Moreover, the term "blueprinting" embraces a tremendous range of engine building skills. Even the most experienced professional engine builder continually discovers new tricks and techniques that will make his motors more powerful, more reliable, or more affordable.

Blueprinting is a constantly evolving science. Any sharp automotive machinist will agree that before a motor has earned the distinction of being blueprinted, the block must first be square and true, the crankshaft straight, its clearances correct, and the cylinder heads completely reconditioned. These are the basics of engine blueprinting, and they'll be covered in detail on the following pages. But there's much more to precision engine building than just covering the basics. The details make the difference—the

alignment of the intake manifold with the cylinder head ports, the carefully matched rocker arm ratios, the endplay of the distributor shaft. You probably couldn't pay a professional builder enough money to double-check every possible detail in an engine—but in many instances, you can do the work yourself for free. And while you'll undoubtedly have to send out some pieces for major machine operations (like boring and surfacing), most of the critical "massaging" of small parts can be done on a garage workbench with simple hand tools. By the time you have trial assembled an engine several times—checking and rechecking each component at every step in the process—you will have developed a unique understanding of the mechanics of motor building.

The cardinal rule of engine blueprinting is really simple: NEVER ASSUME ANYTHING. Copy this quotation on the biggest piece of cardboard you can find and tape it over your toolbox. Whenever the words "I'm sure it's okay" pass your lips, remember this rule!

When it's late on Saturday night and you are putting away the tools, even though you know you should have checked the piston-to-valve clearance, remember this rule! If you do check the part in question and it passes your scrutiny, then your time has been well spent. But if you blindly bolt together odd pieces on the belief that someone else has already done the critical measurements and blueprinting work don't be surprised when you fire the engine for the first time and nasty chunks of piston material rain into the oil pan. And don't be beguiled by shiny new parts in fancy packages; since so many "hot rod" engine pieces are custom-made, the odds are high that some slight manufacturing variations may be present. Once you learn these facts of engine-building life, you will understand that engine blueprinting is really an art.

TOOLS FOR BLUEPRINTING

Deep in his heart, every car enthusiast secretly lusts for a six-foot-high tool cabinet, its drawers heavy with one of every item in the Snap-on catalog, its cubbyholes bursting with micrometers, gauges, and calipers. Anyone who has spent time around automobiles quickly realizes that it is impossible to have "too many" tools. But for all the appeal of a well-stocked tool chest, the fact is that a simple assortment of hand tools and a few precision measuring tools is all that's necessary for most basic blueprinting operations. Naturally, you can't expect to perform precision machine work with hand tools; but the average backyard mechanic, with modest tools and a little common sense, can

accomplish quite a bit of the preliminary preparation work and this will better prepare you to tell your machinist exactly what you want (which greatly increases the chances of getting what you need).

If your automotive endeavors have progressed to the point that you are considering an engine blueprinting project, you have probably already accumulated a fairly complete selection of wrenches, ratchets, sockets, and screwdrivers. However, if you haven't already added a torque wrench to your tool supply, then this item should unquestionably be the first item on your shopping list.

There are two common types of

torque wrenches: (1) beam wrenches, which indicate torque loads by deflecting a flexible shaft, and (2) click-type wrenches, which produce an audible "click" when the torque resistance has reached the specified setting. Even though the click-type torque wrenches are unquestionably easier to use and "sexier" than an old-fashioned beam wrench, they have several drawbacks. First, they are several times more expensive than a beam wrench. Second, any sort of rough handling can cause them to read inaccurately—and wrenches have been known to take a tumble off a workbench. Since there is no simple way to test the accuracy of a click-type torque wrench, it must be

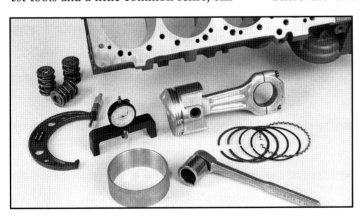

Learning how to use precision tools is an essential part of engine blueprinting. Every component should be checked and re-checked before final assembly.

Treat your torque wrench like a dear friend – your success at engine building will depend on it. Click-type torque wrenches are convenient to use, but must be recalibrated occasionally to ensure continued accuracy. A beam-type wrench is less glamorous, but dead reliable.

returned to the manufacturer for adjustment. Beam-type torque wrenches, on the other hand, are dirt cheap and dead reliable. Since the beam is nothing more than a steel spring, there are no moving parts to break or go out of kilter. Probably the best solution is to own two torque wrenches—a click-type for tedious chores like tightening head bolts, and a beam-type for double-checking the torque readings of crucial fasteners, like rod bolts and flywheel fasteners.

PRECISION TOOLS

A revolution has taken place in the precision tool market within the past 10 years. Until recently, micrometers and other measuring tools were English, difficult to find, and expensive. Now that's all changed. Like cameras and stereo sets, the vast majority of precision tools are now imported from Japan. They can be ordered from dozens of mail-order tool suppliers, and the prices are a fraction of what they used to be. Even large department stores, such as Sears, carry a wide array of precision tools at reasonable prices. In general, the accuracy and dependability of these inexpensive measuring tools are completely satisfactory for most engine blueprinting operations.

Engine rebuilding is only an occasional pastime for most enthusiasts. In these circumstances, it makes sense to form a "tool pool" with other hobbyists. For example, you might convince

Outside micrometers are the foundation of any precision tool collection. You can add more sizes as your engine-building skills and interests grow.

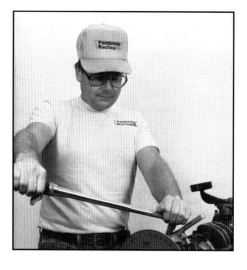

An accomplished engine builder quickly develops a "feel" for his torque wrench. Learn to pull the handle smoothly to prevent erroneous readings.

the car nut next door to buy a set of micrometers, while you invest in dial indicators and magnetic stands. By swapping these tools when a particular measuring task is at hand, you can both have the equipment you need without all the expense. If you need a certain tool only a few times a year, it makes sense to borrow rather than buy.

Although a complete assortment of measuring tools is nice, it is not essential. Throughout this book we'll point out ways to blueprint an engine *without* using anything more exotic than a feeler gauge, modeling clay, and Plastigage. In many instances, this very basic equipment can produce results as accurate as a chest full of micrometers and calipers. Then again, there are times when only the real thing will do. The important thing, however, is to know when to use which tool or technique.

BASIC MEASURING TOOLS

If you ask a professional engine builder which tools he uses most often, he will probably confess that 95 percent of his measurements are taken with just three tools: a 1-inch outside micrometer, a 6-inch dial caliper, and a dial indicator. With a tool budget of only $100—about the cost of an aluminum intake manifold—you can start your precision tool collection with these three essential items.

A *micrometer* is the tool that nearly everyone associates with engine blueprinting. When assembling an engine to close tolerances, there is always a need to know how thick various pieces are—and a micrometer is usually the tool that supplies the answer. For example, measuring the thickness of a head gasket, valve spring shim, or piston ring is a simple chore with a good quality micrometer. Even inexpensive micrometers are accurate to within one ten-thousandths of an inch (0.0001-inch). Usually, though, it's not the price of the tool but the skill of the operator that determines how accurate the measurements are. Becoming proficient with a micrometer is more than learning how to read the spindle. Developing the right touch or "feel" for how tightly to turn the mike is a skill that comes with practice. Two engine builders can measure the same part with the same instrument and come up with slightly different sizes—all because of differences in the feel they have for tightening the micrometer.

When shopping for a micrometer, look for a tool that will read to one ten-thousandth of an inch (0.0001-inch). You may never need to measure anything that accurately, but the extra divisions will help you decide which way to round off a close measurement. Digital micrometers that display the thickness of the part like a calculator are becoming more common. If you are uncomfortable reading a conventional micrometer or plan to use a micrometer very seldom, then the dig-

A good quality micrometer should include a setting standard to check its accuracy. Like all precision tools, micrometers should be stored and used with care.

How to Read a Micrometer

Mastering the art of reading a micrometer is not one of those skills that will cause rich, beautiful women to seek your company. It is, however, a talent that will greatly improve your engine building abilities. The first step is to become familiar with the parts of a micrometer, which are identified in the accompanying photos.

A screw hidden inside the thimble is what gives a micrometer the ability to make precise measurements. This screw has 40 threads per inch. This means that one full turn of the thimble moves the spindle exactly 1/40th of an inch. The decimal equivalent of 1/40 is 0.025-inch, so each turn of the thimble changes the micrometer reading by 0.025-inch. There are 40 lines on the sleeve, so each line that is exposed marks off 0.025-inch. Every fourth line is numbered; these larger lines are tenths of an inch (since 4 times 0.025 equals 0.100). The circumference of the spindle has 25 equally spaced lines. Turning the thimble from one line to the next moves the spindle exactly 0.001-inch.

To read the micrometer, first look at the large lines and numbers on the sleeve. In the example pictured here, the "3" is visible, so the indicated measurement is at least three-tenths of an inch (0.300). Three smaller lines are also exposed after the 3, so you add 0.025 for each line, which equals 0.075. So far the reading is 0.300 plus 0.075, or a total of 0.375-inch. Next, look at the thimble to see which number corresponds to the line on the sleeve. These numbers indicate one thousandths of an inch (0.001). In this example, the "7" is aligned with the line on the spindle, so you add 0.007-inch to the reading. The final measurement, then, is 0.375 plus 0.007, which equals 0.382-inch.

Many micrometers can measure to the fourth decimal place, which is one ten-thousandth of an inch (0.0001). To make this final reading, look at the top of the sleeve. Here you will find a vernier scale, which is a series of lines and numbers. To read the ten-thousandth place, you must find a numbered line that is exactly aligned with a line on the thimble. In the example shown here, the line marked "6" is aligned exactly with a line on the thimble, so the final reading to four decimal places is 0.3826-inch (0.3820 plus 0.0006).

The first few times you use a micrometer, the procedure may seem awkward and difficult. With just a little practice, though, you will soon be taking measurements with a micrometer as easily as you read a ruler.

A micrometer is an indispensable tool for precision engine building. Turning the thimble exposes the numbered lines on the hub. Each line equals 0.0125-inch.

Many micrometers have a vernier scale on the top of the hub, which measures ten-thousandths of an inch (0.0001). To read a vernier, find the line on the hub that aligns with the line on the thimble. In this example, the "6" aligns with the "17."

ital version may be right for you. (Be warned, though, that a digital micrometer can become a crutch. Someday you will be in a shop and have to use a standard micrometer; so avoid the embarrassment of admitting you don't know how to use one by learning the basics.)

High-quality micrometers have a range of only one inch. Thus, a well stocked toolbox should include five different micrometers: 0.0000- to 1.0000-inch, 1.0000- to 2.0000-inch, 2.0000- to 3.0000-inch, 3.0000- to 4.0000-inch, and 4.0000- to 5.0000-inch. This assortment will meet any measurement needs you are likely to encounter during an engine blueprinting project.

Most micrometers have a spring-loaded ratchet on the end of the thimble. Use this ratchet to tighten the thimble until the mike is just snug on the object you are measuring.

You may be tempted to buy a micrometer with interchangeable anvils. These take the place of half a dozen individual micrometers, and allow you to measure anything from 0.0 to 6.0 inches. It sounds too good to be true—and it is. These wide-range micrometers are awkward to use when measuring small items, and changing the anvils is tedious. It is better to add micrometers to your precision tool collection as you find the need for them. For example, start with a 0.0000- to 1.0000-inch micrometer; the next addition might be a 3.0000- to 4.0000-inch micrometer for measuring piston diameters.

Precision tools are available with prices that range from downright cheap to outright expensive. For occasional use, inexpensive micrometers are entirely satisfactory. If you are serious about engine building, you may want to invest in top-quality tools like these Swiss-made Etalon outside micrometers.

Make sure that the micrometer you buy includes a *setting standard.* This is simply a bar of known length that you use to check the accuracy of the micrometer. (A 0.0000- to 1.0000-inch micrometer should read 0.0000-inch when the spindle is closed against the anvil.) You may notice that parts will measure differently at various times of the day. On a hot afternoon, for example, a piston will expand from the heat and measure slightly larger than it did after sitting in a cold shop all night. These differences are too small to affect most blueprinting work—but you should be aware of their existence. If you want to eliminate any chance of error, bring along your micrometers when you deliver parts to your machinist and compare his readings against your own.

DIAL INDICATOR

Once you own a *dial indicator,* you will wonder how you ever got along without one. It is an indispensable tool for degreeing camshafts, checking valve lift, piston deck clearances, crankshaft endplay, and another thousand or so measurements that you will soon discover. Look for a dial indicator with at least one inch of travel, graduated in 0.001-inch increments. Make sure you also get a good selection of extensions ranging up to 6 inches long. These extensions can be joined to allow the indicator to reach into confined areas, such as down a pushrod hole.

There are two dial indicator accessories that are essential for engine blueprinting. The first is a magnetic indicator stand—the stronger the magnet, the better. More than one dial indicator has tumbled off a cylinder

A good magnetic stand greatly increases the versatility of a dial indicator. Select a stand with a strong magnet and clamps that can be operated easily with oily fingers.

head because the magnet wasn't strong enough to hold the setup securely. Look for sturdy arms on an indicator stand, and clamps that are easy to operate even if your hands are covered with oil.

The second vital dial indicator accessory is a bridge. Dial indicators that are sold for use as depth gauges have a removable base that may be used to straddle a hole. This setup works well for measuring piston deck heights when the piston is below the block surface. A U-shaped stand is necessary when the pistons protrude above the deck. These stands are also useful for checking the flatness of a block or cylinder head.

DIAL CALIPERS

A *dial caliper* combines the measuring capabilities of a micrometer with the

Dial indicators are indispensable in engine blueprinting. Dial indicator variations include (left to right) a Starrett "Last Word" finger indicator, a Craftsman 1/2-inch travel indicator, and a Yuasa 1-inch travel indicator.

Camshaft degreeing is easy with this modified dial indicator. It is inserted directly into the lifter bore, eliminating the need for stands and extensions. Rubber O-rings hold it in place.

A depth dial indicator (left) has a flat base, which makes it ideal for checking piston deck heights. A U-shaped bridge (right) allows a standard dial indicator to measure dome heights and to check cylinder head flatness.

Dial calipers are ideal for measurements that don't require absolute accuracy. Dial calipers have two sets of jaws to measure both internal and external dimensions.

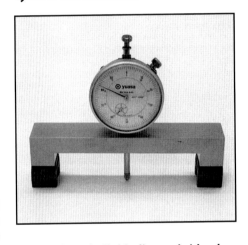

This high-tech dial indicator bridge has magnets to hold it firmly in place on a slippery block.

convenience of a dial indicator. Dial calipers are ideal for taking quick measurements when absolute accuracy is not required. Most dial calipers have both inside and outside jaws. With this setup, you can quickly determine the diameter of a hole or the size of a drill bit. Vernier calipers, which are read much like a micrometer, are less expensive than dial calipers, but they are also less convenient to use.

A 6-inch dial caliper, graduated in 0.001-inch increments, is a good all purpose choice. Better quality calipers have a dust shield over the geared rack that turns the dial; this prevents small metal particles from jamming the mechanism. A good pair of calipers should have no play in the movable jaw. You can check this by placing a thin piece of metal in the jaws. Measure the thickness with the metal close to the rack and then again with the metal out at the end of the jaws. If the measurements vary by more than 0.001-inch, the jaw mechanism is deflecting. Always use care when using a dial caliper—it is a precision instrument, not a clamp. And if you need a super-accurate measurement, put the dial calipers aside and get out a micrometer.

Exotic Tools

A large number of precision tools fall into the category labeled "nice to have, but not essential." Because of the high cost or their limited usefulness, these tools should be considered only after you have given your precision tool collection a good foundation with an assortment of micrometers, indicators, and accessories. These more exotic tools are designed for specialized uses—but when you've got to have one, there is simply no substitute for the right tool.

An *inside micrometer* is most often used to measure the diameter of a hole. Automotive engines are full of holes to measure. Cylinder bores, main bearing bores, and the big ends of connecting rods are all likely candidates for measurement with an inside micrometer. Reading an inside micrometer is just the same as reading an outside micrometer. Using an inside mike does take more skill, however. To measure the diameter accurately, you must find the widest part of the hole. This requires expanding the micrometer while rocking it from side to side and moving it up and down. When the micrometer is adjusted

These dial calipers have been modified to make valve spring installed height measurements quickly and accurately.

Telescoping snap gauges will reach into holes where there's no room for a conventional micrometer.

Spring-loaded snap gauges expand to fit the object being measured. Turning the handle locks the gauge, which is then removed and measured with an outside micrometer or dial caliper.

It takes practice and patience to take accurate measurements with an inside micrometer. The mike must be carefully rocked from side-to-side to make sure that it is recording the true diameter.

properly, you should be able to pull it through the hole with just a slight drag. If the micrometer is loose in the bore or binds as you pull it through, then it is not reading the true diameter.

Inside micrometers can measure holes as small as one inch in diameter when fully collapsed. To measure larger diameters, the micrometer is outfitted with extensions or spacers. For measuring smaller holes, *telescoping gauges* are frequently used. A telescoping gauge is spring-loaded, and after it is inserted in the hole to be measured, the handle releases the gauge, which then expands to the internal size of the hole. Tightening the handle locks the expanded gauge, and after it is removed from the

hole, the width of the gauge can be measured with a conventional outside micrometer.

For serious racers, a *dial bore gauge* is high on the list of desirable tools. In automotive applications, a dial bore gauge has one important function: to check the roundness of the cylinder bores. Although cylinders can be checked with a conventional inside micrometer, a dial bore gauge makes the job substantially easier and more accurate. Dial bore gauges are also excellent for checking the diameter and roundness of bearing bores in main bearing

saddles and connecting rods. Most dial bore gauges can be used in holes ranging from just over 1.000-inch in diameter to 6.000 inches (and even larger) by using various extensions. Unlike outside micrometers with interchangeable anvils, extensions do not adversely affect the accuracy or operation of a dial bore gauge. Engine builders searching for the "Perfect Cylinder Bore" rely on dial bore gauges that are accurate to 0.0001-inch. However, these gauges are rare and expensive. Most currently available gauges are graduated in 0.0005-inch increments, and when used properly these gauges are more than adequate.

A *bevel protractor* can be very handy if extensive piston modifications are required. Among other things, a bevel protractor can be used to determine the precise angle of the valve heads, and will help ensure that the valve notches in the piston dome are machined at precise angles. This is particularly important when using cylinder heads that have been milled on an angle, since this operation alters the valve inclination relative to the piston dome. A bevel protractor will also reveal how much material should be removed from the intake manifold surface after a cylinder head has been angle milled.

Inside micrometers are used to measure cylinder diameters and bearing bores. Extensions increase this micrometer's range from 2 to 6 inches.

A dial bore gauge is expensive, but it is the perfect tool for checking bearing clearances and measuring cylinder bores for taper and eccentricity. This Sunnen gauge is accurate to 0.0001-inch!

ENGINE ASSEMBLY TOOLS

One item of shop equipment in constant use during any blueprinting project is an *engine stand*. Although it's possible to bolt together a short block by wrestling it around on a workbench or the garage floor, this is definitely not the way to treat an expensive motor. If you are handy with a welding torch, you can probably knock out a home-built engine stand in a weekend. At the price of currently available commercial stands, though, it hardly pays you to buy the materials and do the dirty work. There is a wide range in quality between store-bought stands, however. Look for a stand that has more capacity than you think you will ever need. Even if you plan on building only small-blocks, someday you will need a stand that can hold an iron head big-block—and it better be able to stand up under the weight.

Four-wheel engine stands are more stable than the three-wheel variety. Remember, the center of gravity of an engine stand is high. It is very easy to topple the whole stand when you are cinching down the head bolts with a two-foot-long torque wrench. The larger the casters, the easier it will be to wheel the stand around the garage. Wheel locks are a nice refinement. If you're concerned about a place to store the stand between engine building exercises, then consider a knockdown stand that can be stashed under a workbench.

When it comes time to install the pistons in your blueprinted engine block, a *ring compressor* is essential. Ring compressors are available in several styles. The tapered ring compressors made from machined aluminum are easy to use, and present the least danger of breaking a ring. Their drawbacks: You need a different compressor for each distinct bore size, and there is little clearance for cylinder head studs. Despite these shortcomings, tapered ring compressors are the choice of most professional engine builders.

If you're looking for a more "universal" ring compressor, the best choice is the pliers-type compressors offered by K-D Tools. By inserting different compressor bands in the plier handles,

An inexpensive balance scale with an assortment of weights is handy when comparing piston weights.

Choose your piston ring compressor carefully. A band compressor (rear) is quite inexpensive; a pliers-type compressor (center) is easy to use. Tapered ring compressors (foreground) are the "ultimate" piston installation tools, but you'll need a different compressor for each bore size.

A precision bevel protractor can be used to measure valve angles in cylinder heads that have been angle milled.

Extremely stiff valve springs make a rugged spring compressor mandatory when assembling cylinder heads. This lever-action compressor will overcome the resistance of any racing spring.

With a hard-anodized tapered compressor and low-tension piston rings, you can literally install pistons with your fingertips.

A sturdy engine stand with high quality casters is an excellent investment. This Lakewood stand disassembles for storage under a workbench between engine blueprinting projects. Get one that can handle 1,000 pounds.

Installing a camshaft calls for a degree wheel. This one from Mills Specialty Products has a hub that can be turned with a 1/2-inch ratchet (set the screws to lock the wheel in place after locating top dead center) and a sturdy, adjustable point.

A Word on Planning

Some time spent thinking about what combination of parts to use in relation to what the engine is going to be used for has many benefits. Saving time and money are just two. As of 1997, there is more information and a host of planning tools available to help engine builders. Computer software is now available that enables you to build a motor on your computer. Various engine parts combinations can be tried and it can then predict (with reasonable accuracy) how much horsepower and torque the real engine can make. You can then swap parts, such as the camshaft, heads, valve sizes, or compression ratio

to see what effect these changes have on power production. Some engine dyno simulation software will even generate a power curve graph for the engine.

Other software packages can help predict 1/4-mile ETs and mph for a given engine and vehicle combination. Some software can help you figure out throttle stop and carb adjustments from weather data or clutch adjustments, make gear selections, calculate compression ratios, calculate cam timing information, and much more with available "utility" menus. You don't have to know the math involved, the computer does the calculating for you. Most of the programs are very easy to use, even for beginners.

Be sure to include a high-speed grinder in your tool buying plans. A Craftsman dye grinder will deburr blocks, radius piston domes, and chamfer oil holes. If you plan on doing some serious head porting, invest in a heavy-duty Dumore or Milwaukee grinder. Remember to always wear eye protection when using a grinder!

A tremendous variety of stones and cutters are available for high-speed grinders. Carbide burrs are expensive, but they last a lifetime if they are used with care and are resharpened regularly. Shapes include "trees," "flames," and "teardrops." Use coarse cutters for aluminum, and fine cutters for steel and cast iron.

these tools can be used with engines ranging from Honda Civics to Chrysler Hemis.

One of the advantages of the pliers-type ring compressor is that the piston

can be turned with one hand while you drive it into the cylinder bore. The third type of common ring compressor is the band type. These have been around since the days of Henry Ford—but that

doesn't make them any easier to use or less likely to snag a ring. About the best thing that can be said for band-type compressors is that they're cheap.

Sooner or later, you're also going to need a *degree wheel* to properly install the camshaft. Degree wheels can be plain or fancy, large or small, and cheap or expensive. Regardless of the other characteristics, a degree wheel should have easy-to-read numbers. The larger wheels have the advantage on this point—but a big degree wheel can also block access to the cam gear when you have to install a tiny offset cam button.

Assembling cylinder heads requires another group of specialized tools. A high quality *valve spring compressor* is a good investment. If your engine building efforts will be limited to stock-type rebuilds, a simple lever-type compressor will meet your needs. Compressing the stiff springs commonly used with racing and high-performance camshafts

A piston ring expander will save your fingertips when installing rings on pistons – and will reduce the chances of breaking a ring.

The right way to remove a harmonic balancer is with a heavy-duty puller (left) – and the correct way to put it back on is with a damper installation tool like this one from B&B Performance (right).

requires a more substantial tool, however. Several years ago, Sunnen offered an impressive spring compressor with a handle over two-feet long, which really gave you some leverage.

Unfortunately, these super spring compressors are no longer available. Nonetheless, the compound-leverage compressors that can be found at most tool stores or parts suppliers can handle most double- and triple-coil springs.

Finding a glass *burette* may require a visit to a medical or laboratory supply house. A burette is used for such common blueprinting chores as measuring the volumes of combustion chambers or piston domes. Buying a burette from a medical supply can be an ordeal, however. Even if you tell them what you are going to use it for, they are probably convinced that you are going to set up a backyard cocaine laboratory. In that case, your best tactic is to order a complete "cc'ing kit" from one of the mail-order tool suppliers. Ask for a burette with a capacity of at least 100cc's. A burette with a Teflon or plastic valve will be less likely to stick than one outfitted with a ground glass valve. Along with the burette, you'll need a clamp and stand.

A good electric drill has countless uses when building a high-performance engine, from countersinking bolt holes and enlarging oil passages to honing cylinder bores.

Speed Pro's piston ring file makes short work of setting end gaps. Be careful! It's easy to cut too much.

Pneumatic tools are used in production shops because of their reliability and light weights. If you have a compressor with enough air capacity to run them, they are excellent for engine building.

CYLINDER BLOCK

The block is the foundation of any blueprinting project. Every other part in the engine ultimately depends on it. More time, effort, and expense is devoted to preparing the block than to any other single component. If the engine is to perform up to expectations, the block has to be right.

SELECTING A BLOCK

There was a time when any automotive project began with a trip to the junkyard for a suitable core. It's not that simple now. Junkyards are now called "salvage systems" or "ecological recycling centers," and have prices that match the fancy names. More important, many of the cores now available in junkyards are less than desirable from a performance standpoint. In the "good old days," the automakers were quite liberal with their use of cast iron. When metal was cheap, the factories didn't care about the weight of their castings. Their attitude changed dramatically in the Seventies, however. The accountants pointed out that all of this cast iron costs money; and in their search for better fuel economy and mileage, the engineers were working overtime to eliminate weight from cars. The result was the arrival of thin wall castings with flimsy cylinders, skimpy main bearing saddles, and fragile deck surfaces. The

"good" castings—generally those manufactured during the Sixties—have been well picked over by now, especially in the yards surrounding major metropolitan areas. If you want a good block it often pays to head for the country. Many of the engine rebuilding outfits that fill the car magazines with page after page of low-priced engine kits

bring in trainloads of cores from Mexico and the Southwest, where there are still survivors from the Sixties.

NEW VS. "SEASONED" BLOCKS

It used to be that no self-respecting performance enthusiast would consider using a new block. This wasn't simply a

Finding a suitable candidate for an engine blueprinting project is never easy. Approach a used motor with caution unless you are familiar with its history. Cracks and spun bearings may not be apparent until the engine is disassembled and inspected!

The Step-By-Step Guide to Engine Blueprinting

Here's evidence that the automakers are getting serious about performance again. Chevrolet has introduced Bow Tie big-block and small-block castings with all the features any racer could want; Ford and Chrysler offer similar heavy-duty pieces. For a strong street engine, however, Sixties-vintage iron is usually a better (and cheaper) choice.

Chevrolet engine codes are stamped on a pad just above the water pump. This code may help you to identify an engine with a forged crank and big-valve cylinder heads. For more information on identifying blocks, heads, and other engine parts, CarTech® publishes high-performance parts interchange books for Ford engines, Chevy small-blocks, and Chevy big-blocks.

matter of money. New blocks just didn't make as much power as well seasoned used blocks. Engine blocks, like football quarterbacks, get better with age. In the case of a block casting, countless cycles of heating up and cooling down help to "season" the metal. When a block is first cast and then machined on the assembly line, it develops internal stresses. The heating/cooling cycle allows these stresses to "relax," until finally the block becomes dimensionally stable. In the opinion of many top ranked racers, an engine does not achieve maximum power output until it has been honed three or four times; it takes that long for the cylinder bores to settle down and hold the perfectly round shape that promotes a "tight" ring seal.

In certain applications, a used block is no longer the best choice, however. The Detroit engineers have realized that thin-wall castings are not really suitable for high-performance applications. That's why all the major automakers are now offering brand new "off-road" castings with the features that racers and performance enthusiasts demand. For example, Chevrolet will sell you both small-block and big-block "Bow Tie" castings with extra-thick cylinder walls, beefy main bearing bulkheads, and reinforced deck surfaces. Ford offers heavy-duty iron and aluminum blocks through the SVO division, and Chrysler makes special versions of the A-engine block available through the factory-backed Direct Connection program.

If you want the features these blocks offer, then you will have to use a "green," unseasoned casting. For a maximum effort racing engine, the advantages of thicker cylinder walls and a beefy bottom end offset the extra effort required to rehone and rebuild the engine several times before it reaches its power potential. If a strong street performance or moderate competition engine is in the works, then a well-used, seasoned block is probably the better bargain. Engine blocks intended for truck use tend to have more desirable features than passenger car versions. Given a choice, then, the

When shopping for a block, look for desirable features such as four-bolt main bearing caps. Trucks, police cars, and taxicabs are likely sources for heavy-duty castings.

best bet would be a mid-Sixties truck block with low mileage and no cracks—if you can find one!

PRELIMINARY INSPECTION AND DISASSEMBLY

Whether your block is packaged in a factory shipping crate or in an inch-thick-layer of grime, a thorough inspection is important. You can save yourself a great deal of grief and expense by looking for fatal flaws *before* investing in any expensive machine work. Most of the points below apply to used blocks, but even factory-fresh castings deserve a careful going over.

Rebuilding an engine that you personally pulled from one of the family cars is a tremendous advantage because you already know whether the engine was basically sound. Buying an engine out of a junkyard, a swap meet, or a dark garage is a riskier proposition. In most instances, you don't have the luxury of hearing the engine run or even seeing the original vehicle from which it was removed. Was the motor simply worn out, or was it filling the oil pan full of water from a crack in a cylinder wall? It's up to you to find out whether the block is worth dragging home.

The first item on your block-inspection agenda is to decide what exactly you are looking at. Don't take the seller's word that the Chevy V-8 he's offering is a genuine 350ci high-performance LT-1. It might be, but it also could be a 283 (if you don't know how to tell the difference). Your best sources of information about an unknown

Two-Piece or One-Piece Rear Main Seal Blocks

In 1986, Chevrolet small-block V-8s began to use a one-piece rear main seal and matching rear main cap in an effort to stop rear seal oil leaks. This required changing the rear crank journal, flywheel and flexplate bolt pattern diameters, the oil pans, pan gaskets, and timing chain covers. Similar changes were made to Chevy Gen. V and Gen. VI 366, 427, 454, and 502 big-blocks in 1991 and 1996, respectively.

Chevrolet and some aftermarket companies make rear seal adaptors that allow the use of early two-piece rear seal cranks in a late model one-piece rear main seal block. Depending on which adaptor you choose, an oil pan designed for a one-piece or two-piece block can be used. These rear seal adaptors are helpful if you have an expensive crank made for a two-piece seal and wish to use it in a one-piece seal-style block. The adaptors come with the required bolts, dowels, gaskets, and instructions concerning the drilling and tapping of holes to mount the oil seal adaptor.

Generation I Chevy small-blocks use one-piece (left) or two-piece (right) rear-main oil seals and matching caps.

motor are the engine code and casting numbers.

In the case of a Chevrolet V-8, the engine code is a series of letters that accompany the serial number stamped on a pad just above the water pump inlet. For example, a block stamped "DZ" is a 302ci 1969 Z/28 engine, while "FB" indicates a two-barrel 327. Be warned that these codes are not always 100 percent reliable, and that the same letter code is sometimes applied to different engines in

succeeding years. If all you are looking for is a sound block then the engine code may not be important. But if you are paying a premium price for a motor with a forged steel crank and big-valve cylinder heads, then the code is a good clue to the true identity.

Unlike engine codes, casting numbers apply to *types* of engines made over a period of years. To again cite the Chevrolet small-block as an example, the casting number reveals the size of

Mark the main bearing caps before removing them. Number the rods and caps with a punch.

Casting numbers are clues to the identity of an unknown engine. Chevy V-8 casting numbers are located on the bell housing flange behind the cylinder head.

the main bearings and whether the block has two-bolt or four-bolt main caps. (Of course, if the engine is already disassembled, your eyes will provide this information.)

The casting number for a Chevrolet V-8 is located on the rear of the block just above the bell housing surface. One of the several standard rebuilding references will help you decipher the casting number.

Even if the engine is encrusted with grime, a visual inspection will give you an idea about its condition. A block that looks covered with mayonnaise has been running with water in the oil. This may indicate a leaking intake manifold gasket or a serious crack in the block or cylinder heads. A valley full of "gunk" is a sure sign that the oil was changed infrequently. If this accumulation is so bad that it prevents the oil from adequately draining back to the pan, the resulting oil starvation may have caused a bearing to spin. If the oil pan has been removed, check for a black burned appearance around the main bearings. This will be visible even in a dirty block and indicates a bearing that was on the verge of failing. The resulting heat could have caused the bearing cap to be out of register on the block, which will require correction when the block is align honed during the blueprinting procedure.

If the heads have been removed, you can check for visible cracks in the cylinder walls. An exceptionally rusty cylinder or a piston top with no coating of carbon is a tip-off that water was getting into the cylinder. You should also check the diameter of the cylinder

Remove the heads and measure the cylinders to determine whether the block has already been over bored. Then measure the diameter under the ridge at the top of the ring travel to see how much metal must be removed to clean up the cylinder walls.

Undersize bearing inserts are a tip-off that the crankshaft has already been reground.

bores. *Look for a block that has not already been over bored.* Scrape away the carbon at the top of the bore and measure the cylinder diameter above the ring travel. A dial caliper is accurate enough for this measurement. If the block you intend to use has an original bore size of 4.000 inches, then a block with bores that measure 4.060 inches in diameter has already been rebuilt at least once. Boring the cylinders again may leave you with thin, fragile walls.

If the block has passed these tests, the next step is to measure the wear in the cylinders. Measure the diameter of the cylinder just under the ridge at the top of the ring travel. This is generally the point of maximum cylinder bore taper. The diameter under the ridge should be at least 0.015-inch *smaller* than your intended final bore size. This will provide enough material for the boring bar and hone to straighten the cylinder wall surface. Ideally, the cylinder bores should "clean up" with a 0.030-inch overbore.

Now it's time to invest some money in cleaning the likely candidate so that a detailed inspection can be performed. Before the block can be cleaned, it must be stripped. *Always mark the main bearing and rod bearing caps before disassembly.* You can use a fancy set of number punches or just a center punch to mark the caps—just make sure you do it. Number the main bearing caps from front to back and mark the rod forks and caps with their respective cylinder numbers. If you forget these simple steps, your machinist

Main Caps

Engine main caps come in a variety of materials and are bolted to the block saddles in a number of ways, most commonly with two or four bolts per main cap. Common gray cast iron, nodular iron, and steel main caps have been used. Some caps are "cross-bolted" from the side of the block skirts, while other blocks use two- or four-bolt straight or "splayed" caps.

Many believe that a four-bolt main cap is the only way to go, but it depends. A sane, street driven engine and even a mild bracket race motor will do just fine with two-bolt main caps. If you need more strength, four-bolt caps are an improvement; splayed-bolt or cross-bolt positions with steel main caps are better yet. On outrageous, very high power blown or nitrous motors, a main cap girdle can help keep the bottom end together.

Two-bolt blocks can sometimes be converted to four-bolt main caps, but the first question to ask yourself should be, "What will it cost?" By the time you purchase the four-bolt main caps, new bolts, or studs, add in the machining costs to properly register the new main caps, locate, drill, and tap the new bolt holes, and then align bore and align hone the crank bearing saddles, you may be approaching or exceeding the cost of a different block with the four-bolt main cap features you want.

Use an acetylene torch to remove stubborn oil gallery pipe plugs. Heat the plug, let it cool down, and then spray it with WD-40.

will charge for the additional time he must spend sorting them out.

Used parts (like pistons, lifters, and bearings) have no place in a blueprinted engine, so special care is not required with these components. However, be respectful of the parts you will be reusing. While removing the pistons and rods, be especially careful to prevent nicks in the crankshaft journals or gouges in the cylinder walls. A supply of coffee cans and margarine cups is essential for keeping the fasteners organized. Six months from now, you will not remember which bolt holds the oil pump in place unless you label it today. You can also get some clues to the engine's past by inspecting the backs

After the plug has cooled, unscrew it with a 1/4-inch ratchet.

Clean out corrosion that has accumulated around the water drain holes with a tapered punch.

of the bearings. If the bearings are undersize, then it is likely that someone has already overhauled the engine (although the factories do occasionally "save" crankshafts that are off-spec by regrinding them and fitting oversize bearings to the block).

CLEANING

Before a used block can be carefully examined, it must be completely degreased. Most American car owners are not very conscientious about observing recommended oil change intervals; so most blocks are encrusted with grease, varnish, and sludge. There are two ways to remove this accumulated gunk: hot tanking and jet cleaning. Both methods are quite effective, and the choice will probably depend on the cleaning equipment your machinist prefers.

The hot tank is filled with a caustic solution that dislodges years of grit and grime. (Larry Hollum keeps his tank at the boiling point!) An overnight soaking will clean the block so you can continue your inspection.

A length of steel rod is an ideal tool for removing soft plugs in the front of the oil galleries. Drive them out with a heavy hammer.

Remove soft plugs by tapping them sideways with a blunt punch. Then lever them out with a pair of water-pump pliers or a seal puller.

There are several steps that will make the cleaning procedure more effective, regardless of which technique your machinist uses. First, the freeze plugs (also known as soft plugs or core plugs) should be removed. This allows the cleaning agent to scour the water jacket, and permits a visual inspection of the outer cylinder walls. Large flakes of rust and corrosion will be apparent in the water passages of an engine that has been used without anti-freeze protection. Although rust in the water jacket isn't cause to reject a block you should be aware that the corroded cylinder walls would be thinner, and therefore weaker, than unrusted walls.

There are several techniques for removing freeze plugs. Most engine builders strike the plug on one side with a dull punch, turning it sideways in its hole, grab the edge of the plug with a

White soda deposits highlight the cylinder wall cracks when the block is dried after hot tanking.

A jet cleaner is considerably faster than a hot tank; high-pressure nozzles will scour a used block in 20 minutes. Here Kip rinses the casting after preliminary cleaning.

pair of water pump pliers, and lever the plug out of the block. Kip Martin, who operates Patterson-Martin Machine in Augusta, Kansas, was our guide to the block preparation pictured here. He uses a Snap-on oil seal tool to remove old plugs quickly. Occasionally you will encounter a soft plug that refuses to

An overheated bearing causes discoloration around the main bearing bores. Even though the bearing may not have spun, localized high temperatures can foster cracks. Examine the bearing saddles carefully, paying particular attention to the bolt holes and oil passages.

This bare block emerges from the jet cleaner ready for a final inspection and preliminary machine work.

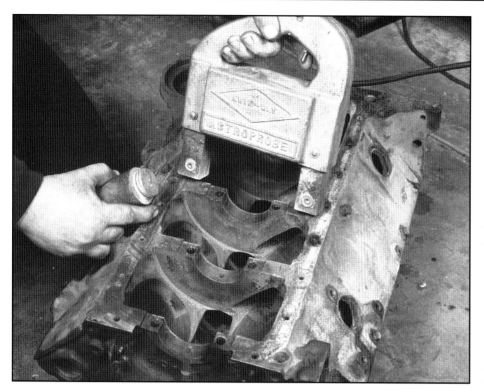

Larry Hollum begins the Magnaflux inspection by magnetizing the main bearing bulkheads, then sprinkling the webs with magnetic powder.

If engine coolant freezes or boils, cracks inside of the water jacket are the likely consequence. Inspection powder highlights the flaws by collecting along the edges of the crack.

cock sideways. This may be caused by a lack of clearance behind the plug, or by rust around the plug hole. In these instances, the only solution is to drive the plug into the water jacket and then fish it out with a pair of pliers. You should also remove the water drain plugs and clean out the holes with a punch or screwdriver.

The small oil gallery passages in most engine blocks are sealed with a combination of soft plugs and threaded pipe plugs. If the plugs are frozen in place—and they usually are—heat from a blowtorch or welding torch will help to free them. After breaking dozens of 1/4-inch drive extensions, Kip discovered a painless way to remove the plugs Chevrolet installs in the back of small-block and big-block V-8s. He heats the plugs with a torch, using a welding tip, and then allows them to cool. After a quick spray with some WD-40 lubricant, the plugs will unscrew with the greatest of ease! After removing these threaded plugs, Kip inserts a three-foot piece of 1/4-inch diameter steel into the oil galleries and drives out the soft plugs behind the camshaft gear with the aid of a small hammer.

If you want a glimpse of what hell must be like, take a look inside a hot tank sometime. Most automotive machine shops have their hot tanks located as far away as possible. They are filled with a caustic soda solution that is heated close to the boiling point. Agitators in the tank

Cracks in the valley can be the result of overheating caused by blocked heat riser passages or inadequate coolant.

keep the solution constantly moving to scrub away the accumulated filth of years of use. The length of time that the block must be soaked depends on the strength of the solution, how hot your machinist keeps his tank, and how dirty the casting might be. Generally, a preliminary cleaning will require a couple of hours in the tank, although a really grimy block might need a stay overnight. Please note, too, that hot tanks are only for iron blocks, since the solution will dissolve aluminum. Leave your Can-Am aluminum Chevy block in a hot tank overnight and it will simply disappear!

An alternative to the hot tank is a jet clean booth. As its name implies, a jet cleaner sprays the block with degreasing solution under high pressure. The block rotates on a carousel during the cleaning process to expose all its surfaces to the cleaning spray. Jet cleaning is much faster than hot tanking—even the dirtiest block will be ready for inspection in less than half an hour. Machinists who prefer the old-fashioned hot tank point out, however, that the jet cleaners aren't as effective at cleaning out the small oil passages in the block. At this point, however, you are not trying to make the block "squeaky clean." Rather, you just want to remove the grease so that you can take a closer look at the casting surfaces.

FINAL INSPECTION

Your two eyes are the best tools for a final block inspection. Most cracks that are cause to reject a block are visible to the naked eye—providing you know where to look. If the block has been hot tanked, the soda solution will often pinpoint a cylinder wall crack by forming a white crust along the fault.

Either overheating or freezing causes most cracks. These cracks are most common in the water jacket above the oil-pan rail and in the lifter valley. If the heat-riser passages in the cylinder head or intake manifold were blocked, there may be localized overheating in the valley. Stress cracks are most often found around the head bolt holes in the deck surface and nearby the oil holes in the main bearing saddles.

Dry *Magnaflux* inspection is often used to pinpoint cracks and flaws. A large U-shaped electric magnet is applied to the test area, which is dusted with magnetic powder. Cracks in the block surface disrupt the magnetic field, causing the powder to form lines that highlight the flaws. A thorough Magnaflux inspection should include both sides of the block, both sides of the lifter valley, and all the main bearing bulkheads. And don't overlook the main bearing caps while you're searching for flaws. Larry Hollum, who operates Hollum's Racing Engines in Fremont, California, performed the block inspection for our camera.

If there are any suspicious cracks or evidence of water in the oil pan, then a *pressure test* is usually in order. The block is prepared for pressure testing by installing new freeze plugs, bolting steel plates to the deck surfaces, and covering the water pump inlets. The water passages are then pressurized with compressed air and the entire block is submerged in a vat of water, or sprayed with a solution of soapy water. Air escaping from the water jacket through a crack will create a telltale stream of bubbles.

You should also examine the block carefully for *porosity*. "Porosity" is the result of air pockets being trapped when molten metal is poured into a casting mold. When a block is machined later, the cutting tools can expose these voids, which may be as small as pinholes or as large as a quarter. Minor holes in the valley and front cover are nothing to be concerned about, but porosity in the deck surfaces and cylinder walls is a serious problem. Blocks with excessive porosity are often repaired at the factory by welding up the offending holes. These welded areas are much harder than the parent metal, and some machinists may refuse to remachine a welded block because of the damage these hard spots cause to expensive cutting tools.

There is probably no such thing as a perfect cylinder block. The *closer you look* the more flaws you will find. It's up to you to decide whether to accept the inevitable shortcomings. Stripped head bolt and main cap holes can be made better than new with Helicoil thread inserts; on the other hand, there is no sure cure for a crack in the main bearing bulkheads. A rare or limited-production block obviously requires a more forgiving attitude than a garden-variety casting.

SONIC TESTING

High-performance engine building is constantly becoming more sophisticated. Today many shops are able to *sonic test* blocks for cylinder wall thickness. The equipment required for this procedure costs thousands of dollars, but the importance of finding a block with thick cylinder walls has convinced a substantial number of racers and machinists to make the necessary investment. Simply stated, the thicker the cylinder walls, the higher the horsepower potential of the engine. Maintaining the tightest possible seal between the cylinder walls and piston rings is essential to making horsepower. In a sense, cylinders that deform and go out-of-round under stress waste valuable horsepower.

The way the block material is distributed around the cylinder bores is also a vital concern. In most automotive engines, the thickness of the cylinder walls is not uniform. The walls are usually thin between adjacent bores to allow coolant to circulate between the cylinders. (Exceptions to this general rule are the "Siamese bore" blocks—such as the 400ci small-block Chevrolet—in which the adjacent cylinder walls are joined.) The walls are also sometimes thicker on the *major thrust surface* to withstand the stress imposed by the piston skirts. The pistons cock sideways as they travel up and down inside the cylinders; this sideways motion is called "piston thrust." These loads are highest during the power stroke, when the piston is exerting maximum pressure on the connecting rod. The highest thrust occurs on the wall opposite the big end of the rod as the piston moves down the bore. In a V-8, this is generally the outboard side of the right and the inboard side of the left cylinder banks.

This block demonstrates how core shift can affect cylinder wall thickness. The outboard side of the cylinder wall measures 0.327-inch thick; the inboard wall is much thinner, with only 0.168-inch of metal.

During the casting process, however, the molds that form the cylinder walls can move out of alignment. This is called "core shift." A block that suffers from core shift will have cylinder walls that are thicker or thinner than they are supposed to be.

Not all core shifts are bad. If the cylinder walls on the side of the bores that are exposed to the major thrust axes of the pistons are extra-thick then they will be stronger. Of course, the sides of the cylinders that bear against the minor thrust axes will be thinner, perhaps to the point of being fragile. The problem is that without a sonic tester, it's impossible to know how thick the cylinder walls are and in which direction the cores may have shifted during the casting process.

Before sonic testing equipment became widely available, there were a number of signs that were reputed to indicate how badly a block had core shifted. Examining the pad around the front camshaft bearing, checking the relationship between the lifter bores and their bosses, and measuring from the coolant holes in the deck surface to the cylinder bores were all supposed to indicate whether a block was "good" or

not. Unfortunately, sonic testing has revealed that these visual clues fall into the category of "old wives' tales." They are simply not a reliable way to determine whether a block has acceptable core shift.

A sonic tester is a high-tech instrument that measures cylinder wall thickness by bouncing sound waves through the metal, much like radar computes distances by measuring the time it takes for radio waves to bounce off a distant object. BHJ Products (Fremont, California) is the source for most of the sonic testers currently used by performance-oriented engine builders. Since the density of various cast iron alloys varies, the BHJ tester includes an assortment of calibrating standards. For example, a block with a high percentage of nickel in the iron alloy requires a different calibration than a block with a relatively low tin content.

Most machinists make a "map" of the cylinder walls when they sonic test a cylinder block. Each cylinder is measured in eight locations—the front, the back, and each side of the bore—with readings taken both at the top and bottom of the ring travel. Machinists who have long experience with sonic testing

report that there is often a substantial variation between cylinder wall thicknesses in the same block. In other words, you can't measure just one hole and conclude that all the bores on that side of the block will have the same wall thickness readings. Kip Martin, who performed the sonic test, pictured here, reports that the number-8 cylinder tends to be the worst hole in a small-block Chevrolet.

The question naturally arises, "how thick is thick enough?" The answer depends on both the type of engine and how it will be used. Late-model Fords and 340-type Chrysler engines, for example, tend to be thin; typical cylinder wall thicknesses on these engines may be only 0.150-inch. A small-block Chevrolet, in contrast, may have cylinder walls over 0.200-inch thick. Kip advises that he wants to see at least 0.180-inch of wall material on the major thrust side after the block has been bored to finished size. Larry Hollum concurs; his general rule is that any small-block with a performance goal of 500 horsepower or higher should have cylinder walls at least 0.200-inch thick.

Sonic testing a block is expensive because of the cost of the equipment involved, but it provides valuable infor-

Sonic testing is the most accurate means of determining cylinder wall thickness. The BHJ Products ultrasonic tester is first calibrated with metal of a known thickness, and then the probe is applied to a cylinder wall. Readings are taken at the front, the rear, and both sides of the bore.

mation. It allows you to reject a block with thin cylinder walls before investing a lot of time and money in machine work. Also, the wall-thickness diagram allows a sharp machinist to relocate the cylinder bores to provide the greatest possible wall thickness on the critical major thrust. It may be possible for him to adjust the bore location as much as 0.030-inch during the boring operation. Without a sonic examination, the machinist must rely on the existing bore location and hope for the best.

Is sonic testing absolutely necessary? For a high-performance street motor, sonic testing is certainly a high cost luxury. On the street, it's not essential to extract the very last horsepower. But for a maximum-effort racing engine, sonic testing should be considered an indispensable step in the engine building procedure!

DEBURRING

If your block has passed this series of tests, it's time to get to work. The first item on the list of things to do is a thorough *deburring*. Deburring is essential for both cosmetic and structural reasons. The aim of deburring a block is to grind off all the sharp edges and casting burrs. These sharp edges are "stress risers" that can give cracks a starting point. Eliminating these flaws will also save you from collecting countless cuts and nicks on your hands while working on the engine.

Begin your deburring work with a hammer and a long punch or chisel. Usually the cam gallery and oil drain passages are full of sharp ridges and casting flash formed by joints in the block molds. Use the punch to knock off this metal residue. Then go over the main bearing bulkheads, lifter valley, and front cover, eliminating any excess metal that looks like it could break off the casting and eventually wind up in the oil pan. Before you put the punch and hammer away, it's also a good idea to take a tour around the outside of the block to knock off excess casting flash.

The next step is to break out the high-speed grinder and attack every sharp edge on the block. Plan on spend-

The casting process leaves numerous sharp edges and hiding places for core sand. Concentrate your deburring efforts in the camshaft gallery, under the oil pan rail, and alongside the main bearing bulkheads.

ing a full Saturday afternoon on this project, and remember to wear eye protection when the chips are flying. You can use either grinding stones or carbide burrs for this chore, although the carbide cutters will make less of a mess.

The idea is to simply round off all the sharp edges on the internal and external surfaces. It is not necessary to meticulously radius every corner, although the finish block will look better if you do (possibly a consideration if the engine is

A hammer and a long punch are essential for removing casting flash from the cam gallery and other inaccessible areas.

Smooth edges along the pan rail will help the oil return to the sump, reducing windage and improving lubrication.

Before you hang up the hand grinder, radius the main oil passage on the Chevy rear bearing cap.

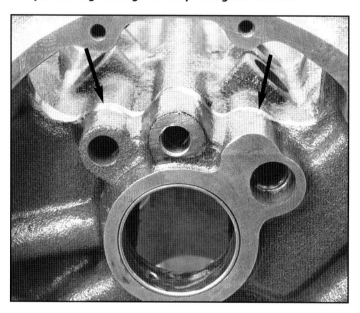

Casting flash is common around the oil drain holes in the lifter valley. Ridges can break off and cause damage by scuffing piston skirts or jamming the oil pump; remove them with a high-speed hand grinder.

destined for a street rod or ski boat).

You should also concentrate on chamfering the oil drain holes. These passages are often full of casting flash that can break loose and find its way into the oil pump. By gently rounding the edges of these holes, you'll encourage the lubricant to return quickly to the sump.

It's possible to get carried away with this operation. Some novice engine builders don't stop until the entire lifter valley is practically polished. These misdirected efforts may actually cause more harm than good, since cleaning out all the grit left from grinding the engine is virtually impossible. The slightly rough surface of the block cast-

Deburring the outside of a block denies cracks a starting place, and saves your hands from cuts and scratches.

Deburr the lifter bores with an extra-fine-grit brake-cylinder ball hone.

Shiny spots on main bearing caps are evidence of "cap walk," or movement, between the caps and the block under load.

Kip Martin begins his align honing operation by cleaning the main cap parting lines with a fine file.

ing helps transfer heat to the oil, which can account for almost 60 percent of the engine cooling.

ALIGN HONING AND BORING

Align honing or *align boring* the main bearing saddles should be the first major machine operation. All the block machine work that follows will be based either directly or indirectly on the main bearing saddles, so it is crucial that this first step be done properly.

As a matter of course, the main bearing bores of every high-performance engine should be align honed or align bored. On the assembly line, engines are routinely fitted with specially selected main bearings to make up for imperfections in the main bearing saddles. Once these bearings are replaced, the alignment is lost. Also, as a block ages and the cast surfaces relax, the main bearing bulkheads can distort. Since this is a slow process, the bearings and crankshaft wear to accommodate this movement. But when new bearings or a blueprinted crankshaft are installed on misaligned bearing saddles, rapid failure can result. Many of the standard backyard tests, such as placing a straightedge on the main bearing saddles or installing a crank to see if it turns freely, are not reliable. For example, these checks will not reveal whether the main bearing bores have become egg-shaped as a result of the main bearing caps distorting. Of course, if a main bearing has spun or if special steel main bearing caps are being installed, the main bearing saddles *must* be realigned.

File marks highlight the irregular contact between the caps and the block. Align honing increases the area of block-to-cap contact.

A Sunnen precision grinder removes a small amount of metal from the cap parting line. This trues the cap surface and reduces the vertical diameter of the main bearing bore.

The most critical part of align honing a Chevrolet V-8 is cutting the wide rear main bearing cap. If this cap is cocked, the thrust bearing will be overloaded on one edge.

Main cap bolt holes are chased with an undersized tap to clean the threads without removing any metal.

Caps should fit tightly in the block. If the caps are loose, Kip peens the block with a blunt chisel to improve the register.

After grinding, the mating surfaces of the main bearing caps are flat and uniform.

The parting line of the main caps is deburred by drawing the cap across a fine file.

The chisel point is rounded with a bench grinder for peening chores.

Main cap fasteners are cleaned, lubricated, and torqued to recommended specifications before align honing begins.

The discarded oil pump housing bolted to the rear main cap simulates the distortion that occurs when the pump is installed; credit Larry Hollum for this refinement.

With the preliminaries finished, honing can begin. The honing stones are constantly flushed with honing fluid to carry off block material and abrasive. A drill motor rotates the hone as the operator strokes the mandrel back and forth in the bearing bores.

Kip constantly checks the diameter of the bearing saddles with a dial bore gauge. The size of the bores is critical if the bearing inserts are to have the proper crush.

A long honing mandrel is centered in the bearing bores with aligning pins. Martin prefers the greater precision provided by the dial indicator.

There is still considerable controversy about the advantages of align *honing* versus align *boring*. In align honing, the main bearing bores are straightened with self-centering abrasive stones. Align boring uses a steel pilot with a single-edged cutting tool. In theory, align boring has the advantage of allowing the machinist to remove the majority of material from the main bearing caps, which leaves the relationship between the crankshaft and camshaft undisturbed. (Only the heavy-duty Tobin-Arp machines have this capability, however. The small, block-mounted boring bars frequently found in machine shops work much like an align hone, removing material equally from both the cap and block saddles.) In practice, however, the skill of the machinist counts for more than the type of equipment he uses. In skilled hands, an align hone can produce results that rival align boring.

Sunnen is currently one of the major manufacturers of align-honing machines, and the widespread popularity of Sunnen brand equipment means that most automotive shops can now align hone blocks. And since most align hone operations are performed on similar equipment, *the difference between a first-rate job and a mediocre effort usually lies in the setup and the preparation.* Few performance enthusiasts have the opportunity to witness the align honing procedure from start to finish. That's why you are now invited to follow along as Kip Martin takes us step-by-step through an align honing job.

Kip begins by running a file over the parting surfaces between the caps and block. This spotlights the high spots on the surfaces and underlines the fact that many main bearing caps are not flat when they leave the factory. Before returning the file to the toolbox, he deburrs the sharp edges on both the cap and saddles. The main cap bolt holes are then chased with an undersized GH-3 tap. This small tap cleans the threads *without removing any metal,* which would weaken them. The bolts are put aside in a can of carburetor cleaner while Kip readies the caps.

Preparing the caps properly is critical to the success of the align honing operation. The caps must be square when the parting-line surface is being prepared. This is especially important on the thrust bearing (the rear main on Chevrolet V-8s). If the cap surface is not ground on a true plane that is parallel with the crank axis, the cap will be cocked when it is reinstalled on the block and this will cause the thrust bearing to wear unevenly. In severe cases, the thrust loads are concentrated on a small part of the bearing surface area, which causes the bearing to fail prematurely. (This is extremely critical if the engine will be used with a manual clutch that has very heavy spring pressures.)

A special Sunnen main-cap cutter precisely grinds material from the parting surface of the cap. Kip removes only enough metal from the cap to produce a smooth, flat finish. (This is one of the overlooked advantages of align honing, since resurfacing the main caps increases the block-to-cap contact.) Trimming several thousandths of an inch of metal from the main caps means that the bearing bores will not be round when the caps are reinstalled on the block. Thus, the hone also resizes the portion of the main bore that lies in the block main webs, much like a connecting rod is reconditioned.

The main caps should fit tightly in the alignment notches. If the fit is sloppy, Kip peens the block alongside the main cap register with a blunt chisel. He also lightly chamfers the parting-line edge of the cap bore by drawing the edge across a fine file. This breaks the sharp edge, which can scrape material off the backside of the bearing shells when they are inserted. The clean main cap bolts are retrieved from the carb cleaner, washed in solvent, and lightly oiled. The caps are then bolted to the block and the fasteners tightened to the recommended torque reading.

Kip prefers to set up the align hone with a dial indicator instead of the usual centering pins. This helps ensure that the bearing bores will be perfectly round. He adjusts the dial bore gauge (which measures the diameter of the bearing holes) to the nominal size listed

in the manufacturer's specifications. Undersize bearing bores are to be avoided, since they will cause the bearing clearance to be too tight. A bearing bore that is slightly larger than the manufacturer's specifications is acceptable—as long as the bearing still has the proper "crush"—because performance engines are generally set up with generous bearing clearances. The Sunnen align hone has a built-in lubrication system that bathes the stones with honing oil to carry away worn abrasive. After several strokes with the hone, Kip checks to make sure that the bearing bores are being cut evenly. If not, the caps are removed and trimmed slightly in the cap grinder.

DECKING

Decking the cylinder block accomplishes several important results. First, it makes the block "square." This means that if you measure from both deck surfaces to the crankshaft centerline at the front and rear of the block, all four dimensions will be equal. If a BHJ Blok-Tru is used, decking will also "index" the block. In most V-8s the decks should be exactly 90° to each other. If you imagine a line between the crank centerline and the camshaft centerline, it should divide this 90° angle between the decks into two equal 45° angles. In the real world of engine building, it's not unusual to find that the decks are slightly cocked, and that the camshaft is somewhat off center.

The third aim of decking a block is to establish the *deck height.* Deck height is measured when the installed piston is at exact top dead center (TDC) and is defined as the distance from the flat quench area of the piston to the deck surface of the block. Deck height is a critical dimension in engine building. If the deck height is too small, the pistons can hit the cylinder heads; if it is too large, the compression ratio may be reduced considerably.

Unfortunately, there is no "ideal" deck height. The thickness of the head gasket must be considered when computing the total clearance between the piston and cylinder head. For example,

The cylinder head decks of most V-8s should be machined 90 degrees to each other.

A BHJ Blok-Tru fixture centers on the main bearing bores and the camshaft bearings. It provides accurate reference points when surfacing the block to correct factory machining mistakes. Conventional V-8 decks should be at precisely 90 degrees to each other.

if the flat part of the piston is 0.020-inch below the deck surface at TDC and a head gasket with a compressed thickness of 0.020-inch is installed, then the final piston-to-head clearance is 0.040-inch. This is only a static measurement; when the engine is running, the actual operating clearance will be much less. In fact, the goal of most engine builders is to have the piston-to-head clearance as close to zero as possible under *actual operating conditions*. When an engine is running at high rpm, the connecting rods stretch, the pistons rock, and the wrist pins flex slightly. All of this reduces the actual clearance between the pistons and cylinder heads.

Engines that operate at very high rpm require more deck height and more piston-to-head clearance than low-rpm motors, since the loads on the engine components increase greatly with speed. Also, the connecting rod material must be considered; aluminum rods stretch more than steel rods. Finally, the clearance between the pistons and the cylinder walls has to be considered. When the pistons are fitted loosely (as is common in high-rpm engines) they will, in effect, tip over more sharply at the top of the stroke—when the crank stops pushing the piston upward and begins to pull it down. This causes the piston decks (along the major thrust axis) to approach the cylinder heads

A two-inch-diameter steel bar supports the block on the main bearing saddles; this ensures that the deck surfaces will be parallel to the crankshaft. A screw jack supports the bar to prevent the weight of the block from deflecting the bar. The block is securely clamped to the worktable before surfacing begins.

A machinist's bubble level is used for the preliminary block set-up. A bubble level is not accurate enough for the final alignment, however.

Final leveling adjustment is made with the dial indicator attached to the cutter wheel. The needle must not move as the indicator travels across the top edge of the Blok-Tru fixture. By milling both sides of the block parallel to the fixture, the decks will be at the desired 90-degree angles.

more closely. And, if any of the pistons accidentally tap the cylinder head, the top ring groove can collapse and pinch the piston ring, greatly reducing the ring seal and power output.

Determining the absolutely correct piston-to-head clearance can be a long trial-and-error process. For most applications, however, the following recommendations can be followed with reasonable confidence. For a high-performance street engine with steel connecting rods, 0.035-inch piston-to-head clearance is the absolute minimum. For a racing engine with steel rods, 0.045-inch clearance is required; aluminum rods require increasing the clearance to at least 0.060-inch (and even more if there is evidence of the pistons contacting the heads). Remember, these are total piston-to-head clearances; the thickness of the head gasket *must be subtracted* to arrive at the desired deck height. In some instances, the block may not be tall enough to produce the desired deck height; in this case, the pistons must be milled.

So how much should the block be milled to arrive at the desired deck height? Well, if your machinist happens to own a BHJ Products Blok-Tru fix-ture, the answer is easy. A Blok-Tru is a precisely machined steel plate that provides consistent reference points for block machining. Once registered in the main bearing saddles and camshaft bore, the Blok-Tru gives an automotive machinist two flat surfaces that are precisely 90 degrees apart. This allows him to set up his mill or

The head dowel pins must be removed from the block before surfacing begins. You can use a vise grips pliers or a punch; Kip prefers this slick Kent-Moore dowel puller that yanks the pins out in seconds.

grinder so that the block will be indexed perfectly, regardless of how slanted or cocked the deck surfaces might be as they came from the factory. Also, since the height of the Blok-Tru fixture is fixed, the machinist can measure from the deck surfaces of the block to the top of the fixture to determine just how much metal must be removed to produce the desired deck-height dimension.

It works like this. To compute the block height from the crank centerline to the deck surface, use the following formula:

**deck height +
piston compression height +
center-to-center rod length +
(crank stroke ÷ 2) = block height**

If you fill in the blanks using the typical dimensions of a 350ci Chevrolet, the numbers look like this:

**0.015 + 1.560 + 5.700 + (3.48÷2) =
9.0152**

This means that the block should measure 9.015 inches from the center of the crank to the deck surface. The BHJ Blok-Tru fixture measures 7.500 inches from the center of the bearing bores to its deck reference point. Subtracting this 7.500-inch figure from the desired block height of 9.015 inches leaves 1.515 inches. The machinist simply measures from the Blok-Tru to the deck surface, then mills the block until a micrometer reading taken from the deck to the fixture reads 1.515 inches. The result? The right deck height on the first try!

The Blok-Tru is a "state-of-the-art" machining fixture, and not every shop has one. Don't despair; there are other ways to come up with the right block height. A large micrometer can provide the answer. The desired block height dimension is computed as in the example above. Then the block is measured from the main bearing saddles to the deck surface. Adding one half the diameter of the main bearing bore gives the existing block height dimension. Subtract the desired block height from the present block height and you are left with the amount that must be machined

If the block height dimension – the distance from the crank centerline to the deck surface – has already been finalized, then the depth of the cut is easy to calculate. The fixture plate measures exactly 7.500-inch from the crankshaft centerline to the top edge. If the depth micrometer reads 1.500-inch from the deck to the fixture plate, then the total block height is 9.000 inch. The machinist can then compute how much material to remove to produce the required piston-to-head clearance.

off the deck surface. The only shortcoming of this method is that it does not allow the machinist to correct the angle of the decks if they are not at 90 degrees—although that may be a problem that only concerns the most fanatic engine blueprinters.

Finally, there is the do-it-yourself method that has been used by generations of engine builders. All it requires is a dial indicator or depth micrometer. First, the short block must be preassembled, using the same pistons, connecting rods, and crankshaft that will be installed in the engine. (If oversized pistons are used, the cylinders will have to be bored before the deck height can be checked.) Each piston is brought up to TDC, and then the distance from the deck surface to the piston top is carefully measured and recorded.

If the pistons have flat tops, this measurement should be taken at the center of the piston. Domed pistons require

The final step in decking the Chevrolet V-type block is to trim the intake manifold mating surface after both of the decks have been cut.

The block height can also be measured with a large micrometer or a specialized tool like this one. After setting the gauge with a standard, the distance from the main bearing saddle to the deck surface is measured as shown. The round ball provides an accurate reading against the curved main bearing bore.

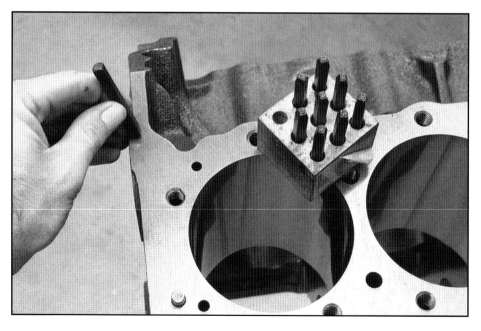

Record the final deck height dimension on the block with number punches. You can refer to this dimension years later when selecting head gaskets to provide the necessary piston-to-head clearance.

a little more effort, since the domes usually interfere with the depth micrometer. You'll have to measure the deck height on the flat part of the piston, which is called the *quench area.* To obtain an accurate deck height figure, rock the piston all the way over to one side and note the deck height. Then rock the piston to the other side and take a second measurement. The average of these two readings should be used as the piston deck height dimension.

Even if you don't have a depth micrometer or dial indicator, you can still check the piston deck heights with an acceptable degree of accuracy. Simply place several small balls of modeling clay on the piston quench surface, put a drop of oil on the clay to prevent it from sticking to the head, and rotate the crankshaft until the piston is halfway down its cylinder bore. Place a head gasket with the same thickness as the one you intend to use for final assembly on the deck surface; then install the head, and torque down the bolts. Rotate the crank through two revolutions, and then remove the cylinder head. The measured thickness of the compressed clay indicates the actual piston-to-head clearance.

The precise thickness of the head gaskets can be measured using a similar technique. It is important to know the compressed thickness of the particular type of head gasket you intend to use. Composition "sandwich" gaskets must be clamped between the head and block before the true compressed thickness can be determined. Similarly, the embossed beads on steel shim gaskets add slightly to the thickness, even after these gaskets have been compressed. To determine the compressed thickness, place the gasket on the block deck surface and then position a BB-size piece of lead shot on the block wherever a hole in the gasket exposes the deck surface beneath it. If there are no places where the deck surface is visible around the gasket, then cut a hole in the gasket. Install the cylinder head, torque the fasteners, and then remove the head. Measure the thickness of the compressed lead ball with a micrometer to learn exactly

The piston deck height and the compressed head gasket thickness determine the total piston-to-head clearance. Measure the deck height with a dial indicator and bridge as close to the center of the piston as possible. Then, take measurements at several points around the circumference of the piston as shown. Rock the piston back and forth to obtain the average deck height dimension.

how much the head gasket will compress under actual conditions.

After all the piston deck heights have been measured, you may notice a pattern. For example, the deck heights may increase from one end of the block to the other. This indicates that the deck surface is tapered. Another possibility is that the deck heights for two pistons that share the same crank throw may be noticeably higher or shorter than the other pistons; the crankshaft stroke on that particular throw may be the culprit. Occasionally one or two random pistons may be higher or lower than the rest. This usually means that the wrist pin holes were bored inaccurately, or that the center-to-center lengths of the corresponding connecting rods are too long or too short. Often these problems can be corrected by swapping connecting rods and pistons until the deck height readings are consistent.

After you have come up with a good match of pistons and rods, you can decide how much metal should be machined off the deck surfaces. For example, if the goal is a minimum deck height of 0.020-inch, and the existing heights range from 0.030- to 0.033-inch, then you would ask your machinist to

mill 0.010-inch off the deck of the block. And remember, the stock deck heights of the right and left cylinder banks of a V-type engine will vary

somewhat, so both must be measured and correspondingly larger or smaller cuts may be required.

You should expect some variation

To measure the compressed thickness of a head gasket, crush a piece of lead shot or modeling clay between the head and the block with the gasket in place, then measure the gasket's thickness with a micrometer.

Although grinders are not as common as mills, they can also produce good results. This Kwik-Way 860 surfacer is approximately the size of a small car, and considerably heavier.

Adapter rings allow the block fixture to be used with various main bearing diameters.

in *piston deck heights.* Most conscientious engine builders will accept a spread of 0.002- to 0.003-inch between the highest and lowest deck heights. It is difficult to get perfectly accurate deck height readings when rocking a piston, so this much variation falls within the range of normal measurement errors.

It's important, however, that none of the pistons have less than the minimum deck height needed for your particular engine. If you are cutting the piston-to-head clearance close, it is better to give away a little compression than risk letting the pistons hit the heads. Also remember that head gasket thicknesses

can vary several thousandths of an inch over a period of time (due to manufacturing tolerances).

Block surfacing machines fall into two general categories: mills and grinders. These types of equipment differ considerably in the way they remove material from the engine block. The

The block is leveled by measuring from the top of the grinder to the bar at both ends of the block.

The next step is to level the block from side-to-side. The grinding stone is perfectly parallel to the Blok-Tru when the indicator reading remains constant as it is moved across the top edge of the fixture plate.

As with the mill, the amount of metal to be removed is determined by measuring from the fixture to the top of the block. The grinder removes only a few thousandths of an inch of material with each pass, leaving an extremely smooth surface.

mills have a large rotating wheel that is outfitted with several dozen sharp cutting tools. The grinders, in contrast, use a heavy abrasive stone that literally wears away the deck surface. The weight and mass of the machinery is important in both types of surfacers. Making a perfectly flat cut over the two-foot span of an engine block demands an extremely rigid and precise tool. Among machinists, the Storm-Vulcan Blockmaster is generally the top-rated mill, while the Kwik-Way 860 gets the high marks among grinders. You may encounter other types of milling machines in your search for a good machinist, but beware of light-weight surfacers. The small equipment simply can't produce the consistent, high quality results that careful blue-printing demands.

Mills and grinders produce distinctive finishes on the deck surfaces. Assuming that the cutting bits of a mill are sharp and properly aligned, the surface finish left by the cutting wheel will be slightly rough. A grinder, in contrast, produces a surface that is so smooth it seems to be almost polished. The grinder removes material very slowly, typically only 0.002-inch or so of metal on each pass. Mills can take much larger cuts, although the final pass is usually a clean-up run that removes only 0.002- to 0.005-inch of metal. There is some controversy about which is the "better" surface finish. Machinists who prefer mills point out that the slight texture left by the cutters gives the metal microscopic "teeth" to grip the head gasket. Advocates of grinding contend that the smooth finish left by their technique maximizes surface contact between the block and head gasket.

BLOCK FILLING

In some street applications and in some race engines, the water jackets in an engine block are filled with a liquid material that hardens after it is poured in. These block fillers can help strengthen cylinder barrels and reduce cylinder distor-

tion, which in turn improves ring seal and engine power. The hardened block filler supports the lower half of the cylinder barrels. Street operated motors can be "half filled" allowing some coolant to circulate through the block. Motors are usually filled up to the lower edge of the water pump core passages, but some are filled right up to beneath the block decks leaving little room for coolant circulation through the block. The weight of the block filler material is offset by the weight of the coolant it displaces from the block. The filler has expansion properties similar to cast iron so that the filler stays put. Block filling isn't for everyone, but can be used in motors with high levels of power, alcohol motors, and some motors with thin cylinder barrel walls, all in an attempt to reduce barrel distortion and improve ring seal.

If you decide to fill your block, you need to do it after the block has been thoroughly cleaned and before the block is bored.

Patterson & Martin Machine uses this block-mounted boring bar. Since the deck surfaces have already been milled parallel to the crank, the block-mounted bar will bore cylinders perpendicular to the crankshaft centerline.

BORING

Overboring the cylinders is one of the most common automotive machine operations. It is also the task most often bungled. During a typical "quickie rebuild" the machinist sets up a boring bar on the block, centers the cutter on

After the block has been surfaced, it must be leveled in the boring stand. The dial indicator must move across the deck surface without a change in the reading.

This Kwik-Way machine at Hollum's Racing Engines supports the block by the main bearing saddles; the boring head mounts on a flat work table above the block.

Hollum's inserts brass shims between the block and the support bar to level the block under the boring bar.

Three equally spaced pins align the tool spindle with the center of the existing cylinder bore.

the existing cylinder bore, and then quickly enlarges the cylinder diameter to within a hair of its final size. In engine blueprinting, however, each one of these steps must be done carefully and thoughtfully. After all, it is the "*roundness*" and the "*straightness*" of the bores that determines how well the cylinders will be sealed.

There are two common types of boring equipment. The first mounts on the deck surface of the block while the second attaches to the main bearing saddles of the block. Regardless of which kind of machine is used, the objective is to bore the cylinders exactly perpendicular to the crankshaft centerline. In theory, if the deck surfaces have been machined parallel to the crankshaft centerline, then a block-mounted machine should bore the cylinders perpendicular to the crankshaft. As with many machining operations, the skill and care of the operator counts as much as the type of equipment he uses.

When a cylinder is bored, the cutting tool leaves a rough surface on the

cylinder wall. Even the sharpest machine tool produces tiny rips and tears in the metal. This is why the machinist does not bore the cylinder to the final finished diameter. Instead, he intentionally bores the cylinder slightly smaller than the desired final diameter. For example, if a block were to have a finished cylinder diameter that is 0.030-inch oversize, then the machinist would bore the cylinders only 0.024-inch oversize. The remaining 0.006-inch of mate-

rial will be removed during the honing operation. This effectively eliminates the tiny pits and gouges left by the tool bit of the boring machine.

The traditional way to overbore an engine block is to center the cutting tool in the existing cylinder bore. This is not always the best location for the cylinder, however. A block with core shift (the casting cores were misaligned slightly when the block was cast) may have thin walls on one side of the cylin-

A micrometer gauge sets the diameter of the cutting tool. The cylinder is bored to within 0.010/0.006-inch of the final bore diameter; the remaining material will be removed with a cylinder hone.

If sonic testing reveals that the cylinder wall is thin on one side of the bore, the cylinder can be offset bored by placing a shim under the boring bar centering pin. The amount of offset is limited by how much the bore is being enlarged, since the boring tool must remain in continuous contact with the cylinder wall.

The final step in the boring operation is to lightly chamfer the top of the cylinder with a 60-degree tool or sanding drum. This makes the piston ring installation easier and eliminates bloodshed caused by the sharp edges of the cylinder.

The sharp edge at the top of the block can disrupt airflow in the combustion chamber. The cylinder bore should be notched or chamfered to match the chamber contour.

Semi-finished heavy-duty blocks have rough-bored cylinders when they leave the factory. Since these bores are not accurately located, a fixture like this BHJ Bor-Tru must be used to position the boring bar when preparing one of these racing blocks. The Bor-Tru plate properly locates the dowel pins and cylinder bores in relation to the other critical block dimensions.

ders, as described in the section on sonic testing. In these instances, you may want to instruct the machinist to *offset bore* the cylinders. Using the "map" of cylinder wall thicknesses produced during sonic testing, a sharp machinist can actually relocate the centerline of the cylinder slightly. Inserting a shim

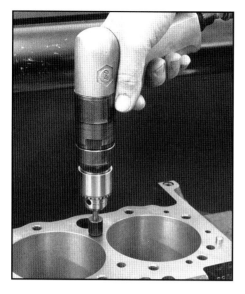

Before honing the block, chamfer the top thread of the head bolt holes with a 60-degree countersink.

Block threads should be cleaned with a bottoming tap to ensure accurate torque readings.

Install freeze plugs in the block before honing the cylinder walls; a socket and short extension work well to drive the soft plugs into place.

between the cylinder wall and the centering pins of the boring machine can cause the cutter to remove more metal from one side of the bore than the other. Naturally, there are limits to how far the bore can be moved; but in building a maximum effort engine no advantage can be overlooked.

The arrival of "racing-only" blocks from the automakers presents a new challenge to machinists. The Chevrolet Bow Tie (high-performance) small-and big-block castings, for example, have rough-finished cylinder bores. This allows the engine builder to bore/hone to stock or over-size bore diameters and

still maintain the thickest possible cylinder walls, but it also presents some problems. The cylinder bores in these semi-finished Bow Tie blocks are not accurately located, so a special fixture is required to put the holes where they belong when the block is finished. Most shops use BHJ Products' Bor-Tru for this important chore. The Bor-Tru plate bolts to the deck surface, providing an accurate reference point for locating the cylinder bores and head-dowel holes. This fixture locates the cylinders from the crankshaft thrust surface, ensuring that the cylinders are precisely centered over the crank throws.

The final step in boring a block is to

Examined under a microscope, the freshly bored cylinder wall has a jagged, torn surface left by the boring bar bit. The honing operation must remove enough material to reach the undisturbed block metal.

lightly chamfer the tops of the cylinder bore. This can be done with either a conical sanding drum or a 60-degree cutting tool inserted in the boring machine. Breaking the sharp edge at the top of the bore prevents damage to the honing stones, and allows the piston rings to slip into the bore more easily during final engine assembly.

HONING

Honing is both an art and a science. Certainly a great deal of the credit for recent improvements in engine performance is due to advances in cylinder wall preparation. The engine produces power because of the pressure exerted on the piston tops by the expanding gases in the cylinders. If less of this pressure escapes past the piston rings, more usable power will be produced. This means that the cylinder bores must be as *round* and as *straight* as possible. Careful honing makes the difference.

If you examine a cylinder wall under a microscope, after it has been bored, you will find hundreds of jagged peaks and valleys left by the boring tool. During honing, these irregularities are cut away, leaving a smooth, uniform finish. During the honing process, radial pressure is exerted against a series of rotating abrasive "stones" that are continuously passed back and forth through the bore. The bonding agent in the stones breaks down, exposing fresh abrasive, and a constant stream of honing oil flushes away particles of the cylinder wall and worn abrasive.

If the stones simply skim across the surface of the metal without cutting, they will lay over the tiny peaks of metal left by the boring tool. This is called *burnishing*, and it should be avoided at all costs. A cylinder that has been burnished will wear out piston rings very quickly and can destroy the piston skirts in short order. But a competent machinist can easily avoid this problem by selecting the proper grade of abrasive stones and correctly adjusting the pressure applied to the stones.

The optimum surface finish on the cylinder walls depends on the type of piston compression rings that will be used. The two most common ring face materials are chrome and molybdenum. Chrome-plated compression rings have an extremely hard surface that is resistant to abrasion caused by dirt. The chrome plating is uniform (microscopic cracks account for only about 2 percent of the surface area); and the hard, smooth surface of a chrome compression ring requires a relatively rough cylinder wall finish. Most piston ring manufacturers specify 280-grit finishing stones for use with chrome-plated rings. The small grooves left in the cylinder walls by these relatively rough stones provide important oil reservoirs that lubricate the ring face.

Compression rings faced with molybdenum can use a much finer wall finish. Approximately 20 percent of the surface area of a moly-coated ring is made up of tiny voids that effectively trap lubricant; and because of this "micro porous" surface, it is possible to use very fine finishing stones. Also, moly rings are lapped in long metal cylinders during manufacturing, so they require virtually no break-in period. For these reasons, cylinder walls are often finished with 400-grit honing stones when moly rings will be installed. In fact, many builders of all-out racing engines prefer "mirror finish" cylinder walls for moly rings. To produce these extremely smooth finishes, the final honing passes may be made with cork-bonded stones designed for honing aluminum cylinder blocks (linerless) or with 400- or 600-grit wet-or-dry sandpaper wrapped around the hone stones.

HONING WITH TORQUE PLATES

Even though an engine block seems to be a rigid mass, in fact, it is quite elastic. A decade ago, engine builders discovered that they could increase engine output by honing the block with *torque plates* bolted to the deck surfaces. A torque plate is simply a two-inch-thick slab of metal that simulates the distortion created when the heads are torqued down. The force exerted by the cylinder-head fasteners (whether bolts or studs) pulls the bores out-of-round when the heads are mounted to the block. For example, a cylinder surrounded by five head bolts will be pulled into a pentangle shape when the heads are torqued up tight. The effect isn't great, but it is measurable. And

Any block destined for racing or high-performance applications should be honed with torque plates. Thick steel plates simulate distortion of the bores, which occurs when the cylinder heads are installed. Use the same type of head gasket when plate honing that you intend to use when assembling the engine.

The goal of plate honing is to recreate the conditions that are present when the heads are torqued on the block. Stands under the head bolts allow fasteners to stretch just as they do when clamping the head in place. The bolts should be tightened to recommended torque specifications.

Since different types of bolts have different elasticities, use the same bolts when plate honing that you plan to use when assembling the engine. The bolts should extend as far through the torque plate as they do through the cylinder head. Adding and removing washers under the fasteners adjusts the thread engagement.

A 1/2-inch drill, a Sunnen hand hone, and a selection of stones are all that's required to hone a block at home. An accurate dial bore gauge will make it easy to check the progress of your work.

since the top of the bore is where the cylinder seal is most important during the compression and power strokes, anything an engine builder can do to improve the effectiveness of the seal will increase horsepower.

When a block is honed with torque plates, a head gasket should be used between the block and plate. If you plan on using a composition head gasket, then make sure that you (or your machinist) install the same type and thickness of composition gasket between the torque plate and cylinder head. The same goes for steel shim gaskets—use the same type and thickness that will be installed when the engine is assembled for the final time.

Remember, the object is to duplicate the same stresses and distortions during honing that will be present when the engine is running.

Some engine builders go to elaborate lengths to simulate these forces. For example, they will bolt engine mounts to the sides of blocks, water pump housings to the front, and bell housings to the back. Some even circulate hot water through the coolant packages while honing the cylinder bores! In some classes of competition, such as Stock Eliminator drag-racing where attention to detail separates the winners from the losers, such practices may be somewhat justified. For most applications, though, these efforts are probably overkill.

HAND HONING

We mentioned earlier that honing was partially an art, partially a science. The artistic side of honing is most apparent when a cylinder block is honed by hand. Before automatic honing machines were developed, all cylinder blocks were finished with hand-held hones. And it takes a lot of practice and a sensitive touch to feel a slight taper in a cylinder bore. This human element is precisely why some engine builders prefer to hone by hand. The results can rival anything done by a high-dollar automated hone!

The equipment required for hand honing is not elaborate. A hone is a necessity, obviously, and so is a honing tank. The honing tank can be any container large enough to accommodate an engine block—old bathtubs and sheet metal basins have been used with success. The tank is filled with several gallons of honing oil, which a pump circulates through a filter and sprays into the cylinder during the honing procedure. A selection of fine- and medium-grit stones will also be required, and a dial bore gauge is needed to check the results.

However, honing a block by hand is a tedious task. If the block was bored properly, there will be 0.004- to 0.006-inch of metal left to remove from each cylinder to reach the final bore size. The usual progression for conventional moly-faced piston rings would be to use 280-grit (AN 500) stones to enlarge the cylinder to within 0.0015-inch of the final diameter. The next 0.001-inch of metal would be removed with 400-grit (M27-J85) stones, and the last 0.0005 with 500-grit (M27-J95) stones.

The final passes with 600-grit (MM33-CO5) extra-fine stones—or with sandpaper wrapped around the stone set—remove a negligible amount of material, but do provide the desired mirror finish on the cylinder walls. At several points in the process the cylinder must be measured carefully with the

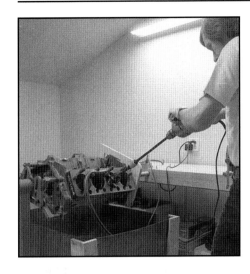

A sheet metal box, a plastic shipping crate, or even an old bathtub can be pressed into service as a honing tank. An electric pump circulates and filters five gallons of Sunnen honing oil. The cylinders should be constantly flushed with oil to wash away abrasive grit as the honing stones wear.

A Sunnen CK-10 Cylinder King automatic hone has become standard equipment in high-performance machine shops. Here Kip adjusts the pressure applied to the honing stones and sets the length of the hone stroke.

dial bore gauge to check for taper (from top to bottom) and for any signs that the cylinder is not finishing to a perfectly round shape. It's no wonder that precision honing a V-8 block can be an all-day job!

Very few professional machinists can justify devoting this much time to a customer engine, which is why close tolerance hand honing is becoming a lost art. The cost of a complete hand honing setup (including a 1/2-inch or larger drill motor to spin the hone) is a tiny fraction of the price of an automatic hone. Depending on the going rate for a professional hone job (with torque plates and all), it may pay you to invest in the equipment needed for honing at home, especially if you plan on blueprinting engines regularly.

AUTOMATIC HONING

It is unlikely that many readers will rush out to purchase a $20,000 automatic hone after digesting this section, but understanding the honing procedure may give you an insight into what your machinist is doing with your precious engine block. The Sunnen CK-10

Honing stone selection is essential for a proper cylinder wall finish and a good ring seal. Molybdenum piston rings work best with a super-fine finish, while chrome-plated rings require a relatively rough surface. Like sandpaper, honing stones are available in a variety of grits. Progressively finer stones are used as the bore size approaches the final diameter.

An automatic hone eliminates tedious hours of hand honing. A metal bar inserted through the main bearing saddles clamps the block in place; the block can then be raised and lowered with a hand crank. Note the stepped torque plate, which eliminates the need for spacers under the long head bolts.

The Sunnen CK-10 floods the stones and cylinder walls with filtered honing fluid to carry away grit and metal particles as the bore is enlarged. The hone automatically strokes up and down to produce the desired crosshatch pattern.

A micrometer fixture adjusts the dial bore gauge to read zero when the cylinder bore is at the desired final diameter (including piston-to-wall clearance).

Bores are constantly checked for "taper" or "bell mouthing" during the honing operation by measuring the diameter at the top and the bottom of the cylinder. The Sunnen dial bore gauge is marked in 0.0005-inch increments; this hole has no measurable taper.

If the cylinder bore is too small at the bottom, the CK-10 operator can press the "Dwell" button, which signals the hone to make an extra revolution at the bottom of the bore on each stroke. The load meter on the automatic hone indicates the pressure against the stones. By reducing the pressure on the final strokes, the machinist can produce an extremely fine surface finish – but he must be careful not to "burnish" the cylinder walls by applying too light a load.

A slight crosshatch pattern should be visible in the finished cylinder wall surface. These microscopic grooves retain oil to lubricate the ring faces during the break-in.

Cylinder King is the standard of the industry, and the machine you are most likely to encounter in a well-equipped shop. The CK-10 gives its operator complete control over the stroke and pressure of the honing stones. By watching a load meter on the machine, he can quickly detect whether the bore is bell-mouthed on the top or tight at the bottom. The CK-10's recirculating pump provides a virtual flood of honing oil to wash away block material and used abrasive, and there is an enormous selection of stone sizes and grits available. An important feature for a professional machinist is the speed with which a complete engine block can be honed on the CK-10. A cylinder bore that may demand an hour to hone properly by hand can be finished in a matter of minutes on a Sunnen machine.

As with hand honing, the stone grits become progressively finer as the cylinder bore is made larger. For example, Kip Martin, who is pictured on page 46 with his trusty CK-10, starts by bringing the bore to within 0.001- to 0.0015-inch of the final diameter with EHU-525 stones, maintaining a 40 percent reading on the load meter. Then he switches to finer JHU-625 stones and hones at slightly less pressure until the cylinder is within 0.0005-inch of the intended diameter.

The last bit of bore stock is removed with a JHU-800 stone, at a relatively light 20 percent load. If the customer has specified a mirror finish, the last six strokes are made with ultra-fine cork-bonded stones normally used for finishing Vega silicon/aluminum blocks. Our second consulting machinist, Larry Hollum, follows the same general plan, although his choice of stones varies slightly. Also, when the engine will be used in a racecar or when extra effort is invested to gain maximum ring life and seal, he prefers to use an assortment of 400-or 600-grit wet-or-dry sandpaper for the final finish.

O-RINGING BLOCKS AND HEADS

O-ringing the block and head deck is not appropriate for every application. However, if you are planning a very high output motor with high cylinder pressures, deck O-rings around each cylinder barrel can help seal the cylinders. Head gasket failure may become a problem with large amounts of nitrous oxide or in extreme blower or turbo applications.

To O-ring, a skilled machinist cuts shallow grooves around the cylinder barrels in the block deck or head deck, and then inserts a wire into the groove. The groove depth and wire are sized so that when inserted, part of the wire will extend above the deck. A solid copper head gasket is used so that when the head

Wrapping 400/600-grit wet-or-dry sandpaper around the honing stones for the final strokes produces a super-fine wall finish. This last step is usually reserved for maximum-effort racing engines.

is bolted to the block, the wire O-rings are imbedded into the head gasket. In a variation of this, matching grooves are machined into the head deck only, and then a "Loc Wire" composition style gasket, available from Fel-Pro, is used. This Fel-Pro gasket features raised wire rings built into the gasket that surround each cylinder barrel. As of late 2004, the "Loc Wire" gaskets are available for Buick V-6, Ford 302/351W, and small-block and big-block Chevy V-8s.

BLOCK PAINTING

Painting the inside of an engine is strictly a matter of personal preference. On the plus side, painting the block helps to seal the surface and trap any tiny particles of grit that might have escaped the cleaning process. Also, it is easier to spot small metal flakes in a painted block, and picking up bits of used gasket material is simpler. A painted block may help the oil return to the pan more quickly, although this is a debatable point.

There are, however, two definite drawbacks to painting the inside of the block. First, the metal surfaces must be scrupulously clean or the paint will not stick. Paint chips can clog an oil pump pickup or oil filter element, so it is important that the paint stay where it

The block surface must be scrupulously clean before painting begins. The paint seals the pores in the metal and may speed oil return to the sump.

belongs. Also, painting an engine block properly is quite time-consuming. To do the job right, all the machined surfaces—lifter bores, main bearing saddles, cylinders, etc.—must be carefully masked. Currently most professional engine builders feel that the minor advantages of painting the interior of a block hardly justify the considerable work required to do the job correctly.

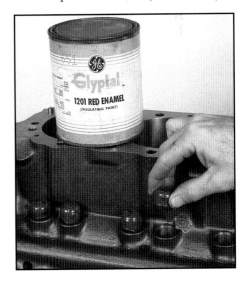

It takes a tough paint to survive inside an engine block. Glyptal and armature winding paints are highly resistant to acids and oils. Rubber plugs used on metal chair legs are useful for masking the lifter bores.

Restrictor plugs limit the oil reaching the lifters and rocker arms in Chevrolet V-8s; they should only be used with solid lifters and roller rocker arms.

RESTRICTING OIL PASSAGES

An engine block that is destined for the racetrack can often benefit from restricting certain oil passages. Racing rocker arms outfitted with roller-bearing trunnions require much less lubrication than conventional rockers. The oil that would normally be pumped to the rocker arms can be redirected to the main bearings, where it will do a lot more good. There are several ways to accomplish this in Chevrolet V-8s. In production big-block and small-block Chevys, the oil passages that feed the lifter galleries are 0.250-inch in diameter.

Moroso and other manufacturers sell oil restrictor plugs to limit the flow of oil to the top end. These are 0.3125-inch (5/16) socket head set screws with 0.060-inch holes drilled through the centers. If you have a drill press, you can make similar restrictor plugs in five minutes.

This modification is quite simple. The oil passages leading from the rear cam bearing are tapped and the restric-

Drain holes in the small-block Chevy lifter valley are blocked with 1/4-inch pipe plugs to prevent oil from splashing on the spinning crankshaft assembly. Note the debris screens over the drainback holes behind the lifter bores.

tor plugs can be inserted through the gallery openings in the block. Or, you can buy special gallery plugs (Moroso types shown here) that have extensions that seat inside the gallery passage, restricting the amount of oil admitted to the gallery. These restrictors can simply be screwed into the block in place of the standard 0.250-inch pipe plugs.

Please note that this is a modification intended only for engines equipped with roller-mounted rocker arms and solid or roller lifters. Since the amount of oil reaching the lifters and rockers is cut to the bare minimum, there is not enough lubrication supply for hydraulic-type lifters or stock ball-pivot rocker arms.

Even if you have limited the oil reaching the top end, there is still a significant volume of oil that eventually must find its way back to the pan. In a small-block Chevrolet, much of this

lubricant drains back through holes drilled alongside the lifter bores. It drips onto the spinning camshaft, which in turn flings the droplets onto the rotating crank assembly. While splash lubrication is useful, it is to be discouraged in a racing engine because all those oil droplets slinging around cause windage losses, which is a fancy name for less horsepower. Fortunately, Chevrolet drilled these oil drainback holes just the right size to accommodate a 0.250-inch pipe tap. Simply thread the holes and screw in a handful of pipe plugs. Forever after, the oil will have to return to the crank via the front cover and rear oil drain.

DEBRIS SCREENS

One fact of life for everyone who builds or races engines is that eventually something is going to break. It is unavoidable—or you're not going to win many races—and the best way to prepare for this certainty is to make sure that whatever fails does not take the rest of the motor with it. Valvetrain components are usually the most fragile pieces inside an engine. When springs, rockers, or pushrods give up, the debris can circulate throughout the engine, causing further damage. Many engine builders epoxy wire screens over the oil drainback holes to catch broken pieces before they can reach the oil pump or crankshaft assembly. You can buy kits that include pre-formed screens and epoxy, or you can make them yourself in an afternoon. Just be certain that the block surface is absolutely clean before apply-

Wire screen epoxied over webs in the big-block Chevrolet lifter valley catches the broken valvetrain parts before they can cause further damage.

ing the epoxy. If the screens break loose they can cause as much damage as the pieces they were meant to catch!

ROD AND CRANK CLEARANCE

If the engine will be assembled with a stock-stroke crankshaft and the original factory connecting rods, then interference between the rods, crank, and cylinder block will not be a problem. If, however, you have opted for a stroker crank or aftermarket connecting rods, chances are that they are going to hit the block someplace. The most likely locations for this collision are the oil-pan rail and the bottom of the cylinder bores. The only way to find out with certainty exactly where there is insufficient clearance is to install the crank assembly. Of course, if you plan to use oversize pistons, this will have to wait until after the block has been bored. But, hold off on honing the cylinder bores until *after* the crank and rod clearance has been checked. This will prevent ruining the cylinder wall finish if you should slip with the hand grinder!

The amount of metal to be ground away depends on how far you have strayed from the stock components. Aluminum rods, for example, are much bulkier on their big ends than most steel rods, and will require more grinding before the crank can turn without interference. Usually the rod bolt heads are the biggest offenders.

If you can slide a 0.050-inch-diameter drill bit between the block and the connecting rods, the clearance is adequate.

When you need more operating clearance the best approach is to grind just enough material off the block so the crank assembly can rotate without interference. Then go back over the areas you have ground and cut away enough metal to allow a 0.050-inch drill bit to slide between the block and the connecting rods or crankshaft. This provides enough "running clearance" to prevent collisions when the pieces start whipping around at high rpm.

Whenever you are cutting on a cylinder block there is always the danger of hitting water. Some heavy-duty castings, like the Chevrolet Bow Tie blocks, have coolant passages relocated to reduce the chances of breaking through into the water jacket. With a standard production block though, you are on your own. The problem becomes most acute when using a long-stroke crankshaft with aftermarket connecting rods. In these instances, you may need to direct some of the metal-removal efforts to the rotating assembly. For example, the bolts on the connecting rods can be ground down slightly, and the bottom of the connecting rods can be profiled to reduce interference problems. These tactics can be risky, though, since you may be weakening highly stressed components. When Chevrolet engineers expanded the small-block V-8 to 400 cubic inches, they were forced to redesign the connecting rods to accept shorter bolts. The 400's poor reputation for durability was one result of this decision. You can learn from this, and use caution and common sense when it comes time to make all the parts fit in the engine.

OIL HOLE ALIGNMENT

The block preparation regimen must include a thorough check to

Long stroke crankshafts and racing connecting rods may require extra block clearance at the bottom of the cylinder bores and the oil pan rail. The grinding marks should be polished out to remove stress risers.

Make sure that all oil passages in the block are unobstructed. Use a long drill bit to remove burrs and to open up undersize holes.

Here's an example of the extreme block clearancing required to build a 600-cubic-inch Pro Stock motor! Water passages are relocated in the Chevrolet heavy-duty Bow Tie block to allow such extensive grinding.

Enlarge the holes in the bearing inserts if they are not aligned with the oil passages in the block.

ensure the proper alignment between the oil holes in the block and the main bearing inserts. In most engines, the oil passages in the bearing saddles are larger than the holes in the bearing inserts, which helps compensate for any small mismatch. The rear main bearings on Chevrolet V-8s deserve special attention, since the oil holes intersect the bearing bores at an angle. You may need to elongate the hole in either the block or the bearing shell to gain an unimpeded flow of oil. Some engine builders advocate enlarging the oil holes in the bearings to match the passages in the block. Although this is not really necessary in most applications, make sure that you thoroughly deburr the bearings if you decide to open up these holes. Also, check that machining chips or other obstructions do not block the oil passages. In some early Chevy small-blocks, the holes between the main oil gallery and the camshaft gallery are only 0.1875-inch (3/16) in diameter; use a long 0.250-inch drill bit to open these passages until they match the size of the holes connecting the camshaft gallery to the main bearings.

BLOCK CLEANING

When all the machining, honing, and grinding is finally done, it's time to wash the block. The object of this exercise is to remove all the grit, dirt, and machining chips that have accumulated in the block during the blueprinting process. To do the job properly you must scour the block with solvent and hot, soapy water. This is definitely a

It takes gallons of solvent, soap, and hot water to scrub a block clean before assembly. Pressure sprayers and stiff brushes will help dislodge the grit and machining chips.

Cylinder bores should be absolutely spotless before assembly begins. Protect them from rust while washing, and then clean them with automatic transmission fluid and paper towels.

High-Tech Coatings

In recent years, the use of high-tech coatings on parts has grown and become available to anyone. Various types of coatings are used and perform different functions. Some coatings help prevent the migration of heat and others reduce friction or corrosion. There are coatings that help a part shed oil in an effort to reduce crankcase windage. Some coatings are used on ferrous metals such as cast iron or steel, while other coatings are used on non-ferrous parts such as aluminum. A number of coatings actually penetrate the surface of the material, while some coatings are added to the surface of the part and do not penetrate the surface.

There are some power gains to be had with these coatings. The main advantages, however, seem to be resistance to corrosion and heat-caused fatigue. The fatigue strength of parts is increased because many of the coatings reduce the absorption of heat and reflect it away from the surfaces. Let me give you some common application examples. Exhaust tube headers can be coated both inside and out to reduce corrosion, smooth surfaces, and pick-up efficiency. Piston tops are coated to reflect heat back into the combustion chamber and to help keep the piston tops cooler. Piston skirts are treated to a different coating that can reduce friction on the skirts and cylinder walls. Valve head surfaces and combustion chambers can be coated to reflect heat into the chamber and reduce heat absorption. Crank counterweights and connecting rods can be coated with an oil-shedding surface to help reduce windage. The bottoms of intake manifolds can be coated to reduce heat absorption and help prevent engine heat from migrating to the intake runners and induction. Using a coating that reduces heat absorption can increase valve spring life.

One thing to keep in mind is that some coatings penetrate the surface of the part being coated, while some coatings are applied to the outside surface of the part. Outside coatings may increase the dimensions of the parts and affect the clearances used during the blueprinting and assembly of the engine. In addition, if the part was coated with reduced heat absorption in mind, the part may not expand as much when heated as an uncoated part. You may then be able to reduce the clearance used.

Make sure that you speak with the coating manufacturer about clearance changes that may be possible or advantageous. Some parts may be available already coated; others require that you ship the part to them for processing. Most companies offer a very quick turnaround on parts shipped to them. There are even some coatings that can be applied by the end user.

These Hooker "Super Competition" tube headers are available with ceramic coatings, which tolerate high temperatures, resist corrosion, scratches, chipping, and flaking, and are very easy on the eyes.

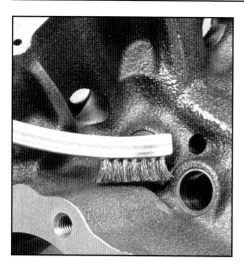

Scour new block surfaces with a stiff wire brush to loosen the casting sand.

chore that is best left for a hot afternoon, because you are going to be drenched by the time the job is completed.

Throughout the block washing process, care must be taken to prevent the machined surfaces from rusting. It is extremely important to protect the cylinder bores against corrosion. When the walls have been scrubbed clean, they can develop a layer of oxidation in an instant unless they are immediately sprayed with a rust-inhibiting agent (like WD-40). If you can enlist an assistant, the block-washing chores are more likely to be successful. One member of the cleaning team can spray the metal surfaces with the rust inhibitor, while the other follows up with paper towels and compressed air.

A large, paved driveway is an ideal place to wash the engine block. You'll need access to a supply of hot water. Attach a garden hose to a laundry sink or kitchen faucet. Open the cold-water tap, then increase the flow of hot water until it reaches the desired temperature.

Be careful. Hot tap water may exceed 160 F degrees! Hot water is good for washing, but tap water can be hot enough to scald human skin. An air compressor, although not a necessity, will make drying the block much easier. In a pinch, you can even use a vacuum cleaner with the hose attached to the exhaust so that it blows hot air.

You will also need a bucket, laundry detergent, an assortment of scrub

brushes, paper towels, and a spray can of rust inhibitor. A solvent gun or a high-pressure sprayer designed for washing cars is helpful for blasting out the oil passages.

The local do-it-yourself car wash is a good place to wash a grimy block. These car washes usually have high-pressure sprayers that do a fine job of blasting away machining grit.

However, the one drawback to cleaning your block at a car wash is the lack of compressed air to dry it thoroughly. Unless you have a portable air compressor and a source of electricity, you must spray down the cleaned block with rust inhibitor oil or automatic transmission fluid to prevent it from rusting until you can get it back home to your garage.

Both Mr. Gasket and Moroso Performance sell brush kits specifically designed for cleaning engine components. A selection of brushes with various bristle diameters is useful for dislodging dirt from the nooks, crannies, and oil passages. Long-handled rifle cleaning brushes are well suited for cleaning out deep oil galleries. Interchangeable brushes are available for bore sizes ranging from 0.22-caliber rifles to huge shotgun barrels.

Begin the cleaning by dousing the block with solvent. Using a stiff brush, scrub every part of the block that you can reach to loosen the metal filings and grinding dust that has accumulated. If you have a solvent sprayer, blow out the oil galleries, lifter bores, and cylinder bores.

Don't scrub the cylinders yet, since the grit may scratch the wall finish. If you are cleaning the block on an asphalt driveway, protect the pavement with a drip pan to prevent the solvent from breaking down the asphalt.

The next step is to scrub the block with soap and water. Dissolve several cups of laundry detergent in a pail of hot water, and prepare to get wet. Once you begin scrubbing an iron block you must keep it constantly wet to prevent rust from forming on the machined surfaces. While your partner directs a steady stream of hot water on the block you should scour the block

with stiff brushes.

Then clean out the lifter bores and oil passages with the small diameter brushes. After the rest of the block has been cleaned, wash the cylinder bores with a soft rag soaked in soapy water. When you have cleaned the entire casting, rinse off the soap, and get ready to start drying.

Rust will begin to form the instant that your partner stops spraying the block! Immediately begin coating the cylinder walls with oil or a rust inhibitor. The oil solution will cause the water to bead up and run off the wall surface. Flip the block over and spray the main bearing saddles and the lifter bores. Once these machined surfaces have been protected, you can start drying the block with compressed air (or your reverse-flow vacuum cleaner). Spray the remainder of the block with rust inhibitor to prevent rust forming on the rough casting.

After you have blown off all the water droplets, check your work by running your finger over the block surface. Pay special attention to the places where dirt and grit can hide on the block, such as underneath the oil pan rail and in the corners of the cam gallery. If you can still find casting sand, abrasive, or grinding dust on your fingertip, the block must be cleaned again. It may require two or three sessions before a freshly machined block will pass the fingertip test.

After the block has been cleaned to your satisfaction, the cylinder walls still require further attention. Removing the last traces of honing abrasive is an important step in ensuring long ring life and good cylinder seal. Saturate a paper towel with automatic-transmission fluid (ATF) and scour each cylinder wall thoroughly. The ATF will loosen tiny particles of abrasive; they will be apparent as dark spots on the towel.

Keep scrubbing until a fresh paper towel wetted with transmission fluid shows no traces of dirt when it is rubbed against the cylinder wall. When all the cylinders pass this test, coat them with clean motor oil to prevent rust, and cover the block with a plastic trash bag while you work on the other engine components.

CRANKSHAFT

The crankshaft is the most highly stressed component in an engine. It converts the frantic up-and-down motion of the pistons into a rotating force that can be readily harnessed to move the car forward. Every ounce of torque travels through the crankshaft, while the pistons do their best to alternately push the crank out through the bottom of the oil pan and pull it toward the cylinder heads. Is it any wonder that the crankshaft warrants your attention during a thorough engine blueprinting?

SELECTION AND INSPECTION

During the Sixties, you could be almost certain that any high-performance engine had a *forged steel* crankshaft. This is no longer the case. Because of manufacturing and raw material costs, the automakers have adopted *cast iron* crankshafts. A forging has a much denser molecular structure and a grain pattern that flows through the crank much like the grain in wood. A casting, in contrast, has a random pattern of molecules, and may have microscopic

holes or "voids." Obviously for high-performance applications, a forged steel crankshaft is superior. If forgings are available for your engine, it's worthwhile to hunt one down.

So how do you spot a forging when you find one? Simple. Look for the forging marks. As the photos on page 55 point out, a cast iron crank has a very distinct *parting line*. This is formed where the two halves of the mold meet. Compressing the metal under extreme heat and pressure, in contrast, creates a forging. The die marks left by this

You may have to go on a scavenger hunt to find a suitable crankshaft core. Shops that specialize in crankshaft repairs are usually good sources, since they buy used cranks in quantity. Most late-model motors are equipped with cast iron cranks because of the higher production costs of forged cranks. You're more likely to find a steel crank in an engine manufactured during the Sixties.

Stroker Motors

The use of longer stroke crankshafts to build larger cubic inch motors is fairly common, even in street driven vehicles. A longer stroke not only increases engine size, but it also can alter where power is made in the rpm range. Mopar, Ford, and GM V-8 motors offer a number of production crank interchanges that make longer strokes possible in production size blocks. For the most part, these stroke increases are fairly easy and economical. Just use the appropriate rod length and piston pin height in order to arrive at the available total block deck height.

You can calculate how much block deck height you will need by dividing the stroke length in half and adding the rod center-to-center length and the piston pin height to get the total block deck height needed. The piston deck-to-block deck clearance (if any) can also be added to this formula.

The block may need special attention when you increase the crank stroke or use longer rods or beefy aluminum rods, because there may not be enough room for the rotating assembly. Some machining or grinding on a production style block can be done, but only up to a certain point. Block water jackets, oil galleries, cam tunnels, cam lobes, and oil pan rails (on the block or oil pan) may limit the amount of clearance you can safely add.

GM, Ford, Mopar, and a number of aftermarket companies offer race blocks, which often make it much easier to build and clearance "mega" cubic inch motors. Small-block and big-block versions are available with many features that are not

This Chevy Bow Tie aluminum small-block can be used to build 430+ cubic inches, and offers a considerable weight savings over a cast iron version.

Buying a complete rotating assembly (like this Lunati set) is a good idea when you're building a stroker motor. Matched parts help you avoid problems with bob weight and interference between parts.

found on production bare blocks. Aluminum and cast iron blocks are made with wider oil pan rails, raised cam bores, taller deck heights, and machined main bulkheads. Many have stronger bottom ends with splayed or cross-bolted steel main caps. Block water jackets and oil galleries are relocated away from areas that may need to be machined, cut, or ground, reducing the chances of a breakthrough. Additional head bolt bosses and thicker deck surfaces are provided. Many of these blocks are factory machined to tighter allowable tolerances than production blocks. While these race blocks are more expensive initially their features cut down the amount of time and money spent machining or clearancing. Many have been designed with very large cubic inch displacements from long stroke cranks as a consideration. The increased strength, ability to swallow large stroke cranks, and other race features make the use of a race-designed block something to think about when you are doing the initial planning of your engine buildup.

430+ cubic inch small-blocks and 700+ cubic inches from a big-block are possible. All it takes is good planning, the right parts, and a deep pocketbook.

This before-and-after comparison illustrates how a sound core can be turned into a race-ready crank. The finished crank (right) has been inspected, cleaned, deburred, shotpeened, reground, polished, and straightened.

It's easy to spot the difference between a cast and a forged crank. If there is a distinct parting line on the rod throws and counterweights, the crank is made of cast iron (right). A wide, raised dye mark indicates a forged steel piece (left).

process are typically 0.375- to 0.500-inch wide, and appear as a slightly raised surface. Look for these telltale marks on the front and rear crank throws.

Forged cranks are not available for all engines. Don't despair; many high-performance street motors have lead long and productive lives with cast cranks. If you plan on 10,000-rpm engine speeds, then you should also plan on buying a crankshaft carved out of a *solid steel billet.* Production cast iron cranks often have extra-large bearings or other features that compensate for the reduced strength of the crankshaft material.

Once you have found a likely crankshaft candidate, measure the rod and main bearing journals to determine if they have already been turned *undersize.* Many crankshaft grinders mark the front counterweight with a notation such as "M20-R20," which would indicate that both the main (M) and rod (R) journals have been ground 0.020-inch undersize.

There's nothing inherently wrong with an undersize crank; providing, of course, that the work was done properly and that bearings are readily available. In fact, some racers in the Stock classes (drag racing) have their crankshafts turned 0.040- or .050-inch undersize as a matter of course. They feel the smaller bearing diameter creates less drag, which in turn frees up a few more horsepower for the rear wheels.

The evidence of a spun or burned bearing will be obvious. The journal in question will usually turn dark blue, and the bearing surface will be pockmarked and scored. Even though such damage looks irreversible, many crankshafts with spun or burned bearings can be

A quick visual inspection will reveal obvious problems such as spun or burned bearing journals. A discolored journal is a sure sign that a bearing has overheated, usually from a lack of lubrication. Unless the crank is cracked, grinding, welding, or chroming the journals can usually repair such damage.

A Magnaflux inspection is mandatory for any used crank. It is pointless to invest money in the crank work until you know that your core is free of cracks in critical areas.

The crank inspection procedure begins by magnetizing the crank, as demonstrated here by Larry Hollum.

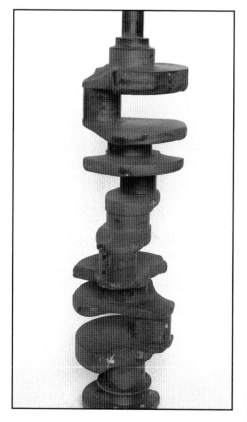

The first step in crank preparation is to strip away the layers of varnish and grime with a pressure cleaner or hot tank. After cleaning, examine the core for stripped bolt holes, broken or chipped counterweights, and other flaws.

saved. If the pockmarks or scores are not too deep, and if the crankshaft is not cracked, turning the journals undersize or adding new material by *welding* or *chroming* can restore the crankshaft to better-than-new condition. These repairs are not cheap, of course, and you will have to decide whether it is worthwhile to repair a damaged crank. If you were using a common crank like a 350 Chevy forging, it would be foolish to try to rescue a damaged crank when you can probably find another inexpensive core.

If the crank passes your visual inspection, then have it hot tanked or jet cleaned to remove all varnish and

The magnetized crank is then saturated with Magnaglo solution; make sure all the main and rod journals are thoroughly covered by the Magnaglo.

Under a black light, cracks appear as bright green lines. A deep crack is easy to spot, but smaller fissures in the journal fillets require a sharp eye to detect. Experience and patience help when inspecting a crank core.

grease. The next step is absolutely essential: have the crank *Magnaflux inspected!* Do not pass go, and do not spend another dime on the crank until it gets a clean bill of health from the Magnaflux man. Unlike the dry Magnaflux powder used to detect cracks in an engine block, a crankshaft is saturated with a magnetic solution. This fluorescent *Magnaglo* liquid reveals any cracks or imperfections in the metal when the crank is examined under an ultraviolet black light. Cracks show up as a bright green line, but it takes a sharp eye to spot them.

Small stress cracks around the oil holes are nothing to be concerned about, but cracks in the fillets between the bearing journals and the throws are usually fatal. To put it as bluntly as possible, there are no effective repairs for a cracked crankshaft. Throw it away and go look for a replacement.

DEBURRING

If the crankshaft core is sound, then the next step is to detail and deburr it. A crankshaft must be deburred for the same reason that blocks and cylinders are detailed: Sharp edges are stress risers

that foster cracks and catastrophic failures. If you intend to use the crankshaft without regrinding the bearing journals, then these surfaces must be protected from the metal particles flung off the abrasive wheel when you are grinding off the sharp edges and casting flash. Wrap heavy masking tape or duct tape around the journals to protect them from pits. A body grinder or an abrasive wheel attachment on a hand drill will make quick work of die marks and parting lines. Crankshafts are both heavy and awkward to work on, so a work stand fabricated from scrap lumber can be helpful when you are working over a forging.

Take the time to clean out all the crankshaft threads. Chase the holes in the flywheel flange and the front snout with a tap, checking carefully for stripped or cross-threaded holes.

SHOTPEENING AND STRESS RELIEVING

Shotpeening and stress relieving are two operations that can improve the life expectancy of a high-performance crankshaft. Both jobs must be performed by a crankshaft service, but you should know what you are paying for. When a crankshaft is *shotpeened,* it is

bombarded with small steel balls—somewhat like a sandblasting process, only with tiny ball bearings. This compresses the metal on the surface of the crank depriving potential cracks of a starting point. Both the size of the steel shot and the air pressure used to propel them are important to the success of the shotpeening process.

Stress relieving is a technique that helps a crankshaft to "relax." The forging process is very traumatic for a crank. Almost all domestic V-8 cranks are forged flat, with all the rod throws in one plane. Before the crank can cool, it is literally twisted to place the rod journals at 90° angles.

Naturally, this only adds to the stresses already created by the hammering and heat of forging. When a crank is stress relieved, it is heated in an oven to a temperature that permits the molecules of metal to rearrange themselves. This "baking" process is similar to what occurs as a new engine block becomes seasoned with use, since it helps stabilize the metal structure. Stress relieving is not a necessity for most street and drag racing crankshafts, although it is a lifesaver for cranks intended for circle track and heavy-duty marine applications.

If the crank passes inspection, the next step is to deburr and detail the rod throws and counterweights. Crank shops often use a body grinder and coarse abrasive discs for this chore. Use caution when grinding near the journals!

Shotpeening is done inside of a large metal cabinet with a rotisserie-like device inside. Peening compacts the surface of the metal by bombarding it with small steel balls. A smooth, uniform surface denies cracks a starting place.

CRANKSHAFT GRINDING

When the bearing journals of a crankshaft are reground, several things happen simultaneously. First, of course, the diameters of the rod and main bearing journals are reduced. How much material is removed depends on the condition of the crankshaft core. If the crank has had only normal wear, and if the journals are not badly pitted or scored, then a "clean up" grind of 0.010-inch will usually restore the bearing surfaces to like-new condition. In cases where the journal has been badly scored by a spun or burned bearing, the crank grinder must remove more material to produce a smooth surface.

When the rod bearing journals are reduced in size, they are also indexed and stroke equalized. *Indexing* simply means that the interval between throws is brought into spec. In a conventional V-8 engine, for example, the rod throws should be exactly 90-degrees apart. Although it is relatively rare to encounter a production crank that has misindexed rod throws, mistakes do happen. Factory cranks with unequal strokes are much more common.

While checking piston deck heights, an engine builder will often find a piston that is noticeably higher or lower in

Grinding a crankshaft is not a job for beginners. It takes expensive machinery and skill to do the job right. Here a technician at Chrome-A-Shaft (Memphis, Tennessee) regrinds the rod journals on a small-block Chevy crank. This operation simultaneously indexes the rod throws and equalizes the strokes on each journal.

the block than the others. If the compression height of the piston and the center-to-center length of the rod are all right on spec, the culprit is the crankshaft stroke for that particular piston, and if throw is way off spec, the only solution may be to have the crank reground with all of the stroke lengths equalized.

A high-performance crankshaft should have the largest possible radius between the bearing journals and the crank cheeks. This is an area of extremely high stress where most crank failures originate. Most performance oriented crankshaft services use grinding stones with generous radiuses to form this critical junction. Beware of cranks sometimes included with cheap rebuild kits; the journals may have sharp edges or distinct corners. The only drawback to a crank with extra-large fillets is the necessity of checking for *interference* between the bearing inserts and the journal radius. If the edges of the bearing contact this radius, the flow of oil across the bearing surface can be cut off. Further, the load on the bearing is concentrated on the outside edges. Both conditions contribute to early bearing failure.

CROSS DRILLING

Cross drilling is a modification that provides "full-time" oiling to the rod bearings. In most stock crankshafts, a single oil passage connects the main and rod bearing journals. Although this system works well for a low-rpm powerplant, it may not meet the lubrication needs of a high-performance engine. When a crankshaft is cross-drilled, two intersecting holes are bored through the main bearing journals at right angles. When used with a standard half-grooved main bearing, this modification guarantees that the rod journal oil passage is always exposed to full oil pressure.

Cross-drilling the crank has several advantages over other schemes intended to provide fail-safe rod oiling. It is superior to grooving the main bearing journals or using full-groove bearing inserts. When either the crankshaft or bearing insert is grooved, the load-carrying capacity of the bearing is reduced con-

Large fillets between the journals and the crank cheeks make a crankshaft stronger. If this radius is too generous, though, it can interfere with the rod and main bearings. The edges of the bearing inserts must not contact the fillets; if there is minor interference, chamfer the bearings with a sharp deburring knife.

siderably. Instead of distributing the loads evenly across the face of the bearing, these loads are concentrated in two narrow bands.

Some engines—notably the small-block Chevrolet V-8—do not require cross drilling except for endurance racing applications. In other instances, the factories have taken the initiative and cross-drilled the main bearing journals—high-performance big-block

Chevrolet cranks, for example, are cross drilled on the assembly line. Cross-drilling the mains is a modification that can never hurt—and it can definitely help.

CHAMFERING OIL HOLES

Chamfering the oil holes on the rod and main bearing journals is a simple procedure that can be done on your

Cross-drilling the main bearing journals is a better way to achieve constant oil flow to the rod bearings than grooving the mains or installing full-groove bearing inserts.

garage workbench. When these passages are drilled at the factory, the bits often leave sharp, ragged edges where they break through the surface of the journal. A small grinding stone will readily deburr and radius these openings. Don't get carried away; all that's needed is a gentle depression around the oil hole. This will act as a small reservoir to help distribute the oil across the bearing and journal surfaces, while also denying cracks a starting point. To complete the deburring process, the journals should be well polished after this chamfering operation.

COUNTERWEIGHT MODIFICATIONS

During the early Seventies, *windage* became a trendy theme among engine builders. Windage is simply the drag on the spinning crankshaft assembly caused by the whirlwind of oil droplets inside the crankcase. If you have ever ridden a bicycle in a rainstorm, you are

Chamfer the oil holes in the crank journals with an abrasive hard roll or a small grinding stone. Don't dig a hole with the grinder – just break the sharp edges.

certainly aware of the impact that a million tiny drops can have. Most of the attention was devoted to keeping this oil mist under control. Windage trays, oil pan screens, and exotic dry-sump oil systems all helped reduce the volume of oil suspended in the crankcase. Then engine builders started looking at ways to reduce horsepower losses by streamlining the crankshaft counterweights. And with that, the "knife-edged" counterweight was born.

A knife-edged counterweight is ground to a sharp "V" on the leading edge. To our knowledge, no one has ever tested whether sharpening the counterweights provides any real benefits (aside from the obvious advantage of lightening the rotating assembly). On the face of it, it seems doubtful. As any textbook on aerodynamics will point out, it is the *trailing* edge of an object, not the leading edge, which accounts for most of the drag. In fact, the "perfect" counterweight shape from an aerodynamic standpoint would be a teardrop, with a blunt leading edge and a long, tapering tail. So, if you really want to spend time shaping the counterweights for a racing engine, it might be wiser to concentrate on the back ends of the counterweights.

Smooth balancing is another trick that developed from the preoccupation that racing-engine builders have for windage losses. A smooth-balanced crank is one that has had all of the bal-

ancing holes in the counterweights covered. Freeze plugs or thin metal straps are welded over the holes, and then ground down so that the circumference of the counterweights is perfectly smooth. Again, the idea is that this will eliminate turbulence and drag as the crankshaft slices through a fog of oil droplets. Does it make a difference? Who knows—but it probably doesn't hurt.

Among all the counterweight treatments for a racing engine, the most useful and practical is to reduce the diameter of the weights. If you are using lightweight pistons and connecting rods, it is almost certain that a great deal of metal will have to be removed from the counterweights to balance the engine. (See the section on balancing in Chapter Nine for a full explanation.) Instead of drilling the counterweights full of holes, it is just as effective to set up the crankshaft in a large lathe and turn down the diameter of the counterweights. This has several benefits. First, it eliminates the need for numerous holes in the counterweights. Second, it reduces the inertia of the crankshaft assembly, which in turn can translate into quicker engine response (a feature that is especially important in oval-track competition and road racing). Use restraint, though, when cutting down the counterweights. If you go too far, you may have to add weight with expensive heavy metal.

These counterweights have been "knife-edged" to reduce drag as the crank spins in a heavy oil mist. There is some controversy about whether streamlining the counterweights is really beneficial.

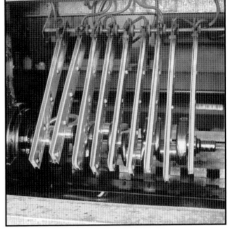

Hard chroming is an industrial plating process that makes the crank journals extremely resistant to wear. Chrome-A-Shaft chromes hundreds of cranks every year for fuel-burning engines, sprint car motors, and super-speedway engines. The first step in the process is to mask the journals and coat the crank with a thick layer of wax.

After the masking tape is removed, anodes are placed on each crank journal. Chrome will not be deposited on the parts of the crank that are covered with wax.

HARD CHROMING AND TUFFTRIDING

There are several ways to improve the surface hardness of the bearing journals. The most popular methods are *nitriding* (Tufftriding) and *hard chroming*. The goal of both these processes is to produce a tough, wear-resistant finish on the bearing surfaces. For most street and drag racing engines, the untreated steel or cast iron surface is perfectly satisfactory. An engine that will see long hours of severe-duty service can, however, benefit from these treatments. Some of the premier performance engines of the Sixties, such as the high-winding Chevrolet Z/28 small-blocks, were equipped with Tufftrided cranks when they left the factory, which indicates the engineers' high regard for this process.

When a crankshaft is Tufftride heat treated, it is heated to 800 F degrees and dunked in a bath of cyanide salt. Ideally, the treatment should penetrate approximately 0.200-inch into the metal—but in fact, the hardening can be very shallow in spots. In some areas, the hardening may be so thin that simply polishing the crank can remove it! Crankshaft shops may be reluctant to work on Tufftrided cranks because of this inconsistency in hardness. Also, the equipment required for the process is quite elaborate; so few shops offer this service.

Chroming, in contrast, is much easier to obtain. Chrome is an extremely hard metal. When a crankshaft is chrome-plated, the aim is not to improve the appearance, but to improve the durability. Chroming can also be used to repair a damaged crank by building up the journals with a layer of chrome. This makes it possible to use standard bearings even with a crank that has suffered a spun or scored journal.

The initial steps in preparing a crank core for chroming are similar to regrinding a crankshaft. The journals are first ground and indexed, then covered with masking tape. The crank is immersed in a vat of hot wax, which coats the counterweights and all surfaces that will not be chromed. The tape is removed, exposing the journal surfaces. The crank is then placed in the chroming tank, with an anode resting on each bearing journal. It remains in the tank for several hours (or several days, depending on the thickness

The crank is then lowered into the chroming tank and slowly rotated. The crank remains in the solution for hours or days, depending on how thick of a layer of chrome is desired.

When the crank is removed from the chroming tank and the wax is stripped off of the counterweights, the chrome that has been deposited on the journals is quite apparent. If a damaged crank is being repaired, it's possible to chrome a single bearing journal.

of the chrome to be plated). During this time the crank is constantly rotated, building up layer after layer of chrome molecules.

After chroming, the journals are ground and micropolished. If the chrome is applied properly, it becomes part of the crank, and should never peel or chip.

After the crank is removed from the chroming tank the journals are again ground and polished. This leaves a super-hard surface. If the chrome has been applied properly, there is virtually no danger of it peeling off. However, a chromed crank cannot be checked for cracks using the Magnaflux inspection procedure. Also, the chroming process may cause *hydrogen embrittlement,* a condition that further increases the problem of surface cracking. For these reasons, hard chroming is generally reserved for crankshafts that will be used briefly in high-load situations and then replaced. Many fuel-burning engines, for example, are equipped with hard chromed cranks.

PILOT BEARINGS

Pilot bearings are usually ignored—ignored, that is, until the transmission will no longer shift. That's when these seemingly insignificant items take on major importance.

Most factory crankshafts rely on bronze pilot bushings. These are pressed into a relief in the rear of the crank whenever a manual transmission will be used. When pilot bushings wear,

the inside diameter becomes galled or egg-shaped. Occasionally the pilot bushing will spin inside the crank. Any of these conditions can prevent the clutch from releasing cleanly. At the very least, you should replace the stock pilot bushing with a new one during the blueprinting procedure. If you don't have a pilot bushing puller, you can remove the old bushing by packing the relief behind it with heavy grease. When you hammer on the end of an old transmission input shaft inserted in the bushing, the grease will force the bushing out of the crank.

For racing and high-performance applications, there are alternatives to the standby bronze bushings. For example, many racers bore the back of Chevrolet crankshafts to accept a roller bearing. Chevy also carries a roller-type bearing for 6.2L diesel engines, which is a direct replacement for the standard bronze bushing.

STROKE CHANGES

There is no reason to limit your choice of engine displacements to the stroke dimensions that the factories happen to offer! There are several common ways to change the stroke of a crank. *Offset grinding* is now a popular and quite common practice. When a crankshaft is offset ground, the diameters of the rod bearing journals are reduced, while the centerlines of the crank pins are moved closer to or farther away from the centerline of the main bearings. Small-block Chevrolets are particularly good candidates for this procedure, since two different rod bearing diameters (2.00- and 2.100-inch) have been used in this engine. By reducing the bearing journal diameter 0.100-inch and regrinding the throw with the maximum possible offset, the stroke can be changed a total of 0.090-inch. Through the miracle of offset grinding, a Chevy small-block crank with a factory stroke of 3.00 inches, for example, can be reground with any stroke between 2.910 and 3.090 inches!

Of course, this modification requires connecting rods with the proper bearing bores to accommodate the smaller diameter rod bearings. In the case of small-block Chevrolets, the use of pre-1968 connecting rods solves this dilemma—although in the vast majority of engines built with offset ground cranks, specialty connecting rods are installed. Remember, too, that a change in crankshaft stroke requires a change in the piston compression heights or the center-to-center length of the connecting rods.

An intriguing variation of the offset ground cranks are the so-called "cheater cranks." In certain racing classes that demand stock engine specifications, the rulebooks spell out allowable tolerances on certain dimensions. In NHRA Stock eliminator classes, for example, the allowable deviation on stroke measurements is 0.015-inch. Naturally, racers who want to take advantage of everything the rulebook allows have their crankshafts stroked exactly 0.013-inch. The difference in final engine displacement amounts to less than two cubic inches, but in these categories, attention to such minute details can mean the difference between winning and losing. A stroke change of only 0.013-inch can easily be compensated for when the block is milled to establish the piston deck heights.

The amount of metal that can be

Chrome-A-Shaft uses this special "submerged arc" welder to repair or add material to a crank journal. Radical stroke changes can be made by building up the rod throws with welding rod and then offset-grinding the journals.

safely removed from the rod journals by offset grinding does limit an engine builder's stroke choices. In instances where a more radical change in crank stroke is needed, *welding* is the only alternative. The welding process adds material to the outside of the rod throw—in the case of a *stroker crank*—or the inside of the journal—if a *destroked crankshaft* is the goal. If the welding is done correctly, the additional material is virtually indistinguishable from the parent metal. Crankshaft welding is usually performed with an automatic wire welder—using a "submerged arc" process, in which a constant shower of iron particles covers the electrode. After welding, the crankshaft journals are ground and micropolished just like an unmodified crank. Using this technique, it is possible to increase the stroke of a suitable core by as much as 0.625-inch (5/8-inch)—although the cost of this operation quickly becomes prohibitive for all but the most

dedicated advocates of big-displacement engines.

MICROPOLISHING

The surface left by the crankshaft grinding stones must be smoothed and polished before it is suitable for bearings. *Micropolishing* performs this important function. A motor-driven abrasive belt is used to dress the bearing surface to a mirror finish. Minor touch-ups can be done at home with nothing more elaborate than a shoelace and a sheet of extra-fine wet-or-dry sandpaper. Cut the sandpaper into strips that are as wide as the bearing journals. Saturate the sandpaper with solvent, wrap it around the journal, and then make one full loop with the shoelace. By "sawing" the shoelace back and forth, the paper will be pulled across the bearing journal. This technique is an ideal way to polish out the minor nicks and imperfections that inevitably result from assembling and disassembling the short block. However, if the crank has been Tufftrided, you must remember that even a light polishing can cut

OFFSET GROUND CRANK

NEW CRANK PIN O.D.
ORIGINAL CRANK PIN O.D.
1/2 STROKE INCREASE
MAIN JOURNAL

Offset grinding the rod journals is an effective way to change the stroke length. The stroke may be increased or decreased by grinding down the rod journal while simultaneously moving the centerline of the rod throw.

An old shoelace or a leather thong will put you in the crank polishing business. Cut a piece of 600-grit wet-or-dry sandpaper to match the journal width. Wrap the sandpaper and shoelace around the journal, and then polish the journal by pulling the ends of the lace back and forth. Lubricate the abrasive paper with solvent.

To check crankshaft straightness, install the crank in the block on the front and rear main bearings. Read the crankshaft runout on the center journal as you rotate the crank.

through the shallow spots in the surface treatment, so don't get carried away!

CRANKSHAFT STRAIGHTENING

Internal stresses, a fall from a workbench top, high engine loads, and heat treating can all cause a crankshaft to bend. After investing considerable time and money in align honing a block, it

Straightening a bent crank is fairly simple if you have the right equipment. Cranks are surprisingly flexible; a hydraulic press and a heavy hammer will straighten a crank quickly.

stands to reason that the crankshaft should be as straight as possible. Checking crankshaft straightness is a simple procedure. Install the crank in the engine block with only the front and rear main bearing inserts in place. Torque down the front and rear bearing caps, and then set up a dial indicator to read the runout (rotational eccentricity) of the center main bearing. Ideally, there should be zero runout—but as a practical matter, readings as high as 0.002-inch are acceptable.

Suppose you discover that your prize crankshaft is bent—then what? While a crank might seem to be a rather formidable mass, straightening a crank is a fairly straightforward procedure for a competent crankshaft shop. The crank is set up in a fixture and then preloaded with a hydraulic jack. When the crank is struck sharply with a heavy hammer, it will yield. A skilled technician can usually bring a bent crank into spec in short order.

STROKE CHECKING

The most accurate way to check crankshaft stroke is with a gauge similar to the one pictured here. This fixture has a long-travel dial indicator

mounted on an aluminum bridge that straddles the main bearing journals. Of course, few backyard engine builders have such an instrument at their disposal. Don't despair, though. There are other ways to check the accuracy of the individual rod throws.

The perfect time to check crankshaft stroke is when the engine has been

This stroke-checking fixture uses a long-travel dial indicator to detect differences between rod throws. The stroke is measured by noting the difference in the indicator readings when the rod journal is at the highest and lowest positions.

preassembled to measure piston deck heights. A dial indicator, a depth micrometer, or even a pair of dial calipers can be used.

Simply run the piston up to TDC and measure from the deck surface of the block to the quench flat on the piston. Then rotate the crank until the piston is at bottom dead center (BDC); you may have to rock the crankshaft forward and backward to find this exact point. Measure again from the top of the block to the piston. The difference between the two readings is the crankshaft stroke.

The accuracy of your measurements will be improved if you take readings as close to the center of the pistons as possible; this helps minimize the problem of piston rock.

Also, if you know that the block is perfectly square, you can check the deck heights in every cylinder using only one piston/rod combination; different readings from one cylinder to another will indicate variations in the crankshaft stroke (but remember this technique is only valid if the block decks are perfectly square and parallel to the crankshaft bore centerline).

BEARING CLEARANCES

Proper *bearing clearances* are critical to engine life. The clearance between the crankshaft journals and the bearing inserts permits a constant flow of oil to pass across the bearing surface.

This oil flow is essential for both lubrication and cooling. If the clearances are too small, the oil supply is choked off; if it is too large, the oil simply washes across the bearing without forming a wedge to support the crankshaft and without carrying heat away from the bearing insert. Just a few seconds of metal-to-metal contact between the bearing and crankshaft can be fatal to an engine!

The most accurate way to measure rod and main bearing clearances is by comparing the outside diameter of the crankshaft journals to the inside diameter of the bearing inserts. This procedure requires both inside and outside micrometers—or, better yet, a dial bore gauge.

To determine the bearing clearances, first measure the diameters of the crankshaft journals. Check each journal at several points to make sure that it is not tapered or out-of-round.

As you check the bearing clearances with this method, you will soon discover that bearings are not perfectly round. Rather, they are slightly elliptical, with the diameter across the parting line somewhat larger than the diameter at 90 degrees to the parting line. The *vertical diameter* is the critical dimension, since the highest crank loads occur in this direction. The increase in diameter at the bearing parting line provides an oil reservoir that lubricates the rapidly spinning crankshaft.

There is an alternative way to measure bearing clearances without precision tools: Plastigage. Although professional engine builders frown on this method, the truth is that thousands of engines have been assembled using this simple technique.

Plastigage is a waxy plastic string. To measure a clearance, a short piece of Plastigage is first placed on the crankshaft journal. The main cap and bearing are installed and torqued. The cap is then removed, exposing the flattened Plastigage. Comparing the width of the smashed string with a chart on the Plastigage package indicates the bearing clearance.

In order for the Plastigage to give an accurate reading, the bearings and journals must be clean and free of oil. The crank must not be turned while the Plastigage is in position. And don't forget to remove all traces of the compressed wax

Then measure the inside diameter of the bearings with the rod cap or main bearing cap torqued in place. Measure the bearing inside diameter at 90 degrees to the parting line. The difference between the journal diameter and the inside diameter of the bearing inserts is the actual clearance.

before starting final engine assembly.

Most high-performance and racing engines are content with bottom end clearances ranging between 0.0025- and .0035-inch. There are exceptions, however, and you should find out if your particular engine is one of them. Crankshafts that are particularly susceptible to flexing may require larger clearances, as will engines with inefficient oiling systems.

If the bearing clearances are within the specified range for your particular engine and intended usage, then you can get to work on other blueprinting projects. But if the bearings are too tight or too loose, you have several options.

You can adjust the bearing clearances by using thicker or thinner bearing shells. To accurately measure the thickness of a curved bearing, you'll need a ball bearing adapter for your micrometer spindle.

Common Plastigage will provide a fairly accurate indication of the bearing clearance if you don't have access to a set of micrometers. After the waxy string has been compressed between the bearing and the crank journal, its width is compared to a chart on the package to determine the bearing clearance.

The first is to buy bearing inserts that will produce the desired clearance. Bearings are commonly offered in 0.001-, 0.002-, and 0.010-inch undersizes. It is more difficult to find bearings that are slightly *oversize* to increase the clearance (although Chevrolet does offer a limited selection of these bearings for small-block V-8s).

Another alternative is to try a different brand of bearing. If, for example, Clevite bearings don't produce the exact clearance you are seeking, try a set of Vandervell or Federal Mogul bearings. Just be certain that the bearings you audition are really made by different manufacturers. Just because they come in different packages doesn't necessarily mean that different companies make them.

Minor adjustments in bearing clearances can be made by "half-shelling" the bearings. As an example of half-shelling, you might combine the lower halves of a set of standard bearings with the upper halves from a set of 0.001-inch undersize bearings.

Even though this solution commits you to buying two sets of bearings for a single engine, you will have enough inserts left over for another complete engine.

The final cure for tight bearings is to reduce the diameter of the crankshaft journals. This can be a risky business, since it is very difficult to polish small amounts of metal off a crankshaft without causing the bearing journals to become crowned.

Many crank grinders prefer to grind the crank a full 0.010-inch undersize to produce the correct clearance, since grinding the journals allows much greater control over the amount of material actually removed.

THRUST CLEARANCE

The *thrust clearance* limits the front-to-rear motion of the crankshaft. The thrust bearing, like the other bearings in the crankshaft assembly, requires clearance to allow for thermal expansion and to permit oil flow across its surface for both cooling and lubrication. The correct clearance varies between engines, but generally a figure between 0.005- and 0.010-inch is acceptable.

To determine the existing clearance, the crankshaft is installed in the block and the main caps are torqued in place. In most automotive engines, the rear or center main bearing controls crankshaft thrust. Before the main cap for the thrust bearing is tightened down, the bearing should be seated by smacking the crank snout and flywheel flange with a soft-headed hammer or mallet.

After all the main caps have been tightened, set up a dial indicator with the plunger parallel to the crankshaft axis (as shown). Pry the crankshaft forward and backward with a long screwdriver and note the indicator readings. The total travel is the crankshaft thrust clearance.

On some engines, it may be possible to measure thrust clearance with a feeler gauge. Pry the crank as far for-

To check thrust clearance, set up a dial indicator parallel to the crankshaft axis and pry the crank forward and back.

On some engines, you can measure crank endplay by inserting a feeler gauge between the crank thrust flange and the thrust bearing.

ward as it will go, and then select the largest feeler strip that will slide between the bearing and the crankshaft thrust surface.

If the thrust clearance is too small, it can be increased by carefully sanding the thrust bearing. A piece of heavy, flat glass is a good low-buck surface plate for this operation.

Place a piece of 600-grit wet-or-dry sandpaper on the glass, and then saturate the abrasive with solvent. Carefully sand the thrust surface of the bearing on the abrasive, using a figure-8 motion to remove material evenly across the bearing face. Concentrate your efforts on the front side of the bearing, which is only lightly loaded when the engine is running.

Occasionally you may find a crank with too much thrust clearance. Usually this is caused by a thrust surface that has been previously damaged and repaired. In extreme cases, the thrust clearance is so large that the entire crank assembly can move far enough to allow the rods or crankshaft counterweights to hit the block.

The only practical cure for this condition is to have a competent crankshaft service build up the thrust surface by welding additional material onto the thrust bearing flange.

Thrust bearing problems are,

If the crank endplay is too small, it can usually be increased by carefully sanding the thrust bearing. Use a piece of thick glass for a surface plate, and move the bearing in a figure-8 as you sand it.

unfortunately, quite common in high-performance engines. In many instances, it is the torque converter or clutch that is at fault, not the thrust bearing itself. If the pressure plate has excessively high spring pressure, or if the converter "balloons," the load exerted against the thrust bearing can cause it to gall or burn.

Making sure that its thrust surface is exactly parallel to the thrust flange of the crank can increase the life expectancy of a thrust bearing. To check this, paint the bearing with machinist's dye

You can check for a cocked or misaligned thrust bearing by painting the bearing with machinist's dye and noting the contact pattern after rotating the crank. An alternate method is to check crank endplay before and after the cap is installed; if the endplay changes, the cap may be cocked.

or a felt-tip pen. Rotate the crank while prying against the end of it with a large screwdriver. Then remove both halves of the thrust bearing and examine the contact pattern where the dye has been worn away. The dye should be worn evenly around the entire circumference of the bearings. If the contact is concentrated in one area, the main bearing cap may have been cocked slightly when the block was align honed.

CONNECTING RODS

Life is never easy for a connecting rod. With every turn of the crankshaft, it is alternately stretched and compressed. The motion of the crank and pistons tries to snap the beam in half, while the big and little ends are baked with intense heat. Considering the environment they live in, the survival rate among connecting rods is remarkably high. Of course, there are steps you can take that will extend the lifespan of any connecting rod used in racing or high performance.

SELECTION AND INSPECTION

The type of connecting rods you choose will depend on how the engine will be used. If you are assembling a high-performance street engine, then it is likely that you will be using production connecting rods. Drag-racing engines are usually outfitted with aluminum rods, when the rulebook allows a choice, while road racing, marine, and circle-track motors depend on specialty steel rods. (Exceptions to these general rules, of course, would be those "limited" classes that restrict competitors to original factory parts.) Each type of connecting rod has distinct advantages and shortcomings that make it best suited for certain applications.

On the street, low cost and ease of installation tips the scales in favor of stock rods. The horsepower levels attainable even with supercharged street engines will not overtax a good forged steel factory rod. Since these rods are designed specifically for the engines in which they are installed, clearance problems between the rods, cam, and block are eliminated (as long as a stock-stroke crankshaft is retained).

In highly modified drag-racing engines, aluminum rods make more sense. Although the fatigue factor disqualifies aluminum for endurance racing, these rods are brutally strong for short periods of time—a characteristic that is ideal for high-rpm drag engines. The price of aluminum rods is not much higher than the cost of preparing a set of stock rods. Also, most manufacturers can supply virtually any combination of

Stock connecting rods can be reworked to perform perfectly in street and certain limited racing applications.

rod length and bearing size, which suits drag racing engine builders who are constantly juggling strokes, pin heights, and bearing diameters in search of a competitive edge.

Until recently, the choices in specialty steel connecting rods were quite limited. For many years the famous Carrillo forged, premium-steel connecting rod had a virtual monopoly on this market. The growing popularity of oval-track racing has enticed a number of companies into manufacturing their own steel rods. Also, the factories have stepped up with their own off-road rods, like the Chevrolet "Bow Tie" forgings. If you are racing a small-block Chevrolet, you have at least six alternatives when selecting steel connecting rods. Of course, if you are planning on running a Morris Minor at Daytona, your choices will be somewhat more limited. The going rate for specialty steel rods is $600 to $1,000 a set—a big check to be sure, but a bargain when you consider how much damage a broken rod can cause. Top quality specialty rods require virtually no preparation. You inspect them (for shipping damage), clean them, and install them.

Getting a set of stock rods ready for assembly is not so easy. The first task is to do a bit of research to determine exactly what you've got. For example, Chevrolet has produced several different versions of the venerable small-block rod, just as Chrysler and Ford have offered various grades of connecting rods for their respective perform-

Growing popularity of oval-track racing has prompted aftermarket manufacturers to introduce new steel connecting rods. Differences in beam sections and big ends are apparent.

Rod Ratios

The rod ratio is determined by dividing the rod center-to-center length by the stroke length of the crankshaft.

An example would be a Ford 302 V-8 connecting rod center-to-center length of 5.090-inch and a stock stroke of 3 inches, which gives a rod ratio of 1.696:1.

ROD RATIO = 5.090 inches ÷ 3.00 inches = 1.696:1.

Different engines have different rod ratios. A 351W Ford has a 3.50-inch crank stroke and a connecting rod length of 5.956 inches, which gives a rod ratio of 1.701:1.

In recent years, it has been increasingly popular to use longer than stock rods to increase the rod ratio of a motor. Many combinations are possible. In a Ford 351W, you could swap the stock 5.956-inch length for a stock length rod from a 400 Ford, which is 6.580 inches. Many Chevy 350 stock rods, which are 5.7 inches in length, are swapped for 6.0-inch rods. (Remember that you must also change the piston pin height to allow for the change in rod center-to-center length.)

You must also have enough total block deck height to fit your planned crank stroke length, rod length, and piston pin height combination. Also, make sure there is enough clearance between the bottom edges of the piston skirts and the crank, and between the piston deck and the head deck.

Generally, increasing the rod ratio reduces rod angularity, which reduces the side loading of the piston against the cylinder wall thrust surfaces.

Aluminum rods are ideal for drag racing. They are reasonable in price, very strong, and available with a variety of lengths and bearing bore diameters. Remember that the low fatigue strength of aluminum demands regular rod replacement.

Black carbon deposits around the big end of used connecting rods are warning signs that the overheated bearing was on the verge of spinning.

If you have a number of stock rods to choose from, favor the rods with small balancing pads. They are likely to have more metal in the crucial beam section!

ance engines. It makes little economic sense, though, to pay more money for features that you won't use. The difference between a premium Chevy LT-1 connecting rod and an ordinary small-block rod, for example, is simply the extra operations performed at the factory. But if you are already planning on polishing, shotpeening, bushing, resizing, and installing new bolts in your connecting rods, then the high-dollar cores offer little, if any, advantage.

Most connecting rod cores come out of well-used engines. Although there is no way of knowing how many cycles a rod may have endured, the instances when a rod simply breaks are rare indeed. Almost all rod failures are caused by a lack of lubrication due to either the fasteners yielding or the bearing spinning. Black baked-on carbon around the big end of the rod indicates that the bearing had overheated and was on the verge of spinning. If your rod cores are still in one piece and they show no signs of spun bearings, then you can proceed with the inspection procedure.

The surest way to find flaws inside a connecting rod is to have it X-rayed. For most applications, however, a simple Magnaflux inspection will reveal surface cracks that could cause problems later. The procedure for Magnafluxing connecting rods is similar to checking a crankshaft.

Each individual rod is magnetized, saturated with magnetic fluid, and then examined under a black light. Cracks show up as bright green lines under the florescent lamp. Our connecting rod advisor for this section, Larry Hollum, notes that relatively few rods are rejected during Magnaflux inspection. He prefers to grind the die marks off the rod beams before inspecting them. This

Larry Hollum begins the Magnaflux inspection by magnetizing the connecting rod.

The rod is saturated with magnetic inspection fluid and examined under an ultraviolet light. Flaws show up as bright green lines.

Forging marks on the sides of connecting rod beams are removed with a carbide cutter.

The rod beams are then smoothed with a coarse-grit belt sander.

The final polishing is done with an abrasive cartridge roll. Polish the beams parallel to the long axis of the rod.

reveals any "cold lap" flaws that might otherwise be concealed.

POLISHING AND SHOTPEENING

Polishing the connecting rod beams is cheap insurance for any high-performance engine. It's a task you can easily do at home with a minimal investment in time and equipment. In some racing classes (notably certain Stock categories), it is not legal to grind away the die marks on the connecting rods. But unless the rulebook prohibits these efforts, your time will be well spent if you clean up the rod forgings. You will deny cracks a starting point, while also reducing the reciprocating weight.

If the beams are particularly rough,

you may want to start by cutting off most of the forging flash with a carbide burr mounted in an electric or pneumatic die grinder. The goal is to remove only the raised forging marks on the beam without cutting into the rod itself. You can also use a wide belt sander to grind off the nastier chunks of metal on the beams.

No matter which method you use, you should always finish up by polishing the beam with an abrasive cartridge roll *parallel to the long axis of the beam*. Don't bother trying to polish the rod to a mirror finish. Instead, concentrate on

A carefully prepared stock connecting rod is slightly lighter than the original forging, and significantly more durable.

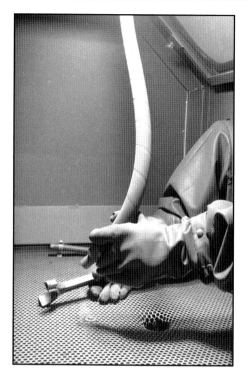

Shotpeening compacts the surface of the connecting rod to deny cracks a starting place.

removing all the grinding marks left by the carbide burr or belt sander.

Most stock connecting rods have a machined shoulder under the bolt head. Remove the rod bolts—you'll be replacing them anyway—and carefully deburr and smooth this area with a small hand file. This is a highly stressed part of the rod; nicks and gouges left here by machine tools can give cracks a place to start.

After the rod has been polished, it is ready for *shotpeening.* As noted in the crankshaft chapter, shotpeening compacts the metal surface by bombarding it with steel balls. This closes up the grain structure, preventing stress cracks from developing.

The detailed technical procedures recommended by Chevrolet engineers for shotpeening suggest using number 230 cast steel shot to obtain an Almen 0.012/0.015 arc height. Good luck finding a shop that can meet these specs! Most shops have a favorite type of shot, a favorite air pressure for the blasting gun, etc., and let it go at that.

ROD BOLTS

The absolute best investment you can make in a high-performance engine is to replace the stock connecting rod bolts with high-strength fasteners. There are many sources for super-quality rod bolts, including ARP, Moroso, B&B Performance, and similar racing suppliers.

Fasteners made by the SPS Company are highly regarded because of their superior material, close quality control, and unique thread angle. If there is a shortcoming to the SPS fasteners, it is the nuts, which should never be torqued more than five times. The SPS nuts are available individually, but you can eliminate this hassle by using stock nuts during the many mock-ups you perform, and saving the good SPS nuts for the final assembly.

In a pinch, you can install new rod bolts yourself. Support the rod with soft jaws in a vise and drive the new bolts into place with a brass hammer. However, a hydraulic press does a much neater job, and you can be sure that the bolts are seated properly if you apply 3,000 pounds of pressure.

Rod bolts are designed to stretch. It is this carefully controlled spring action that keeps the nut tight and provides the clamping force. A torque wrench measures this stretching indirectly by recording the force required to turn the nut. A better way of determining bolt stretch is to measure it directly. Most high-performance bolts have dimples on the head and threaded end to accommodate an outside micrometer with a pointed anvil and spindle. By noting the changes in the overall length of the bolt as it is tightened, the proper "stretch" can be obtained. This method also makes it easy to spot a bolt that has been over

The radius between the beam and the rod bolt shoulder is dressed with a small, round file and then polished with sandpaper to eliminate stress risers.

High strength aftermarket connecting rod bolts are a worthwhile investment for any engine. The unique fasteners made by the SPS Company have special asymmetrical threads and diamond knurled shanks.

A hydraulic press prevents damage to the rod when installing new bolts. The bolt head must be fully seated on the shoulder of the rod.

Patterson Racing uses this gauge to measure the center-to-center length of the connecting rods. A gauge is significantly more accurate than dial calipers.

Rod bolts develop their maximum clamping force at the specified stretch. A stretch gauge provides more accurate readings than a torque wrench.

tightened, because the bolt reaches the yield point and suddenly stretches alarmingly. Since it is difficult to get an accurate micrometer reading inside the narrow confines of a crankcase, several precision tool suppliers are now offering a special rod-bolt stretch gauge, featuring a dial indicator that quickly records changes in the length of the rod bolt.

ROD RESIZING

When the big end of a connecting rod distorts, the rod bearing is in for trouble. The constant, rapid changes of direction can cause the big end to become egg-shaped, unless the mass around the bearing bore is substantial enough to resist these forces. If the bore does distort, the bearing clearances change dramatically. The edges of the bearings at the parting line can actually become metal "squeegees," shearing off the oil film that protects the bearing surface. Without a wedge of oil between the bearing and the crankshaft journal, the bearing quickly seizes, and another engine is ready for the scrap pile. Resizing the big end of a rod can help prevent these disasters.

When a production connecting rod is originally forged and machined, it has internal stresses that cause it to be dimensionally unstable, just as a new block goes through a seasoning period during initial use. Combine these internal stresses with the constant loads imposed by the reciprocating mass of the piston and small end of the rod, and the need for rod resizing becomes clear. Like align honing a block, resizing stock connecting rods is an essential part of engine blueprinting.

The first step in rod reconditioning is to trim the rod fork and the cap with a precision grinder. A minimum of material should be removed to prevent shortening the center-to-center distance.

This is how Kip Martin intentionally finishes the big ends of rods out-of-round. Shims are punched out of typing paper, and then inserted between the rod fork and the cap.

Connecting rods are resized on a reconditioning machine. The procedure is very similar to align honing a cylinder block. The rod caps are trimmed slightly on a cap-grinding machine, and reinstalled on the rod fork. The bearing bore is then honed, restoring it to a perfectly round circle with a diameter matching the manufacturer's specifications.

When the big end of a rod is resized by this method, the minimum amount of metal should be ground off the rod caps, which will allow the bore to be restored to the correct diameter. As the caps are trimmed and the bearing bore honed round again, the center point of the big end is effectively moved closer to the small end. Usually a 0.003-inch cut is sufficient. If a cap requires more trimming, then the center-to-center length of the connecting rod will be changed significantly. This can cause inconsistency in the piston deck heights.

Measuring the center-to-center length of a connecting rod is difficult without the proper equipment. Dial calipers can give a ballpark figure. Measure the distance between the bores on the big and small end. Then measure the diameter of the pinhole and the bearing bore, and divide both of these dimensions in half. Add all three numbers and you have the center-to-center length of the connecting rod.

Most engine builders are more concerned with the consistency of the connecting rod center-to-center lengths than the actual dimensions. You can quickly check rod lengths by installing the same piston on each rod and then measuring the deck height in the same cylinder bore. A change in the deck height indicates that the rod is shorter or longer than its companions.

Some specialized Super Stock (drag-racing) engines require factory connecting rods with big ends that are intentionally finished "out-of-round." Machinist Kip Martin explains that by increasing the bore diameter at the bearing parting line, the bore will become round under actual operating conditions. Just as a torque plate is used to

The rod and cap are held in a special vise while the bolts are torqued. Never hold the rod by the shank when tightening the fasteners.

A reconditioning machine resizes the big end of the connecting rod with a precision hone.

Kip reserves one set of finishing stones for each rod bore size so that the stones will always have the proper arc.

stress the cylinder bores to duplicate the conditions that exist when a head is torqued down, Kip's out-of-round Super Stock rods assume the proper shape only under a load.

Rod bearing inserts, like main bearings, are not perfectly round when installed; the inside diameter is larger at the parting line than at the vertical axis (the axis parallel to the beam of the rod). This slightly eccentric shape allows the bearing to pick up lubrication as the parting line passes over the oil hole in the crankshaft journal. When the big end of the connecting rod stretches under a severe load, the bore draws in at the sides, cutting off this vital oil supply. But if the diameter of the bearing bore is intentionally increased 0.0025-inch at the parting line, the oil flow will not be cut off even when the bore distorts. In fact, Kip reports that the rod bearing clearances can be reduced 0.001-inch with this technique, since the effective clearance is adequate even when the bore distorts under the stress of racing.

In order to produce a bearing bore with the proper eccentricity, Kip places 0.004-inch shims between the cap and rod. The bolts are then torqued and the rod resized normally. Kip hones the bearing bore to within 0.001-inch of the finish size with a set of roughing stones, then switches to special finishing stones for the final pass. Each set of finishing stones is reserved for a single bearing bore size. This means that Kip has one set of stones for small-block Chevy rods with 2.125-inch bearing bores and another set for rods with 2.225-inch bores. Thus, the honing stones always

Jets spray the inside diameter of the bore with honing fluid as the operator strokes the rod back and forth on the mandrel. It takes skill to prevent the bore from becoming "bell mouthed" or "tapered."

A gauge measures the diameter of the resized rod-bearing bore to 0.0001 inch.

Semi-finished connecting rods are manufactured with blank small ends. Reher-Morrison Racing Engines uses this special machine to bore a pinhole while maintaining the correct center-to-center distance.

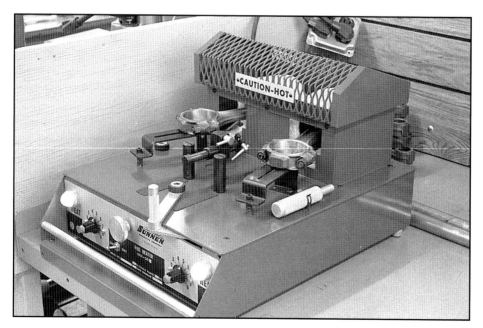

have the proper arc for the rod bore they are sizing. This produces bearing bores that are smooth and straight, with no trace of "bell mouthing" at the sides of the rod. When the shims are removed and the cap reinstalled, the bearing bore has the desired eccentricity.

PIN FIT

Up to this point, the big end of the connecting rod has received most of our attention. It is the small end of the rod that takes care of the important business of supporting the piston, however. There are two ways to hang a piston on a connecting rod: with pressed pins or with full-floating pins. Floating wrist pins have a racier image than pressed pins, a reputation that may not be completely warranted.

The real reason that racers prefer floating pins is convenience. By their very nature, racing engines are overhauled frequently. Full-floating pins make it easy to assemble and disassemble piston and rod pairs. Most production line engines, in contrast, rely on the less glamorous press-fit pins. In an engine that may go over 100,000 miles before a rebuild, ease of disassembly simply is not a consideration.

More and more racers are beginning to recognize the virtues of pressed pins, however. In a well-equipped shop, having to press apart the pistons and rods is not a great hardship. Pressed pins eliminate the constant worry that free-floating pins will start floating too much! None of the pin retaining devices—Tru-Arcs, Spirolox, and buttons—is totally reliable. In contrast, when you press a pin into a rod with a 0.0015-inch interference fit, you know that pin is going to stay put.

Very few press-fit pins are actually pressed into rods these days. The preferred installation method is to heat the

Very few press-fit pins are actually pressed into the connecting rods. Instead, an electric oven heats the small end of the rod, and expands the bore diameter. A pin is pushed through the small end, and then locked in place as the rod cools.

rods in a special oven. This expands the pinhole and allows the pin to slide through easily. As the rod cools and contracts, it grips the pin tightly. The mismatch in the diameters of the pin and the small end of the rod is critical. Although an interference fit of 0.001-inch is adequate for a stock engine, a high-performance motor requires at least a 0.0015-inch difference in diameters to lock the pin firmly in the rod. Piston pins are commonly available in 0.0015- and 0.003-inch oversizes to provide the proper interference fit in rods with larger-than-normal pin bores.

Unless your connecting rods were originally designed to accommodate floating pins, they will have to be modified if full-floating pins are part of your engine building plans. Some small-block Mopar and big-block Ford connecting rods have factory-installed bronze bushings in the small end. This is an ideal bearing material for floating pins. Stock small-block Chevrolet rods, in contrast, were never offered with pin bushings. Chevy rods intended for use with floating pins had a microscopic layer of babbitt plated inside the pin bore.

The small end of the connecting rod is honed on the rod reconditioning machine to provide clearance for the full-floating piston pins.

For years it has been a common engine building practice to bore the small end of the rod and install a bushing when floating pins are used. This

Super Stock drag-racing engine builders often bush the small end of Chevy connecting rods to accept the light 0.875-inch wrist pins in place of the stock 0.927-inch-diameter pins.

Floating wrist pins need 0.001-inch of clearance in the connecting rod.

The chamfered oil hole in the top of the connecting rod supplies lubrication for the floating pin.

also allows the engine builder to correct minor differences in center-to-center length by offset boring the small end bushing. Unfortunately, this practice leaves the wall thickness surrounding the pin bore very thin. That is why many Chevy engine builders now eliminate the bushings altogether. Instead, they hone the pin bore to provide 0.001-inch clearance and assemble the pin and rod combination "steel-on-steel." As long as the pin has adequate lubrication, this method works well.

Regardless of whether the small end of the connecting rod is bushed, a floating pin requires constant lubrication. The "correct" way to oil the pin is always a matter of controversy. Currently most engine builders prefer to drill a single 0.125-inch hole through the top of the rod with a generous 45° chamfer around the hole, which acts as a funnel to channel oil to the wrist pin.

Until recently, however, Chevrolet recommended drilling two holes underneath the wrist pin, angling toward the rod centerline. Carrillo and other specialty connecting rods use this type of pin oiler, but it has been blamed as a contributing cause of rod failure in stock connecting rods. Certainly it is easier to drill oil holes through the top of the rod—and probably safer as well.

ROD-TO-CAM CLEARANCE

When you combine a long-stroke crankshaft with specialty connecting rods and a radical high-lift camshaft, what do you get? Sometimes you get a collision between the rods and the cam lobes.

Providing clearance between the rods and engine block requires grinding some strategic reliefs in the block, but ensuring that the rods and cam lobes don't come together is a little more difficult. Specialty aluminum and steel connecting rods are generally stronger than stock rods because they are bigger than stock connecting rods. The extra material makes them more resistant to distortion, but it also makes them more likely to interfere with other parts inside the engine. This isn't just a problem with V-8 engines; inline sixes and fours that have their cams mounted in the block also have to be checked for interference between the cam and connecting rods. In general, any small-block Chevy equipped with a 3.48-inch or longer stroke and non-stock connecting rods should be checked. And if you are using the 3.750-inch stroke (400cid) crank, don't even dream of not checking.

What makes this procedure tricky is the fact that the cam rotates at half crankshaft speed. In other words, it takes two revolutions of the crank for every one revolution of the camshaft. Thus, there can be adequate clearance on one stroke—but on the next cycle, the rods may hit the cam. In fact, the cam lobes that operate the valves for adjacent or opposite cylinders may be the cause of interference problems, depending on the particular engine layout and the relationship between the lifter bores and the rod centerlines.

The easiest way to check for rod-to-cam clearance is to cover the rod shanks with a 0.125-inch-thick layer of modeling clay. Preassemble the engine with the pistons, rods, and crank in place. Install the cam and timing chain you plan to use—it's not necessary to degree them in precisely, although the cam should be reasonably close to the final phasing. Then rotate the crank-

Clearance between the small end of the connecting rod and the piston pin bosses must be checked when the engine is preassembled. Not all connecting rods are centered under the pistons; the rod must be narrowed or the pin bosses relieved to eliminate rubbing.

shaft at least four full revolutions. If the engine stops turning, don't force it. Get an inspection light and find the problem. Even if the crank turns freely, you are not finished yet. Remove the piston and rod assemblies, and then look closely at the clay on the rod shanks and around the bolts for impressions left by the cam lobes.

If you find marks in the clay left by the lobes, carefully section the clay with a sharp knife or razor blade. If the clay is at least 0.050-inch thick there is enough clearance to keep the rods and cam from colliding when the engine is at full speed.

If the thickness of the clay reveals that the cam and rods are too close for comfort, there are two solutions—neither of which is totally painless. You can either relieve the rod and bolts with a grinder, or install a cam with a smaller base circle.

If you choose the first alternative, remove the minimum amount of metal that will provide the required clearance. Remember, the rod shank and fasteners are highly stressed in a performance engine, and they may fail if the grinding weakens them. Always deburr and polish the areas where you have removed metal to prevent stress risers from forming.

If the cam-to-rod clearance problem is severe, a cam with a smaller base circle may be the only alternative. These specially ground cams have a smaller minor diameter than a standard cam. This means that the lobes are smaller, even though the lift and duration figures are unchanged.

Small-circle cams have their drawbacks, however. These cams usually have to be custom ground, which adds expense and limits your selection. The smaller base circle requires longer pushrods to restore the proper valvetrain geometry. Finally, the tappets project farther out of the bottom of the lifter bores. In extreme cases, this can cause a massive internal oil leak when the reliefs in the lifters unmask the oil gallery passages. Certainly part of the art of blueprinting is solving the problems that your other "solutions" may have created.

PISTON-TO-ROD CLEARANCE

If you are using stock pistons and stock rods, you can skip this section. But if you have changed either or both of these components, then you must check the clearance between the small end of the connecting rods and the underside of the pistons. Make sure there is room between the top of the rod and the underside of the piston deck to allow the rod to pivot freely. Aluminum rods require careful scrutiny, because they generally have a greater wall thickness around the pin bore than steel rods. The balancing pads on the top of factory rods can sometimes hit the underside of non-stock pistons, especially when the pistons have a relatively short compression height.

You should also check the clearance between the small end of the rod and the pin bosses. Just because the rod has room to slide back and forth between the bosses when it is on the workbench does not mean that the clearance will be adequate when the rod and piston are installed in the engine. In many engines, including the Chevy V-6 and big-block Chevy V-8, the connecting rod beam is not centered under the piston. If the small end of the rod rides against the pin boss, it will cock the rod and overload one edge of the rod bearing. The usual result is a spun bearing and a broken rod. Again, aluminum rods are most likely to have extra-wide small ends, which can create these problems.

Check the rod-to-piston clearance when the engine has been preassembled. Turn the motor upside down on the stand and watch the small end of the rod move back-and-forth between the piston-pin bosses while the crankshaft is rotated. You should be able to move the small end of each rod from side-to-side without contacting the pin bosses. If the rods are rubbing against the pin bosses, you have a problem that must be corrected before final assembly. The pin bosses can be milled or the small end of the connecting rod narrowed. If the rods are offset slightly in the engine, only one of the piston pin bosses or one side of the rod may need to be machined to provide enough clearance.

ROD BEARING CLEARANCE

The rod bearings are often the last to receive lubrication, yet they operate under the most adverse conditions. Providing plenty of cool, clean oil at the correct pressure and with the proper clearances is the secret to rod bearing survival.

Rod bearing clearance is measured just like main bearing clearance. The diameter of the crankshaft journal is measured with an outside micrometer. Next, the bearing shells are inserted in the rod and cap, the fasteners are torqued, and the inside diameter of the bearing is determined with a micrometer or dial bore gauge. The difference between the two readings is the bearing clearance.

Whenever the rod bolts are tightened, the cap and rod should be held in

Long crankshaft strokes and bulky big ends may cause interference between the rod and the camshaft lobes. Impressions left in the clay on the rod shank indicate where the lobes are too close.

To check the rod bearing clearance, measure the crankshaft journal diameter, and then measure the vertical diameter of the bearing shell after the fasteners are torqued. The clearance is the difference between these two dimensions. The bearing diameter will be larger at the parting lines.

alignment with a vise. Engine shops have special rod clamps for this purpose, but a standard workbench vise works well if you protect the rods with soft jaws. Clamp both the rod fork and cap in the vise when you torque the fasteners; never hold the rod by the shank. A long torque wrench provides considerable leverage, and you may inadvertently twist the rod beam.

Rod bearings, like main bearings, are not always perfectly round. The diameter is generally largest at the parting line, where the bearing picks up oil as it rotates around the crank journal. When measuring the bearing clearance, it is the vertical diameter (90 degrees from the parting line) that is important. The highest loads occur in this direction, caused by both combustion pressure and the stretching forces as the piston changes direction at the top of the stroke. If precision tools are unavailable, rod bearing clearance can also be measured using Plastigage, as described in the crankshaft chapter.

The rod bearings should also be checked for interference with the crankshaft fillets. When a crankshaft is reground for performance or racing use, the radius of these fillets is often increased to add strength at this critical area. In some instances, however, the radii extend into the bearing surfaces on the journal. Installing a bearing insert in the rod and pushing the rod firmly against the crank cheek can check this. Usually the amount of interference is minor and can be corrected by chamfering the outside edges of the rod bearing with a deburring knife. In extreme cases, however, the rod bearings will have to be narrowed. The usual procedure is to make a fixture from a discarded rod; and when the bearing shells are mounted in this makeshift fixture they can be precisely chamfered in a lathe.

ROD SIDE CLEARANCE

The rod bearing clearance is adjusted by selecting thicker or thinner inserts. A ball bearing is used on the micrometer spindle when measuring the curved bearing shell.

Connecting rod side clearance is a factor in controlling the amount of oil circulating through the engine. If the rod side clearance is too small, the flow of oil across the bearing surface is restricted. This oil flow is vital, since it both cools and lubricates the bearing. Further, the centrifugal force of the spinning crankshaft throws the oil onto the cylinder walls, piston skirts, wrist pins, cam lobes, and other moving components. This "splash system" is the only source of lubrication for many parts, so it is vital that the rod side clearance be correct!

Measuring the width of the rods and then comparing this dimension with the distance between the crankshaft cheeks on both sides of the journal can check rod side clearance.

An alternative method is to assemble the rod (or rods, in the case of engines in which a pair share the same journal) and then measure the side clearance with a common feeler gauge. Make sure the rod caps are aligned squarely with the rod fork and then tighten the fasteners.

Keep trying progressively thicker gauges until you find the one that will just slip between the rod pairs or between the rod and crank cheek. The thickness of this feeler gauge equals the rod side clearance.

If the side clearance is tighter than the recommended specification for your engine, there are several ways to increase it. First, you may be able to correct the clearance by swapping rods between journals, or by pairing up different sets of rods.

For example, you may have two rods that are slightly larger than the rest installed on a rod journal that is slightly narrow. By rearranging the rods, you may be able to gain the required side clearance.

The second alternative is to sand down the sides of the rods. This is actually easier than it sounds. You will need a thick piece of plate glass to use for a surface plate, and several dozen sheets of emery paper. Place the abrasive on the glass and sand the side of the rod by moving it in a figure-8. This technique works well if you need to remove only a few thousandths of an inch of metal; taking a larger cut will require dozens of sheets of sandpaper and hours of arm work.

To check the rod side clearance, measure the combined width of the connecting rod pairs – if two rods share a common journal – and then subtract this dimension from the width of the crankshaft journal.

When the rods must be cut substantially to correct the side clearance, they will have to be machined or the crankshaft reground to widen the journal (an expensive and sometimes impractical solution).

Occasionally you may find that the rod side clearance is larger than the recommended specification. Unfortunately, there is no easy solution to this problem, short of obtaining new rods or a replacement crankshaft.

Excessive rod side clearance increases the amount of oil flying around in the crankcase, which can lead to higher windage losses and oil control problems on the cylinder walls. Neither of these conditions is necessarily fatal to performance, however. As long as the rods are not banging around on the journals, a little extra side clearance is acceptable.

For reasons known only to rod manufacturers, most aluminum rods are much narrower than factory steel rods. Consequently, many engine builders discover that the side clearance may be in excess of 0.040-inch (for a pair of aluminum rods).

Although aluminum does expand at roughly twice the rate of steel, these enormous clearances are not necessary. In fact, many successful racers run aluminum rods with side clearances more often associated with steel rods, ranging from 0.016- to 0.020-inch. They report no detrimental effects, and note that the combustion chambers have noticeably less oil contamination than before they reduced the side clearances.

The dowel pins in the aluminum connecting rods must not protrude above the bearing surface or they will score the crankshaft journal.

PISTONS

Aluminum pistons are really rather amazing. They are alternately seared by the heat of combustion, and then blasted by a jet of cold air with every intake stroke. They are accelerated and decelerated at tremendous speed with every turn of the crankshaft, while withstanding side loads that try to weld the piston skirts to the cylinder walls. Everything that an engine builder does to increase performance, from installing a hot-rod cam to porting the heads to bolting on a blower, is intended to do just one thing:

increase cylinder pressure. And, of course, the more pressure there is in the cylinders, the higher the loads the pistons must endure.

Much of the work devoted to piston preparation is required by the special characteristics of aluminum. Since aluminum expands at approximately twice the rate of steel, clearances that are correct at room temperature can change dramatically when the piston tops are heated to over 500 F degrees. Forged aluminum pistons have a much

denser molecular structure than cast pistons, so heat transfers through the forged material more quickly. Also, different parts of the piston expand at different rates. There is more metal around the pin bosses than in the skirts, so these two areas grow to different sizes when heated. This is why an engine that is noisy when first started on a cold morning can run quietly after it has warmed up. As the pistons are brought up to operating temperature, they expand to create the proper clearances.

PISTON-TO-WALL CLEARANCE

The right clearance between the piston skirts and the cylinder walls is absolutely essential. If the *piston-to-wall clearance* is too large, the pistons rock back and forth in the bore. This prevents the rings from sealing the cylinder properly, and can crack the skirts as the piston slaps from side to side. If the clearance is too small, the piston will literally stick in the bore, scuffing the skirts and destroying the wall finish. There's a thin line between too much and not enough, but providing the correct running clearance pays dividends in both durability and horsepower.

There are two piston characteristics that affect the clearance. The first is the *cam grind.* All good quality pistons

TYPICAL TEMPERATURE DISTRIBUTION

CAST — 550°F, 500°F, 450°F, 350°F, 300°F, 350°F, 275°F, 200°

FORGED — 450°F, 425°F, 415°F, 300°F, 250°F, 375°F, 300°F, 200°F

This diagram illustrates the heat distribution in cast and forged aluminum pistons. The densely packed molecules in the forging allow it to conduct heat away from the piston top quickly.

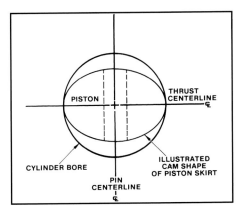

Piston skirts are slightly elliptical when measured at room temperature. This oval shape is the piston's "cam grind."

A "barrel face" piston has a skirt that bulges outward in the center. Because of this complex shape, it is essential to follow the piston manufacturer's instructions when setting the piston-to-wall clearance.

have skirts that are not perfectly round. If you were to cut a piston in half horizontally through its pin bore and then examine the skirts, you would discover that the skirts are slightly elliptical or oval. The eccentricity is hardly noticeable—usually between 0.020- and 0.040-inch—but it's important. The skirt diameter perpendicular to the pin

Piston Materials and Applications

Cast pistons have been the standard automotive pistons for decades. They are inexpensive and easy to produce. They have a thermally stable crystalline grain structure and often incorporate cast-in steel expansion struts that allow them to fit tightly in the bore for optimum stability and ring seal. Under normal use they will stand up well to tens of thousands of miles of use. However, they have limited speed, thermal, and detonation resistance. They should only be used in moderate performance engines where speed is limited and detonation is strictly avoided.

Hypereutectic pistons are castings, but they have nearly 2-1/2 times the silicon of a standard cast piston for increased hardness and greater resistance to higher temperatures and cylinder pressures. They are dimensionally stable and require very little skirt clearance. In some instances they can be operated with less clearance than standard cast pistons. This feature keeps the pistons and ring package well stabilized in the bore and improves sealing and blowby control. While Hypereutectic pistons are well suited to street performance applications, they do not have the detonation and temperature resistance of forged pistons. They should not be used with more than very light nitrous-oxide injection loads, nor with high-pressure turbo- or supercharging systems.

Forged pistons are manufactured with a forging dye from a solid slug of heat-treated aluminum alloy. They possess the dense grain structure and metallurgical properties to stand up to severe use, including a degree of detonation resistance. However, forged pistons have less dimensional stability and require greater skirt clearance for reliable operation. Forged pistons remain the top choice when strength and durability are required for racing, turbocharged, supercharged, or nitrous-oxide-injected applications.

(Photo courtesy of Federal-Mogul Corp.)

Proper piston-to-wall clearance is essential to protect the skirts from scuffing. Measure the piston diameter at the point specified by the manufacturer.

Inserting a feeler gauge between the skirt and the cylinder bore can also check the piston-to-wall clearance.

the primary ingredient, the amounts of silicon, magnesium, manganese, nickel, copper, and other elements vary between the different alloys. These differences in turn affect the expansion characteristics and wear properties of the piston.

The design of the piston skirts also must be considered. Stock cast aluminum pistons, for example, often have steel struts inserted in the pin bosses. These struts hold the skirts in a permanently expanded position, so the piston-to-wall clearance can be greatly reduced. Also, slots behind the oil rings in these pistons effectively isolate the piston head from the skirts, creating a heat dam that prevents the transfer of heat below the ring band. These features produce a very quiet engine, which is ideal for an everyday commuter motor. Forged pistons, in contrast, do not have struts, so the piston-to-wall clearance must compensate for thermal expansion. Also, high-performance pistons frequently rely on holes drilled in the back of the bottom ring groove (instead of a wide slot) to drain oil away from the cylinder walls. Thus, the heat at the top of the piston can travel downward to the skirts, where it causes the aluminum to expand.

Engine speed also determines the optimum piston clearance. High-rpm racing engines require more piston-to-wall clearance than street motors. Piston noise is not a consideration when you are running with wide-open exhaust headers, so racing engines have decidedly looser piston clearances to prevent skirt scuffing under the heat and pressure of competition.

With so many variables to consider, the best advice is simply to follow the piston manufacturer's recommendations—precisely! The piston maker will be familiar with the expansion characteristics of their piston material and skirt design. Measure the piston diameter exactly where the instructions tell you to take the readings. And don't talk yourself into believing that a "little extra" skirt clearance is a good thing. More clearance than is necessary simply makes the engine noisier, oilier, and less reliable.

of the skirt tangs than it is at the piston pin hole. The amount of taper is very slight, typically between 0.005- and 0.010-inch.

Since the range of piston-to-wall clearances for high-performance pistons runs from 0.0015-inch all the way up to 0.015-inch, piston taper can have a tremendous impact on the actual clearance. Some pistons have an even more complex skirt shape called a *barrel grind*. Barrel ground pistons have skirts that bulge outward beneath the oil ring groove, then taper back inward as you move toward the tangs at the bottom of the piston. Regardless of how the piston is shaped, it is extremely important to know *where* on the skirt the manufacturer wants you to measure the clearance!

Most piston makers call for measuring the piston diameter perpendicular to the wrist pin when setting the piston-to-wall clearance. There are exceptions, however. Some racing pistons are measured just below the oil ring groove, while others are miked at the tangs. These differences depend on the particular cam and taper that the manufacturer has chosen.

Other factors also affect the clearance. There are several different aluminum alloys commonly used by piston manufacturers. Although aluminum is

bore is the widest part of the piston, becoming smaller as you move around toward the pin axis. Why? The answer again lies in the different expansion rates of various parts of the piston.

The second piston characteristic that must be considered is *taper*. If you measure that skirt diameter at several places between the top and bottom, you will probably discover that the average piston is wider at the bottom

RING GROOVES

The vast majority of automotive pistons have three ring grooves—two for *compression rings* and one for an oil ring. Although some racing engines pare this assortment down to a single compression ring, and some heavy-duty diesels add an extra one, three seems to be the magic number for piston rings.

Ring grooves are machined with great precision. The tops and bottoms of the grooves must be as smooth as possible to provide a sealing surface for the rings. Whenever the engine is pre-assembled or the pistons are being worked, the ring grooves should be protected by wrapping masking tape around the ring band. This protection is crucial if the pistons are glass beaded; unprotected ring grooves will be pitted, destroying the smooth surface that is essential if the rings are to seal tightly to the piston grooves.

Unlike piston skirts, the ring lands have no cam grind—they are always perfectly round. The diameter of the lands, however, is somewhat smaller than the diameter of the piston. This prevents the lands from contacting the cylinder walls when the piston "rocks over" at top dead center. Reducing the diameter of the ring lands ensures that the skirts alone will handle the thrust loads. The diameter of the ring lands may be stepped, with the land between the top and second ring slightly smaller than the land separating the second ring from the oil ring. On some pistons, the land diameters are tapered, with a constant cut from the oil ring upward.

The location of the ring grooves relative to the top deck of the piston can vary by the type of piston material used and the intended use of the engine. A hypereutectic aluminum cast piston, because of its high silicon content, will reflect more heat from the piston deck into the chamber and not run as hot or expand as much as a forged piston. The ring groove position could be moved upwards slightly. On the other hand, a motor with high doses of nitrous or large amounts of boost from a blower might need the piston grooves placed lower on the piston, and thicker piston decks.

Using a longer than stock connecting rod requires that the piston pin hole be higher in the piston. This in turn may require that the ring grooves be moved higher and closer to the piston deck in order for everything to fit. Most piston makers have "off the shelf" pistons for various non-standard crank stroke and rod length combinations. If you are looking for something other than what is on the shelf, custom pistons can be machined for your application. When ordering pistons, make sure the manufacturer knows not only what compression ratio you are trying to achieve, but the parts combination you have, what you plan to use for fuels, cam data, and the intended use of the engine.

VALVE POCKETS

Almost all overhead valve engines require *reliefs* or *notches* in the piston tops to provide clearance for the valves. Without these notches, the valve lift would be severely limited. Installing a camshaft with longer duration and higher valve lift increases airflow through the engine, allowing the engine to produce more power. As the valves move farther off their seats and are held open longer, the location and depth of the valve pockets in the piston tops become more important.

The valve notches found in stock pistons are usually the wrong sizes and in the wrong places. Factory flattop pistons for a small-block Chevrolet, for example, have four equal-size valve reliefs—even though each combustion chamber has only two valves with unequal head diameters. With four notches, however, the pistons are "universal"—they can be installed in any hole on either bank of cylinders, and there will always be a valve pocket where it's needed. High-performance and racing pistons yield more compression by eliminating the two "extra" valve reliefs. And once the size of the pockets is reduced to fit the exhaust and intake valve heads precisely, then each piston must be assigned to a cylinder with the same valve layout.

If you are using a high-performance camshaft, specialty pistons, or oversize

A punch made by sharpening a valve stem (or a length of drill rod) is the perfect tool for locating the center of the valve relief on a piston.

valves, the location of the valve reliefs must be checked. This requires a sharpened punch that you can insert through the valve guides. (Cutting the head off a discarded valve and sharpening the stem to a point in a lathe or drill press can make a tool.) Preassemble the crank rods and pistons in the block, and then attach a degree wheel to the crank snout and adjust it to indicate TDC for the number one piston. (See the camshaft chapter for a full explanation of this procedure.) Place head gaskets of the same type that you intend to use on the block, and then bolt down the bare heads (without valves). The point when the exhaust valve is closest to the piston generally occurs at 10 degrees *before* TDC; intakes are closest at 10 degrees *after* TDC. To mark the exact center point of the valve pockets, bring the number one piston to 10 degrees before TDC. Insert your punch into the exhaust valve guide and tap the end with a hammer. Remove the punch, rotate the crank to 10 degrees after TDC, and mark the center point of the intake valve, following the same procedure. Repeat this procession for the remaining cylinders, marking the valve locations at 10 degrees before and after TDC. (If your particular cam grind differs greatly from the norm, then you may have to adjust the point at which you punch the pistons.)

You will find a pair of punch marks on the top of each piston when you remove the cylinder heads. These punch marks correspond to the exact center of the valve stem when the piston and valve are closest. To determine if the valve notches are large enough and in the correct location for your engine combination, scribe the valve head diameters on the piston top, using the punch marks as the center of the circle. When scribing these circles, add 0.080-inch to the radius of the valve heads to allow for piston rock and valve float. If the circles you have scribed are within the existing valve notches, then the location of the valve reliefs is correct. If not, the valve notches must be machined to provide clearance. But before you start cutting on the piston tops, the *depth* of the valve notches must also be checked.

How brave are you? That's a question you will have to answer before deciding how much *piston-to-valve clearance* is enough. Surprisingly, determining the right piston-to-valve clearance for a full-on racing engine is easier than settling on the clearance for a high-performance street engine. This is because racing engines usually have stiff valve springs, rigid valvetrains, and solid or roller lifters. Street engines, in contrast, often have heavy valves, weak springs, and hydraulic tappets—all of which contribute to *valve float*. When you decide how much valve clearance is enough, you are really trying to estimate the worst case of valve float that your engine could encounter.

If you had an ideal engine in which the valves always followed the camshaft lobes exactly, the piston-to-valve clearance would never have to be larger than the dimension you used for piston-to-head clearance. This clearance would be enough to allow for *rod stretch* and *thermal expansion* of the pistons. But in the real world, piston-to-valve clearance always has to be larger than the piston-to-head clearance—usually two or three times greater. The reason is that the valves *don't always do exactly what the cam profile tells them to do*. Valve float is a danger that cannot be ignored. Even

Flattop pistons with four valve notches may be installed in any cylinder, since the two notches always correspond to the valve location. The "extra" notches reduce compression, however.

Bring the piston to 10 degrees before TDC, insert the punch in the valve guide, and then lightly tap the punch to mark the exact valve location.

if you are so skillful with a four-speed that you never miss a shift, or have an automatic transmission that never allows the engine to over-rev, there will still come a day when the engine rpm goes sky high. Maybe a universal joint will break or the tires will simply lose traction. On that day, you will be thankful that you took the possibility of valve float into consideration.

The exhaust valves are usually the first to hit. If you ever have an opportunity to see one of the cutaway engines that cam makers always display at the shows, you can see why the exhaust valves have such a tough time. The piston is "chasing" the exhaust valve as it closes. If the cam lobe no longer controls the exhaust valve motion, it is quite likely that the piston will smack the valve as it floats freely in the chamber. Valve action is more controlled on the intake side, though. Here the intake valve follows the piston down the cylinder bore. Since the intake valve is opening when it is closest to the piston, the valve spring exerts greater control over the valve motion. This is why cam manufacturers frequently recommend more clearance for the exhaust valves than for the intake valves.

There are several ways to check piston-to-valve clearance using dial indicators and light tension springs, but the best method is still the old-fashioned clay technique. When you check with clay, you eliminate questions about how much the pushrods might deflect against stiff valve springs or whether the rockers will bend as they overcome the valve spring resistance. What you see when you check valve clearance with modeling clay is exactly what you've got.

Once again, the engine has to be preassembled, with the camshaft degreed in and the heads assembled with the correct valves and springs. Before bolting the head on to the block, place a 0.125-inch-thick layer of modeling clay in the valve notches. Dust the clay with talcum powder or a few drops of oil to prevent it from sticking to the valves. Tighten down the heads on the block, install the rocker arms and pushrods, and adjust the valve lash to the recommended setting. (If you are

using a hydraulic cam, you must substitute solid lifters when checking piston-to-valve clearance. Adjust the valves to zero clearance when checking the clearance with a hydraulic cam.) When all these preparations are finished, rotate the crank through four complete revolutions. Remove the cylinder head. The impressions left in the clay by the valve heads will tell you how much piston-to-valve clearance you have.

Section the clay with a sharp knife or razor blade. Measure the thickness of the clay with a dial caliper, or assemble a stack of feeler gauge strips that equal the height of the clay left on the piston. Although every engine and camshaft design differs, the general rule is that *you must have at least 0.080-inch clearance for the intake valve and 0.100-inch clearance for the exhaust.*

There are several tactics that will increase the piston-to-valve clearance. You can install a cam with shorter duration and/or less valve lift. You can change the *phasing* of the cam by *retarding* or *advancing* it; this will increase clearance for one valve while decreasing it for the other. You can regrind the valve seats to sink the valve seats deeper in the chamber (which, unfortunately, hurts airflow). You can also make the valve heads thinner by

Check the valve relief size with the compass set at the valve head diameter (plus the required safety margin). Center the compass in the punch mark and scribe around the valve notch.

taking a cut across the faces in a lathe. Finally, you can have the pistons machined to deepen the valve notches.

Among these possible solutions, deepening the valve pockets is usually

The clay method may not be the most glamorous way to check the piston-to-valve clearance, but it is the easiest and most reliable way. To be accurate, you must use the same springs and valvetrain that you intend to use when the engine is assembled. Coat the clay with oil or talcum powder to prevent it from sticking to the valve, and then measure the thickness with calipers after turning the crank several complete revolutions.

The valve relief in the piston must match the valve angle in the cylinder head. A protractor bevel provides the precise measurement.

the best choice. The compression ratio will be reduced slightly, but that is a small sacrifice to keep the pistons and valves from colliding. When the valve notches are machined, you can add enough clearance to accommodate future cam changes and to compensate for the inevitable timing changes that occur when the timing chain stretches.

Deepening and enlarging the valve notches requires a vertical mill, which means that most amateur engine builders will have to pay a machinist for these services. There are several do-it-yourself tools to cut valve pockets, but the results generally are not as good as paying a professional to do the job right. The most common way to deepen valve notches is with a *fly cutter*. A fly cutter has a single bit that can be adjusted to the diameter required to provide clearance for the valve head. In racing engines, where every last bit of compression counts, the valve reliefs are sometimes *plunge cut.* In this method, a cutter of the correct size is plunged straight downward into the piston dome, leaving an eyebrow of piston material around the valve relief.

Occasionally the angle of the valve pockets must be corrected as well. This is usually required if the cylinder heads have been angle milled, since this modification changes the relationship between the valve heads and the piston tops. If the clay impression produced during the piston-to-valve clearance check measures thicker on one side of the valve notch than on the other, this indicates that the angle of the valve relief does *not* match the angle of the valve heads. This can be checked with a bevel protractor, and the angle corrected when the valve reliefs are machined.

DOME FITTING AND RADIUSING

The best piston dome is no dome at all! A lump of aluminum projecting into the combustion chamber does raise the compression ratio, but it also disturbs the flame front as the flame spreads through the chamber. Almost without exception, it is better to cut the chamber volume in a wedge-type engine in order to increase compression than to increase the size and height of the piston dome.

There are times, however, when a dome is unavoidable. Racing engines, particularly those that burn alcohol, thrive on compression. In these situations, it is important to maximize the benefits provided by the dome, and to minimize the shortcomings. This means that the domes must be fitted carefully to the chambers, contoured to promote flame travel, and shaped to prevent the creation of pockets and dead areas that can promote detonation.

Most "TRW-type" pistons have universal domes. That is, the domes are small enough to fit most combustion chambers without interference, as long as the cylinder heads have not been milled unmercifully. With these mass produced pistons, all that is required is some hand work with a grinder to radius the edges of the dome. By blending and rounding the dome contours, the flame front has an easier time reaching the far corners of the chamber as the piston parks momentarily at TDC at the start of the power stroke.

Custom pistons will require more work. It is usually a struggle to coax maximum compression from a small displacement drag-racing engine. First, the *swept volume* of the cylinders is small in this type of engine, which limits the available compression. Second, these engines are generally fitted with high-lift, long-duration cams that demand deep valve reliefs in the piston tops. These notches reduce the effective dome volume, so again the final compression ratio suffers. The result is that most "universal" custom-made pistons have very large domes, which must be *individually fitted* to the combustion chambers.

To fit the domes to the chamber by hand, you must first mark the exact location of the cylinder bores on the deck surfaces of the heads. Paint the head with machinists' dye, and then bolt it onto the bare cylinder block. Reach up into the cylinders and mark the location of the bores with a long, sharp scribe. When the head is removed, you will have a circle around each chamber that corresponds to the exact bore location.

Lay the head on a workbench with the chambers facing you. Select the piston that you have assigned to the first chamber, turn it upside down, and position it inside the circle scribed on the head. Take care to align the piston pin holes so that the piston is in the same position relative to the chambers as it will be when it is installed in the engine. Hold the quench area of the piston flat against the deck surface of the head and slowly move it around inside the scribed circle. If the piston moves freely within this circle, there is no interference between the dome and the combustion chamber. Since the top ring land is slightly smaller than the cylinder bore, you can be reasonably sure there will be adequate clearance between the dome and chamber when the piston rocks over at top dead center.

If the piston cannot be moved to the edges of the scribed circle, the dome and chamber are hitting. To pinpoint the interference, paint the dome with dye, and then attempt to fit it inside the scribed circle. As you move the piston within the circle, the dye will be rubbed off where the dome is too close to the chamber walls. Examine the dome carefully for evidence of interference, especially in the areas where it meets the piston top.

Chamber Size and Piston Domes

When you are making your engine parts selection plans, keep in mind that the current performance trend is to use smaller combustion chambers and small dome, flattop, or dish pistons. Large volume wedge-shaped chambers usually require large piston domes in order to achieve high static compression ratios. A large piston dome makes it more difficult for the flame front to cross over the top of the piston. Using a smaller piston dome or no dome at all enhances flame travel and speed. Thoughtful planning can still achieve high compression ratios without a big dome piston. Many performance heads are now available with very small chambers. Decking the heads, angle milling the heads and the choices you make in bore, stroke length, valve relief volume, piston deck-to-block deck height, and head gasket compressed thickness all affect the static compression of the motor. You can juggle these factors to achieve the desired ratio.

Keep in mind that if the motor is to be run on unleaded pump gasoline, the compression ratio should be limited to a maximum of 9.5:1 on an iron-headed motor. With aluminum heads the maximum compression ratio can be 10.5:1. These maximum ratios require premium unleaded fuels with 91 to 92 octane ratings.

To mark the bore location on the cylinder heads, paint around the combustion chambers with machinist's dye, and then bolt the head to the block and scribe around the cylinders.

If the dome and chamber walls are too close for comfort, the offending metal must be removed. You can either grind on the pistons or grind on the cylinder heads—or you may wish to remove a little material from both. A carbide burr or grinding stone works well on cast iron chambers; a high-speed steel cutter dipped in automatic transmission fluid or WD-40 will make quick work of aluminum piston domes and chambers. The simplest way to find and eliminate all the tight spots is by trial-and-error. After you trim a little off the dome or chamber walls, paint the piston dome with dye and try again to fit it inside the circle.

Remember that every little bit of piston and chamber metal that you cut away will *reduce* the final compression ratio; if maximum compression is essential (racing), work slowly and carefully to remove the *minimum* amount of metal needed to fit the dome to the combustion chamber.

This method works well with pistons that have large, flat deck surfaces, such as small-block Chevrolets. Engines with smaller piston quench areas (small-block Boss Fords and Hemis, for example) require a different technique. With these types of engines, the piston tops must be covered with clay, the heads installed, and the clay sectioned to reveal tight spots. Any areas where the clay is compressed thinner than the piston-to-head clearance dimension must be relieved.

Another way to check for dome interference is to use a special extra long connecting rod. The total piston-to-head clearance dimension should increase the center-to center length of this rod. For example, if your engine uses rods that measure 5.000 inches between centers and the total piston-to-head clearance is 0.050-inch, you would then need a checking rod that measures 5.050 inches center-to-center. This extra long rod simulates what happens at high rpm when the piston-to-head clearance is reduced to zero by rod stretch, pin flex, and piston rock. You can also make a checking rod by placing a shim between the rod fork and bearing. The thickness of this shim should equal the piston-to-head clearance dimension.

To check for dome interference with this method, install the piston on the long rod in the assigned cylinder. Bolt down the cylinder head without a gasket and then rotate the crankshaft. If the crank stops as the piston approaches TDC, there is interference somewhere between the piston and combustion chamber. Paint the dome with dye and remove material—where shiny spots indicate interference—until the crankshaft turns freely. When the engine is reassembled later with a head gasket in place, the gasket thickness will provide *running clearance* for the piston.

When the piston domes all fit their respective combustion chambers, they must be smoothed and contoured. Start with a 100-grit hard abrasive cartridge roll and polish away the tool marks left by the cutting burr. On pistons used in deep-wedge chambers, like small-block and big-block Chevrolet V-8s, the edges of the dome should be rounded with a 0.250-inch radius. However, this generous radius is unnecessary on a piston designed for a shallow chamber (such as

Scribe marks on the deck surface show the exact positions of the cylinders. The pistons must be able to fit inside of these circles without interference.

Although you can center the pistons in the chambers by eye when fitting the domes, a more precise method is to mark the exact piston centerline using a surface plate. With the piston held on the vertical pin, measure the ring land diameter, divide by two, and then scribe the piston skirt at the center point.

Align the scribe mark on the skirt with the reference point on the cylinder head to center the piston in the combustion chamber.

the Cleveland Ford family); all that is required is to break the sharp edges. Finish up with fine 220-grit rolls or a Scotchbrite wheel.

If the piston has an extremely large dome, it is important to unshroud the spark plug. A "fire slot" tunneling all the way across the piston is not usually necessary, but there must be enough clearance around the plug electrodes to prevent the dome from cutting off the flame front before it can spread evenly and completely across the chamber. An easy way to determine the location of the plug relief is to bring the piston up to TDC, set the cylinder head in place, and mark the piston dome with a scribe inserted through the spark plug hole. The type of plug you plan to use will dictate how much material must be removed for the plug relief. Extended-tip plugs, for example, will require much more metal removal than a regular gap design.

Another goal of piston dome contouring is to eliminate secondary pockets. These are formed when the dome blocks off portions of the combustion chamber. The fuel/air mixture trapped in these pockets may not burn completely, and heat energy is lost. Further, most automotive combustion chambers are

designed to encourage turbulence as the pistons rise and fall. The swirling motion of the fuel/air mixture suppresses detonation and aids combustion efficiency. The carbon traces deposited on the piston tops of an engine that has been run only a short time provide a graphic illustration of the flame travel taking place inside the chamber. Areas that remain clean and shiny have probably been washed by the incoming fuel, or are the result of incomplete combustion in secondary pockets.

Before you put away your hand grinder, the valve reliefs should also be radiused. This eliminates sharp edges that can cause preignition, and helps the intake and exhaust gases move easily through the combustion chamber. The valves are very close to the piston at times during the overlap stroke. Sharp edges on nearby valve reliefs can hinder flow across the valve heads. The intake pocket should have more generous radii than the exhaust, since the incoming fuel/air mixture is moving away from the valve.

CHECKING PISTON THICKNESS

Before any machine work is performed on a piston, the thickness of the deck and valve reliefs should be

The edges of the combustion chamber frequently interfere with the piston dome. Paint the chamber and dome with machinist's dye when trial fitting the pistons; shiny spots highlight where additional clearance is needed.

checked. Even under ideal conditions, the heat and pressure of combustion can burn holes through piston tops that are too thin. If the engine encounters *detonation*, it takes a thick deck to stand up to the hammering.

A fixture to check piston thickness can be assembled quickly on your workbench vise. Set up a dial indicator

After relieving the dome and chamber walls, the piston on the left fits completely inside the scribed circle on the cylinder head; the dome on the unmodified piston (right) hits the chamber wall before the piston fits completely inside the circle.

Rod stretch (at high rpm) is simulated by placing the shim between the bearing and the connecting rod fork. If the engine turns over with the shim in place, then there is adequate piston-to-head clearance.

Some piston domes require grinding to clear the spark plug electrodes. Mark the location of relief by inserting the scribe through the plug hole with the piston at TDC.

The edges of the piston dome should be radiused to remove the sharp edges and to promote flame travel. The size of the radius depends on the chamber and piston design, the desired compression ratio, the plug location, and other factors. Lubricate the high-speed cutter with WD-40 or automatic transmission fluid to prevent aluminum from clogging the burr.

After radiusing the dome, smooth and polish the cutter marks with hard abrasive rolls.

Carbon deposits on this well-rounded dome indicate that the flame front is reaching all parts of the cylinder. Uncolored areas on the piston domes often are signs of incomplete combustion or fuel separation in the chamber.

Valve notches should be lightly radiused to promote flow around the valve heads and to remove sharp edges, which might cause pre-ignition.

After radiusing the valve reliefs with a high-speed cutter, finish with an abrasive spiral roll.

The custom piston is finally ready for installation after fitting the dome to the chamber, blending the edges, cutting the spark plug relief, radiusing the valve pockets, and glass beading.

on a magnetic stand, as shown in the accompanying photos, then zero the indicator against a metal rod clamped in the vise. To measure the thickness of the piston top, insert the piston between the rod and indicator. Note the indicator reading as you move the piston around on the rod, paying particular attention to potential trouble spots at the bottom edge of the valve reliefs and around spark plug notches. Mark the readings you take on the piston top to provide a "map" that will guide your machinist when he deepens the valve pockets or lightens the piston.

The metal thickness required for reliable piston operation depends on the intended use of the engine. Drag-racing engines, for example, can survive with piston tops as thin as 0.080-inch in very small areas; a circle-track or supercharged engine might not last 10 minutes with such thin piston sections. The piston material also makes a difference, since some aluminum piston alloys are stronger than others. The factor that influences piston life more than any other is *detonation*. Any piston that encounters severe detonation is going to fail eventually, regardless of the deck thickness. Similarly, when combustion temperatures climb because of an extremely lean fuel mixture, the super-heated aluminum will soon fail, no matter how thick or thin it may be.

Insert the piston between the rod and the dial indicator to measure the metal thickness. Watch for thin areas under the corners of the valve reliefs, beneath the deck surface, and around the plug notches.

Clamping a steel rod in a bench vise and then centering the dial indicator plunger over the tip creates this simple piston thickness checker.

PISTON LIGHTENING

Lightening an automotive piston requires a delicate balance between weight reduction and durability. Lightweight pistons improve the throttle response of the engine, which is important in certain types of racing. Light pistons reduce the loads on the connecting rods and piston pins, which in turn allow the weight of these components to be further reduced. The lighter reciprocating weight permits the crankshaft counterweights to be reduced, which further aids engine response. At some point, however, an engine builder reaches the point of diminishing returns. Usually he knows he's arrived there when the pistons start falling apart.

When reliability is more important than quick response, lightening the pistons offers no advantages. Street engines and high-speed oval-track motors operate at fairly constant engine speeds, so lightweight pistons are not essential. The situation changes drastically, however, when you are building a sprint-car engine or a state-of-the-art drag-racing motor. In these applications, engine acceleration is all-important, and every gram of piston weight counts!

One piston manufacturer has observed that when you are trying to take weight out of a piston, aluminum is more expensive than gold. If the dyes in which the piston blank was forged are reasonably up-to-date, the only way to remove weight is to machine it away. This is tedious handwork that requires hours of set-up time and specialized tooling. Although an unknowing engine builder might attack the underside of a piston with an ordinary hand grinder in the hope of eliminating excess weight, the only way to really pare down a piston is with a mill and a wide variety of cutters. The accompanying photos illustrate the areas where a savvy machinist can safely cut down piston weight. It is

This is Patterson Racing's piston thickness checker; the long-travel dial indicator makes it easy to insert a piston in the fixture, and the sharpened point on the steel rod reaches into the tight corners.

Sweeping the inside of the skirt with the end mill lightens the piston skirts. The nozzle sprays the tool with water-soluble oil to lubricate and cool the cutter. All lightening work must be done with radiused cutters, since sharp edges invite cracks.

Piston lightening is expensive because of the amount of machine work it involves. In some types of competition –notably drag racing – piston weight is a critical factor in engine performance. In endurance racing, though, it's more important to have a piston that will last, than a piston that is ultra-light.

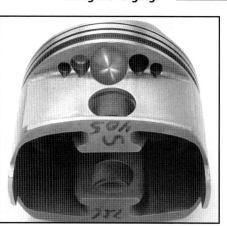

Taking weight out of a piston is never easy. Piston forging design often determines where grams can be trimmed. A ball mill cutter is plunged under the pin boss to remove weight without weakening the forging.

The holes under the ring land must be precisely angled to avoid breaking through to the back of the grooves. After lightening, all edges are carefully deburred to eliminate stress risers.

If you are lightening more than one batch of pistons, accurate records will cut your set-up time. Here's the "log book" that Patterson Racing keeps for each type of piston forging. Entries include the depths and angles of all cuts.

Right: Cuts on the piston struts alongside the pin boss remove weight and allow skirts to flex slightly, reducing cylinder wall distortion. Note the large radius left by the cutter. Lightened pistons must be checked carefully for cracks whenever the engine is disassembled.

Left: A digital position readout for the vertical mill ensures that every piston in a set is machined exactly alike.

The first step in skirt preparation is to deburr the sharp edges left by machining the piston.

Protect ring grooves, ring lands, and pinholes from glass beads with several layers of masking tape. If grooves are glass beaded, the ring seal will suffer.

essential that all lightening work be done with radiused cutters. Sharp corners are natural stress risers that can quickly lead to disastrous cracks.

PISTON SKIRT PREPARATION

Pistons don't just move up and down inside the cylinders. They also try to move sideways as they push against the connecting rod and crank pins. The skirts must stabilize the piston and

absorb these *thrust loads* without distorting or damaging the cylinder walls. The proper cam grind, the right surface finish, and the correct piston-to-wall

clearance can all help the skirts do this job. Detailing the piston skirts will pay dividends in engine durability.

The first step is to thoroughly

Wash the skirts with solvent, and then buckets of hot, soapy water. Scour the grooves with a stiff bristle brush to remove the glass beads and machining chips. Scotchbrite pads work well for scrubbing the pistons.

This engine cutaway illustrates how little clearance there is between the counterweights and the skirts when the piston is at BDC. If you have changed the crankshaft stroke, the rod length, or the piston design, you must check for skirt interference.

Cylinder pressure must be able to reach the rear of the piston rings either through the gas ports drilled from the deck surface or via the ring side clearance. Side clearance is measured by selecting a feeler gauge strip, which just slides between the ring and the groove.

COMPRESSION RING

PISTON

GAS PRESSURE

FACE SEAL

RING TENSION

SIDE SEAL

OIL

Compression rings rely on cylinder pressure to seal the ring face against the cylinder wall. Clearance between the ring and the groove allows this pressure to reach the back of the ring.

RADIAL THICKNESS

WIDTH

SIDE CLEARANCE

deburr the piston skirts. Using a sharp deburring tool, lightly go over all the piston edges and remove the ragged corners left by the factory tooling.

These burrs and nicks can score the cylinder walls if they are not removed. Then carefully round the skirt edges with fine wet-or-dries and paper satu-

HEAD LAND RING

1/8 INCH

1/16 INCH

DYKES RING

0.031 INCH

1/16 INCH

A Dykes or a pressure-backed piston ring has an inside notch that reduces the weight of the ring and improves high-rpm performance.

rated with solvent. Then lightly sand the skirt surfaces with 600-grit paper.

Many engine builders glass bead the piston skirts, but this is still a controversial practice. Those who recommend glass beading claim that a slightly rough skirt texture traps oil and helps lubricate the skirt and cylinder wall. Doubters point out that the small glass particles can become embedded in the skirt material, leading to cylinder scratching.

Certainly custom made-in-California pistons seem less susceptible to galling and scuffing after the skirts have been glass beaded, but you will have to decide for yourself whether the advantages outweigh the risks.

If you decide to glass bead the skirts, the ring grooves and piston pin holes must be protected with masking tape. Use only new, clean glass beads, and set the pressure regulator to 35psi or less. The nozzle should be kept in constant motion across the skirts to prevent concentrating the stream of glass beads in a single spot.

After the glass beading session, wash the pistons thoroughly in clean solvent, and then scour the skirts with Scotchbrite. Finish up by scrubbing the skirts with a stiff brush and hot, soapy water.

SKIRT-TO-CRANKSHAFT CLEARANCE

If you are using specialty pistons, a stroker crankshaft, or non-stock con-

necting rods, you must check the clearance between the piston skirts and the crankshaft counterweights. The bottoms of most piston skirts are scalloped to provide room for the counterweights to pass by when the piston approaches bottom dead center. Occasionally, however, mistakes do happen—especially if the engine has a combination of non-original components.

The skirt-to-crankshaft clearance should be checked visually when the short block is preassembled. As you slowly rotate the crankshaft, look for interference between the bottom of the skirts and the crank counterweights. If they collide, the skirts must be trimmed or remachined to prevent contact.

PISTON RINGS

Piston rings perform a number of vital functions. They seal the gap between the piston and the cylinder wall, preventing combustion gases from escaping into the crankcase. They stabilize the piston as it travels up and down. They cool the piston by transferring three-fourths of the piston heat to the block. They meter the film of oil left on the cylinder walls. What is most remarkable is that they perform all these tasks automatically under the most severe conditions.

There are several ring designs to choose among. Ring materials range from cast iron to ductile iron to stainless steel. Ring facings run from uncoated iron to molybdenum, chrome, or even exotic ceramic coatings. There are rectangular rings in various thicknesses, L-shaped Dykes and headland (pressure-backed) rings, and spacers that allow an engine builder to install one type of ring in a groove machined for an altogether different ring. Yet, despite this wide array of choices, ring selection falls into rather rigid categories. For high-performance street machines and bracket racing engines, the overwhelming choice is a standard 5/64- or 1/16-

Drilling gas ports is a delicate machining operation. The piston is set up in a rotary table on a vertical mill, and the hole locations are marked with a center drill. The gas ports are then drilled with a 0.040/0.060-inch-diameter bit.

inch-wide moly ring. High-rpm drag-racing engines favor 0.043-inch moly rings, while 0.031-inch Dykes rings with either chrome or moly faces are almost universal in Super Stock (drag racing) engines. On the dirt, 1/16-inch chrome plated rings are practically standard equipment.

All compression rings require combustion pressure to work properly, regardless of their material or design. Rings have a certain amount of *radial tension*—the resistance you feel as you squeeze a ring. This radial tension keeps the ring in contact with the cylinder wall when the engine is lightly loaded. When the engine is really making power, though, it is combustion pressure that seals up the cylinders. The clearance between the rings and grooves allows the cylinder pressure to get *behind* the ring, forcing it firmly against the cylinder wall.

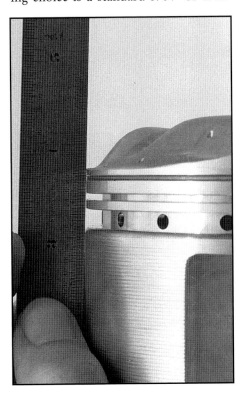

Rings must never stick out of the grooves. To make sure the ring has sufficient back clearance in the groove, hold a straightedge along the skirt and the top ring land; light should be visible between the ring face and the straightedge.

Gas ports eliminate the need for excessive side clearance by ducting the cylinder pressure directly to the back of the top compression ring.

This clearance between the ring and groove is called *side clearance*. In addition to sealing against the cylinder wall, the ring also seals against the groove. Almost all compression rings have a beveled edge or a tapered face. This non-uniform cross-section causes the ring to "dish," just like a dinner plate, when it is compressed. As the ring dishes, it seals against the top and bottom of the groove. To check side clearance, insert the ring in the groove and then find the feeler gauge that just fits between the two. Most compression

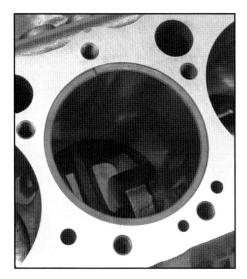

One of the most important engine blueprinting operations is setting the correct piston ring end gaps. Standard rings have large gaps, which allow combustion pressure to leak into the crankcase; high-performance rings are available in 0.005-inch oversizes so that you can tailor gaps to each cylinder. These rings often butt or overlap when first installed in the bores and must be filed to provide the correct gap.

rings require 0.002- to 0.004-inch side clearance to function properly.

The only time that less side clearance is acceptable is when the pistons have been drilled for *gas ports.* Gas ports are a means of applying combustion pressure directly to the back of the ring. When a piston is gas ported, a dozen or more small diameter holes (typically 0.040- to 0.060-inch in diameter) are drilled through the deck and dome to intersect the back of the ring groove. Since these holes supply the pressure that makes the top ring work, the side clearance can be reduced to

This modified K-D rotary ring file is used to carefully trim the end of an oversize compression ring. File carefully to keep the ends of the ring absolutely parallel.

almost nothing. By eliminating the side clearance, the ring has less opportunity to flutter at high rpm, since it is restrained by the groove itself. To take full advantage of the gas ports, a lightweight, narrow faced 0.043-inch ring should be used. Disadvantages? Well,

A fine-toothed file will also cut ring end gaps. Clamp the file in a vise and move the ring along the teeth. Remember to file from the outside of the ring toward the inside to prevent chipping the delicate chrome or moly ring face.

the gas ports will eventually fill with carbon, making the top ring seal ineffective. This is why gas ports are used only on ultra-rpm drag-racing engines. These motors demand the highest quality ring

To measure end gap, insert the ring into the cylinder, and then find a feeler gauge that just fits. Start with a small gauge, and then work your way up to larger ones to make sure that the ring is properly seated in the bore.

The ring should be square in the cylinder when the end gap is measured. You can use a commercially available ring-squaring tool like this one, or a flattop piston inserted upside down into the bore.

After the end gaps are cut, break off the sharp edges with a small whetstone or a fine machinist's file.

Ring End Gaps
for Nitrous and Blower Motors

The increased heat and cylinder pressures generated by the use of nitrous oxide or a blower can cause the top and second piston rings to expand more. You can allow for this increased heat when you end gap the rings for these motors. Speed-Pro makes the following recommendations for end gaps with iron rings.

TOP RING END GAP (ductile iron)

Nitrous Oxide - Street	.006" per inch of bore diameter
Nitrous Oxide - Drag Race	.008" per inch of bore diameter
Supercharged	.006" per inch of bore diameter

SECOND RING END GAP (cast iron)

Nitrous Oxide - Street	.005" per inch of bore diameter
Nitrous Oxide - Drag Race	.0065" per inch of bore diameter
Supercharged	.005" per inch of bore diameter

These are recommendations only! Check with your piston and ring maker for their recommendations when using these types of fuels and inductions. When a motor is freshened or pulled down, always check to see if the ring ends have been butting together. If they have, you must open the gaps more. If there is no evidence of ring end butting, then you can think of reducing the gap. This requires that you keep accurate records of what the end gaps were at the time the motor was built. Be careful! There is some power to be found by getting the ring gaps just right for your particular combination. However, the motor can be damaged if the gaps are too tight.

COURTESY OF SEALED POWER CORP.

RECOMMENDED END GAPS

DUCTILE IRON TOP RINGS
   Supercharged/Injected Engines:

Supercharged/injected nitro engines	0.022/0.024-inch
Supercharged/injected alcohol engines	0.018/0.020-inch
Supercharged/injected gasoline engines	0.022/0.024-inch

   Carbureted Gasoline Engines:

Oval track (rectangular rings)	0.018/0.020-inch
Oval track (head land rings)	0.024/0.026-inch
Oval track (pressure back rings)	0.020/0.022-inch
Modified drag racing engines	0.018/0.020-inch
Stock drag racing engines	0.016/0.018-inch
Street engines	0.016/0.018-inch

PLAIN IRON SECOND RINGS
   Supercharged/Injected Engines:

Supercharged/injected nitro engines	0.014/0.016-inch
Supercharged/injected alcohol engines	0.012/0.014-inch
Supercharged/injected gasoline engines	0.012/0.014-inch

   Carbureted Gasoline Engines:

Oval track	0.012/0.014-inch
Modified drag racing engines	0.012/0.014-inch
Stock, Super Stock drag racing engines	0.010/0.012-inch
Street engines	0.010/0.012-inch

These suggested end gaps are intended only as a guide. Individual engines may require larger end-gap dimensions.

This chart underlines the importance of proper piston ring end gaps to performance. Sealed Power Corporation found that reducing the end gaps from 0.024-inch to 0.016-inch added approximately 30 horsepower to a typical 350ci Chevrolet. Further reducing the end gaps to 0.010-inch hurt power because the ends of the rings were butting. (Sealed Power Corp.)

This fixture is used to reduce the radial width of a compression ring. By machining the back of a top or second ring, the tension – and thus the amount of ring "drag" – is reduced. This requires special shallow ring grooves, and should be considered a trick for serious racers only.

seal, even at astronomical rpm levels, and are rebuilt frequently.

Another crucial dimension for piston rings is *back clearance,* the space behind the ring when the face is flush with the ring lands. For high-performance and racing applications, the back clearance should be as close to zero as possible. When the volume behind the ring is reduced, the gas pressure charges the ring more quickly, which improves the cylinder seal. Ring grooves in many production pistons are much deeper than they need to be. If your pistons have these extra-deep grooves, using steel shim material, sold by Speed Pro and other sources, can reduce the back clearance. The rings must *never* protrude past the lands.

Providing the proper ring end gaps will pay big dividends in performance. A ring must be split to allow it to slip over the top of the piston; the space left where the ends of the ring meet is the *end gap.* This gap also allows the ring to expand as the piston and the combustion gases heat it. Ideally the ring should grow just enough to reduce the end gap to zero. The combustion pressure then has no way to escape, so more of the combustion energy is applied to pushing the piston down the cylinder bore.

You can fashion a dirt-cheap piston ring holder from a scrap of lumber and a handful of nails. This will prevent mixing the rings after they have been assigned to a particular cylinder bore.

Double Tru-Arc or Spirolox pin retainers add an extra margin of safety for a high-rpm engine. Always install Tru-Arcs so that the sharp edge is against the groove in the piston and pin, with rounded edges facing each other.

With perfectly round bores and the right end gaps, blow by—and the lost horsepower it represents—can be cut drastically.

When you buy a standard set of piston rings, the end gaps are invariably too large for best performance. The ring manufacturers recognize that production engine rebuilders don't take the time to tailor the ring end gaps. Consequently most ring sets will have about 0.030-inch of end gap—almost twice as much as is necessary to accommodate normal thermal expansion. Fortunately, top quality ring makers—like TRW and Sealed Power—also realize that minimizing end gaps is an important part of engine blueprinting, so they offer ring sets that are 0.005-inch oversize. For example, you would order 4.035-inch rings for a 4.030-inch bore size. When these rings are first installed in the cylinder bore, their ends may butt or overlap. By carefully filing the ring ends, the engine builder can come up with the exact end gap he wants.

Placing the ring squarely in the cylinder, and then inserting a feeler gauge in the space left between the ends measures ring end gap. Setting the ring end gaps is one of the last steps before the engine is assembled for the final time. The cylinder bores must be honed and cleaned; a change of only 0.001-inch in bore diameter will increase the end gap by over 0.003-inch. When checking the end gaps, it is best to

"sneak up" on the final gap dimension. This means that if you want a total end gap of 0.016-inch, you should start with the 0.013-inch feeler gauge. Then, progressively increase the gauge thickness, going from the 0.014- to the 0.015-inch-thick gauge before finally inserting the 0.016-inch feeler. This technique ensures that the ring is in tight contact with the cylinder wall, and prevents the removal of too much material. If you cut the ring gaps too large, there's nothing to do but get another ring and start over!

You can tailor the end gaps with a circular file made expressly for this purpose or with a standard metal file held firmly in a vise. Regardless of which tool you use, you must always cut from the outside of the ring toward the inside. This prevents chipping the molybdenum or chrome ring face. Check the straightness of your cuts frequently by squeezing the ends of the ring together and holding the ring up to a light. If you can see light seeping through the gap, because one of the ring ends is rounded or angled, carefully file the ends straight again—taking care not to let the total gap (when the ring is installed in the cylinder) become too large. When you are satisfied with all the ring gaps, use a fine whetstone to deburr the edges.

The size of the end gaps depends on the ring location and engine usage. As the rpm range and horsepower climb,

the end gaps must be made larger to compensate for the greater heat they encounter. A general rule of thumb is to allow 0.004-inch of end gap for every inch of bore size for high-performance street engines. Using this formula, rings for a 4-inch bore cylinder should have 0.016-inch end gaps. Since second rings generally run much cooler than top rings, the end gaps can be closed up slightly, to 0.003-inch for every inch of cylinder diameter. The ring experts at Sealed Power Corporation have compiled the accompanying chart of recommended end gaps for typical applications.

You should resist the temptation to run ring gaps that are substantially tighter than these recommendations. If the gaps are too small, the ends of the rings will butt together. As the ring continues to expand, the ring face is forced against the cylinder wall, causing rapid wear. The ends of the rings should always be inspected when the engine is disassembled for overhaul; shiny spots are clear evidence that the ends have butted. If no shiny spots are apparent, the end gaps on the next set of rings can be reduced slightly—no more than 0.002-inch at a time.

End gaps for oil rings are much less critical. Most oil rings have three distinct components: two *rails* and an *expander*. The rails should be inserted in the cylinder bore to make sure that they

A good pair of internal snap ring pliers is essential for installing and removing Tru-Arc pin retainers. Don't invite trouble by reusing Tru-Arcs; replace them at every overhaul! Spirolox are usually destroyed when you remove them, so there's no temptation to put them back into a motor.

have adequate end gaps. Since the oil ring does not seal the combustion pressure, even gaps as large as 0.030-inch are all right.

Many high-performance piston ring sets feature low-tension oil rings. These rings are intended to increase power output by minimizing frictional losses as the rings travel up and down the cylinders. Low-tension rings are created by deliberately mismatching the rails and expanders. For example, a standard tension oil ring for a 4.060-inch cylinder would have two rails and an expander specifically designed for a 4.060-inch bore. A so-called low-tension oil ring has the same rails, but the expander comes from a ring set designed for a 4.030-inch bore, a cylinder that is 0.030-inch smaller. To produce a "super low-tension" oil ring, an expander from a 4.000-inch bore ring set would be substituted.

These low-tension oil rings reduce internal friction, but at the cost of increasing oil consumption. Oil economy simply is not important to most owners of high-performance and racing engines.

What is important, though, is keeping oil out of the combustion chambers, where it leaves deposits and fosters detonation. Engines equipped with low-tension oil rings usually require some kind of crankcase-evacuation system to help slow the migration of oil past the

oil rings. The hoses often seen on racing engines that connect the valve covers, intake manifold, and header collectors are all part of an elaborate crankcase-evacuation system that is designed to improve oil control inside the motor.

You can measure the effects of ring tension with a common fish scale. To check ring drag, install the rings on a piston, then insert the piston into the cylinder bore, upside down. Push the piston to the bottom of the cylinder, and then hook the fish scale to the piston pin. As you pull the piston upward, note the resistance on the scale. Don't be confused by the force needed to start the piston moving up the bore; instead, concentrate on the scale reading as the piston moves at a steady speed.

By comparing the force required to pull the piston through the cylinder with different ring packages, you can quite graphically see differences in ring tension.

PINS

Even though pressed wrist pins have numerous advantages, floating pins have a racier image and are therefore more popular with performance engine builders. Floating pins simplify engine assembly and disassembly, a feature that appeals to backyard engine builders. The trick is making sure that floating pins stay in the pistons until you decide that it is time for them to come out.

Floating piston pins are held in place with either Tru-Arcs, Spirolox, or wire rings. Many performance pistons are machined for *double* Tru-Arcs or Spirolox, based on the theory that a pair of retainers on each end of the pin is less likely to fall out than a single clip. With the aid of a good set of snap ring pliers, Tru-Arcs are reasonably easy to remove and install. Spirolox, on the other hand, require a small, sharpened screwdriver and a great deal of patience to remove. Spirolox retainers are usually destroyed in the process of removing them, which at least removes the temptation to reuse them. Even though you can get a set of Tru-Arcs

A common fish scale measures oil ring tension as you pull the piston through the cylinder. Pull slowly so that the scale accurately records the ring drag and not the force needed to start the piston moving.

out of a piston without harming them, used Tru-Arcs should be discarded at every engine overhaul. These clips lose tension every time they are compressed, making them more likely to pop out on their own.

When you are preassembling the engine to check deck heights, valve clearance, and so forth, balls of masking tape will hold the wrist pins in place. Don't install the pin retainers until the engine is going together for the final time. If the pistons are machined for double Tru-Arcs, snap the two clips into the groove with their rounded edges facing each other. With a single Tru-Arc per side, the rounded edge should be against the pin, leaving the sharp edge to bite into the aluminum of the piston.

CYLINDER HEADS

An engine's cylinder head ports are the pathways to power! The air and fuel that pass through them are the sole source of energy. No matter what standard you apply to engine performance—horsepower, torque, fuel economy, or response—it is the valves, seats, and ports that are finally responsible for how well the motor works.

Differences between high-performance short blocks are relatively minor; what makes one motor superior to another is likely to be the valve layout, chamber shape, and port volumes.

No book can thoroughly explain the mysteries of cylinder head porting. Porting techniques are as trendy as hairstyles and musical tastes; yesterday's hot setup is today's old news. First of all, the design qualities of available head castings have a tremendous impact on what is possible and what is not. And with both the Detroit automakers and the specialty head manufacturers introducing radical new designs and revisions of old ones almost daily, the state of the art in head porting is constantly changing. For these reasons, we will concentrate

The range of cylinder head choices confronting performance enthusiasts has never been greater. Today an engine builder can select from a variety of factory and aftermarket castings in both aluminum and iron.

on the basic blueprinting techniques that apply to *any* cylinder head: Preparing the valves, seats, guides, and springs. And for those who have a compulsion to grind on cylinder heads, we will outline some simple port work that can make a substantial difference in airflow.

SELECTION AND INSPECTION

Selecting and inspecting cylinder heads parallels very closely the steps involved in choosing a cylinder block. Many of the same procedures and cautions apply.

In general, late-model cylinder heads are inferior to older, Sixties vintage iron.

Current production castings have very thin metal sections, and the ports are likely to be extremely restrictive. These small runners promote high mixture velocities, even at low engine speeds, so they are favored by mileage-conscious automakers. Power, though, comes with

Cylinder Head Selection

In 1997, the number of cylinder heads available for your engine was staggering, and the numbers of choices were a little intimidating. Cylinder head design, particularly for high performance and race heads, has ranged far from the factory performance castings of the Sixties and Seventies. Older designs with their attendant limitations and problems have been improved upon tremendously. Aluminum and cast iron performance heads are available in many port volumes sizes, valve sizes, port configurations, valvetrains, combustion chamber sizes and designs, spark plug locations, water jacket locations, spring pocket dimensions, and deck surface thicknesses, and they have better oil and gasket sealing.

Many of the blueprinting and performance-enhancing techniques in cylinder head preparation have been adopted into the newer design racing and street performance heads. These days, you get more cylinder head for your money, more power, less cost, and

wider consumer availability. Many reputable specialty cylinder head shops can prepare heads, flow bench test them, and assemble them with the valvetrain parts you need. "Swirl and Tumble" head technology has even found its way into street head designs, not only to improve cylinder filling and power, but also to reduce tailpipe emissions levels.

One aspect that many of us have to consider is cost. You can certainly use an older style casting and make improvements in port flow, valve size, valvetrain parts, etc. However, you may need to install hardened valve seats to the heads if you are going to use unleaded pump gasoline. By the time you add up the costs of these improvements and include the costs of head cleaning, repairs, seat grinding, guides, install screw-in rocker arms, seals, etc., the costs may surpass the cost of a newer design head that has already incorporated these improvements. Give it some thought before you make your cylinder head choices.

an increase in port volume—which is why you must go back to the ample passages found in older cylinder heads if you are building a serious street performance or bracket-racing engine.

For an all-out racer, however, nothing less than the very latest factory or specialty castings will do. The series of "Bow Tie" cylinder heads developed by Chevrolet, the SVO offerings from Ford, and even the so-called "corporate" small-block heads (for the Chevrolet cylinder block) available from Pontiac all represent the latest thinking in the science of engine airflow. And when both your budget and the rulebook allow specialty castings, the racing-only designs from Dart, Brodix, Brownfield, and other non-Detroit sources are vastly superior to anything you can find in a salvage yard.

If your head choices are confined to used parts, then you must look carefully before exchanging cold cash for cast iron. Cylinder heads, like blocks, are prone to cracking if they have been overheated or frozen during their lifetime. The advent of unleaded gasoline in the early Seventies prompted many automakers to induction-harden the valve seats in cylinder heads. This allows the seats to survive without the lubrication provided by small amounts of lead—but this process also made the seats much more susceptible to cracks, especially on the hot exhaust side. This is another point in favor of early "pre-smog" head castings. Cylinder heads can be checked for cracks with Magnaflux inspection or by pressure testing the water jackets, as discussed in the chapter on cylinder blocks.

A thorough head inspection should also include a close look at the valve seats and guides. If you have a choice, avoid heads that have already had a valve job performed on them. During a typical quick-and-dirty valve job, the seats are ground with little concern for airflow characteristics. The usual result is that the valves are "sunk" in the chambers. This reduces compression, by increasing the combustion chamber volume. In addition, the bumps and ridges left around the seat by a careless machinist can disrupt the flow of air around the

Edelbrock Performer aluminum heads offer good value for those seeking a more modern design street performance head. When you consider the time and money spent altering an older style production cast iron head, the newer designs are comparable in price, but you get more cylinder head for your money with the newer designs.

valve head. It may be difficult to find this telltale evidence of a previous valve job in a cylinder head that is coated with baked-on carbon. When you go head hunting, take along a valve spring compressor and remove several valves. If you find distinct ridges surrounding the seats, chances are good that someone has already worked over—and perhaps ruined—the castings.

A sharp parting line around a seat indicates that at some time in the past it has been repaired with an *insert*. An insert is a metal ring that is pressed into the head to repair a damaged or cracked seat. There is nothing intrinsically bad about a seat insert; after all, most aluminum heads are outfitted with seat inserts at the factory. However, you have no way of knowing if the insert was installed properly or what type of damage it conceals. Unless the casting in question is extremely rare or valuable, it is probably better to continue your hunt than to buy someone else's problems.

A little preliminary research can make your head shopping more successful. Every brand of performance engine has some prized head castings. For example, small-block Chevrolet enthusiasts seek out "fuel-injection," Bow Tie, and "turbo" castings; Mopar fans covet various W-2 and Stage heads, while the Ford contingent stalks Boss and Cleveland components.

Unfortunately, a reputation for high performance is likely to add a premium to the price of a set of cylinder heads. You can, however, cut the high cost of hot rodding by recognizing that the real distinction between a set of high-priced heads and cheaper castings may be only an insignificant difference in valve sizes or combustion chamber volume.

Among small-block Chevy head castings, for example, the early large port heads with 2.02-inch intake valves—usually identified as "fuel-injection" heads—can fetch twice the price of a pair of similar castings with 1.94-inch intakes. In truth, the heads with smaller valves are really the better buy. They have the same ports and chambers as the big-valve castings. And if you upgrade them by installing larger

Non-Adjustable Valvetrains

Many stock production valvetrains are not adjustable for valve lash. Hydraulic lifter flat tappet and roller cams with non-adjustable "net lash" have been used on Ford and many late model Chevrolet motors. The individual rocker studs or bolts, rocker arms, and pushrod lengths on these valvetrains limit the choices you can make with regard to higher lift cam profiles since they will not accommodate much more lift, nor can they be used with solid lifter flat tappet or roller cams that require the use of any valve lash. If you intend to use a cam profile with more lift and duration, and you are going to use a production cylinder head that originally was designed to work with a non-adjustable valvetrain, you will have to change the rocker arm assembly. This change may require the use of a different rocker arm stud, pushrod length, rocker arm, and ball. The head may need to be tapped and threaded for a screw-in stud, instead of a pressed-in stud.

A number of cam companies have the required parts to change over from a non-adjustable rocker arm assembly. Some of these kits do not require any additional machine work and are "bolt on," but some need machining depending on your engine application. Late model Chevy production heads with the "net lash" valvetrains can usually be changed over by using the rocker arm assemblies from pre-1986 valvetrains with replacement screw-in studs.

If you plan to use the non-adjustable rocker arm assembly, with a production head, cam companies have a number of grinds that will improve performance and still work with computer controls and net lash rocker assemblies. Keep in mind that if the block or heads have been decked, or if you are changing the head gasket thickness, the pushrod length may no longer be correct for your application. Check the rocker arm geometry and adjust pushrod length accordingly.

Late model stock Chevrolets use non-adjustable, "zero or net lash" valvetrains and "self-aligning" rocker arms. Many Ford production rocker arm assemblies are also non-adjustable. If you change to a higher-lift camshaft you may also have to change to adjustable rocker arm assemblies with longer slots and different rocker studs.

Casting numbers are the keys to spotting desirable cylinder heads. Heads with the same casting numbers may have different valve diameters, however.

valves, your machinist will have virgin metal to work with when he grinds the critical valve seats. This is just one instance of smaller being better—and a bargain, too.

Before starting work on your chosen cylinder heads, a thorough cleaning is in order. An overnight stay in a hot tank (cast iron heads only!) or some time on a jet-cleaner turntable will remove most of the grease and grime. Carbon deposits in the chambers and ports can be dislodged with a wire brush mounted in a drill. A glass beader will blast the runners clean while simultaneously deburring and smoothing the

Three-angle valve seats have become standard for most high-performance and competition engines. Although the preferred angles and widths may vary depending on the type of cylinder head and the intended use – all three-angle seats have a bottom cut, a seat cut (which seals the valve face), and a top cut.

passages. Use caution, though, if your heads are destined for a racing engine that requires stock cylinder heads; the tech inspectors will be looking for ports that are suspiciously smooth. If you glass bead the heads, take extra care to get all the grit out of the bolt holes and valve guides before proceeding.

HEAD GASKETS

Three general types of head gaskets are made: a solid steel shim gasket, a composition type with different layers of materials, and a third type which is a solid copper alloy. Each type has various qualities, compressed thicknesses, and applications.

Many factory production street motors were built with cast iron cylinder heads, and most of these used a steel shim head gasket when built at the factory. If aluminum heads were used, a composition gasket is utilized. Since a cast iron block and aluminum heads have different expansion rates when heated, aluminum heads want to move around more relative to the cast iron block deck surface. A composition head gasket is better able to maintain a seal between the head and block deck surfaces.

A number of race engines use solid copper head gaskets. The copper is softer than the steel shim and can conform to minor surface irregularities on the decks. Copper also transfers heat well. Copper head gaskets can be cleaned and reused. If a block or heads have been O-ringed, the wire used in the O-rings will embed in the copper gasket and help seal the individual cylinders.

If you use a steel shim or copper head gasket, it must be coated with an appropriate head gasket sealer before installation. A number of spray-on or brush-on sealers are available. Gasket sealers are generally not used with composition head gaskets.

Some head gaskets may require that you "re-torque" the head bolts after the engine has initially been run and reached normal operating temperatures. Make sure you follow the manufacturer's recommended head bolt torquing sequence and torque amounts. If you use an aftermarket head bolt or stud and nut, follow the maker's recommended torque amounts, use of thread lubricants, torque procedures and stages, and final fastener torque amounts.

A number of composition gasket makers have head gaskets with steel rings that surround each cylinder barrel. There are also some with a raised fire ring for use on engines with extreme cylinder pressures (for example, a high dose nitrous motor or very high output blower or turbo engine).

With these raised fire ring gaskets, an O-ring groove is cut into the head deck. These grooves match the raised fire ring in the gasket. Fel-Pro offers their "Loc Wire" ring composition style gasket for these applications. The gasket fire ring then engages and locks into the groove for a tight seal when the head is bolted to the block.

Head gaskets are available in various compressed thicknesses, and you must carefully consider which to use. Minimum clearance between the piston deck and the head deck, when using steel connecting rods, is .040-inch. If you are using aluminum rods, which stretch more, the operating clearance has to be increased.

The head gasket thickness is considered with other factors and engine dimensions. What is the piston deck-to-block deck clearance on your motor? What static compression ratio are you trying to achieve? You also want to maintain the proper minimum clearance between the piston deck and an open valve. You may wish to use a head gasket thickness to lower the compression ratio (thicker) or to increase the ratio (thinner). Some time spent planning before the motor is machined and parts purchased will help you make decisions on head gasket types and the appropriate thickness for your application.

VALVES AND SEATS

The seats are where the valves meet the cylinder heads. Whether the head castings came out of a factory parts box or a station wagon with 100,000 miles on it, the time and effort lavished on preparing the seats properly will be well spent. The seats are the most critical area in the engine in terms of airflow. Every molecule of fuel and oxygen the engine burns must pass through these critical points.

Since air is invisible, it is sometimes difficult for beginning engine builders (and even some experienced ones) to imagine how it moves through a motor. It may be helpful, therefore, to visualize the air as if it were a liquid. If you can picture a wild river brimming with rocks and boulders, you will have a good idea of the obstacles in the pathway of the air/fuel mixture as it winds through the head ports. As the water in this imaginary river rushes downstream, it forms turbulent whirlpools and eddies, as well as stagnant pools where there is little movement. These white-water rapids may be spectacular, but they make river travel difficult. A smoothly flowing river channel seems tame in comparison, but it does a better job of moving large volumes of water. Like the water in a river, the air/fuel mixture that flows through an engine has mass. Obstacles in the path and quick changes in direction cause it to become turbulent; it forms invisible swirls and whirlpools. As a result, fuel droplets, which are heavier than the air molecules that surround them, separate from the main flow and collect in pockets, like driftwood along the banks of a river. Since this upsets the delicate balance of fuel and air that is needed for optimum power, engine performance suffers. So the goal of most cylinder head work is to create the conditions that allow the "river" of fuel and air to move through the ports as smoothly as possible.

Valve seats in factory-installed heads are designed for durability, not maximum airflow. Factory valve seats are ground at only one angle—usually 45 degrees, although some automakers use 30- or 37-degree seats. This single angle causes the air and fuel (or exhaust gases) to make an abrupt change in direction as they flow past the valve head. And, as you might expect, this sharp turn causes

The search for precision has led some cylinder head specialists to use torque plates when grinding the valve seats. Here Darrell Wilke bolts a head to a thick steel plate. This recreates the stresses in the casting, which occur when the head is installed on the block.

Machined reliefs in the torque plate provide clearance for the grinding stones. A head gasket is sandwiched between the plate and the deck surface.

Steel cutters remove material quickly when installing oversize valves or opening up the "throat" just below the valve seat.

Grinding high-performance valve seats requires a selection of stones and pilots. Each stone is cut to produce one distinct angle of the valve job (from left to right: 30-degree top cut, 45-degree seat, 60-degree bottom cut). Pilots for the grinding stones must fit the guides tightly to ensure that the seats are concentric with the valve stems; expandable and over-size pilots are available.

The stones are dressed to the desired angle with a diamond-tipped cutter.

problems. The flow becomes turbulent, restricting the amount of air that can enter or leave the combustion chamber. Fuel droplets fall out of the airstream and collect on the port walls and valve heads, which cause the air/fuel mixture to fluctuate. Surely, you say, there must be a better way to grind a valve seat. And indeed there is. The *three-angle valve job* has become nearly universal among builders of high-performance engines.

Each of the three angles has a distinct function. The *bottom cut* is typical-

THREE ANGLE VALVE SEAT

30° TOP CUT

.030

45° SEAT

.060

60° BOTTOM CUT

.100

A typical three-angle valve job consists of a series of cuts, which will promote a smooth flow of gases between the ports and the combustion chambers.

ly ground at a 60-degree angle; it marks the beginning of the transition from the valve bowl to the combustion chamber. The width of this bottom cut depends on how much metal the machinist has to work with beneath the seat, although a figure of around 0.100-inch is typical.

Instead of using different valve seat grinding stones to cut each angle in a valve seat, many newer seat grinding machines use steel seat cutters. These cutters can be set up to provide seat diameter, seat width, angles, and can cut all three angles simultaneously. In a three-angle valve job, the top cut, valve seat angle, and bottom cut can be made at the same time. It's quicker than using three different grinding stones, each with the appropriate angle.

The actual *valve seat,* which seals against the valve face, is ground at a 45 degree angle. The width of this seat will vary according to the machinist's preferences and the intended usage. Darrell Wilke, the proprietor of Wilke Performance Specialties in Wichita, Kansas, performed the cylinder head and valve work pictured here. His years of experience have shown that 0.040-inch-wide intake seats and 0.055-inch-wide exhaust seats work well with the limited valve spring pressure of a street or bracket-racing engine equipped with a flat-tappet camshaft. With the higher spring pressures that accompany a roller cam, wider

0.060- and 0.080-inch seats are more resistant to "pounding out."

In general, it is good to remember that a narrow seat usually flows somewhat better than a wide seat, but it is not as durable. Also, heat in the valve head transfers to the cylinder head through the seat, so a wide seat helps to cool the valve. This is why exhaust seats are usually ground slightly wider than intake seats.

A *top cut* is the finishing touch for a three-angle valve seat. The angle of this

The first step in performing a high-performance valve job is to clean the guides and insert the pilot. The pilot remains in place until all three angles have been ground.

The stone is mounted on a holder and installed over the pilot.

The grinding stone is spun with a high-speed pneumatic or electric driver.

A machinist constantly checks his progress by measuring the seat diameter with dividers. Seats in used heads are ground until all pits and grooves are removed, and then narrowed with top and bottom cuts. Seats should be as high as possible for the best airflow.

cut can run from a shallow 15 degrees to a relatively steep 37 degrees, depending on the condition of the cylinder heads and the depth of the valve seats. This top cut narrows the seat to match the diameter of the face of the valve head, and eliminates the sharp edge where the seat meets the combustion chamber. If the cylinder head is new, or if oversize valves are being installed, this top cut may be omitted to keep the seat as high as possible.

A *radiused valve* seat is a refinement of the three-angle seat. This type of seat is sometimes used in racing cylinder heads. Actually, the seat itself is not radiused—although it may be narrowed considerably. Instead, the angles above and below it are carefully rounded. The valve seat remains at a 45° angle, but the top and bottom cuts are blended by hand, using a hard abrasive roll in a high-speed grinder.

Some head porters also use specially prepared grinding stones to radius the approaches to the seat. A radiused valve seat has no sharp edges to disrupt the airflow; instead, there is just a gradual transition from the combustion chamber to the port. The cost of preparing radiused seats is usually higher than a simple three-angle valve job because of the skillful handwork required to blend the approaches without disturbing the seat itself. For any street or moderate competition engine, radiused seats are probably an unnecessary luxury.

New valves require very little preparation. The faces are normally premachined to the engine manufacturer's specified angle. If, however, the angle of the valve seats in the cylinder head has been changed, then the valves must be reground. This is required when an unusual seat angle (30 or 37 degrees, for example) is replaced by a conventional three-angle valve job with 45-degree valve seats. Used valves must be refaced in a valve-grinding machine to remove pits and wear marks. Regrinding a valve narrows the margin—the straight

portion of the valve head. As much of the margin as possible should be preserved when refacing valves; if the margin is ground away when refacing a valve, then the valve should be discarded

A valve seat indicator confirms the accuracy and concentricity of the finished valve job.

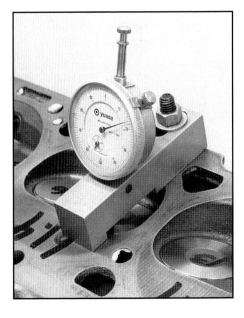

A Moroso valve depth checker allows engine builders to equalize the valve seat heights. This produces consistent valve-to-piston clearances and uniform combustion chamber volumes.

Hardened Valve Seats

By 1997, leaded gasoline at the gas station pump had disappeared along with the gas station attendant who used to pump your gas, clean the windshield, and check the fluid levels and tire pressures for you. Unleaded pump gasoline is the norm, as are lowered octane levels. If you are building a motor to be used on the street that will burn a steady diet of unleaded pump gasoline, make sure the cylinder head castings you use have hard seats. Many of the cast iron heads produced before 1975 had soft seats for use with the leaded pump gasoline that was available everywhere at the time. If your heads are the early soft seat variety, your machinist can add hardened seat inserts to the heads to help the seats, guides, and valve edges survive on unleaded fuel. Properly installed hard seat inserts won't hurt the flow of air through the bowls. Keep in mind that every aluminum head casting uses hard valve seat inserts.

and replaced with a new piece. A knife-edged valve head is weak and the sharp outer edge inhibits flow.

Stock valves can usually benefit from a practice called *back cutting*. Production valves often have excessively wide faces and sharp edges behind the valve heads. Both features restrict airflow.

A valve-grinding machine is used to cut down the underside of the valve head, usually at a 30-degree angle. This both removes the sharp edge and narrows the valve face. The amount of material that can be safely removed depends on the shape of the valve head. The width of the remaining valve face should always be slightly larger than the seat width in the cylinder head. Valves that are designed for racing or high-performance applications generally have much narrower faces than stock valves, and usually require only a slight back cut to narrow their faces to match the width of the valve seats.

VALVE LAPPING

The operations described up to this point—seat grinding, valve facing, and back cutting—all require expensive machinery and considerable know-how. There is one head preparation chore, however, that demands no exotic equipment. *Valve lapping* is a task you can do on a garage workbench. It will provide the best possible valve seal, and will allow you to check the workmanship of your machinist.

To lap the valves in a cylinder head, you will need some extra fine *lapping compound* (Clover 3A to 6A is recommended by many experts) and a valve lapping stick, which is nothing but a wooden dowel with a suction cup on the end. (Most auto parts stores stock these items.) Add a little water to the lapping compound to make a thick paste, and then smear the compound around the circumference of the valve face. Squirt a few drops of oil into the valve guide, and then insert the valve into the head. Wet the suction cup on the lapping stick and apply it to the valve head. Twirl the stick between your palms while lightly pressing the valve against the seat. After a few seconds of lapping, lift the valve and rotate it 90 degrees, then continue lapping.

When you feel the abrasive lapping compound no longer cutting, pull the valve out of the head, wipe off the compound, and examine the face. You will see a light gray ring on the valve face where it was rubbing against the seat.

A valve-facing machine grinds new seats on valve heads. The valve rotates against the abrasive wheel while cutting fluid carries away grit and metal particles. A valve facer can also regrind seat angles and back-cut valve heads.

Intake and exhaust valves are back cut to eliminate sharp edges under the heads, which disrupt the airflow.

Lapping valves is an easy way to check the condition of the valve seats. Mix water with fine lapping compound to form paste, and then apply compound to the valve head.

This ring indicates the point of contact between the valve face and the seat. It should be of uniform width all the way around the valve, and it should be located near the outer edge of the valve face. If the gray ring is inconsistent or disappears entirely on one side of the face, the valve has been faced improperly or the valve stem is bent.

You can also check the valve seat after lapping. The lapping compound will mark the seat with a light gray line where it contacts the valve head. Again, this gray area should be consistent in width, and it should completely encircle the seat. If the ring is narrow or faint in spots, repeat the lapping procedure; then re-examine the seat. If the lap marks still show spotty contact between the valve and seat, then it is almost certain that the valve will not seal properly when the engine is running.

The pressure of the valve spring might distort the valve head enough to seal the seat, but then again it might not. If lapping the valves reveals a problem, it is time to have a heart-to-heart talk with your machinist about the situation.

Lapping the valves is an excellent way to freshen up the valve seal in a rac-ing engine. Lapping allows you to visually check the contact between the valve faces and seats, and will quickly indicate a valve that has bent or a seat that has pounded out. Lapping the valves every time the engine is overhauled will prevent unnecessary valve jobs by allowing you to constantly monitor the condition of the valves and seats. Regrinding the seats should be a last resort, since every valve job sinks the valves a little farther down into the ports, and this will generally hurt flow and engine output.

VALVE GUIDES

If valves moved only up and down, the valve guides would last forever. Unfortunately, a valve also moves sideways a tiny bit as it opens and closes, thanks to the force exerted by the rocker arm as it sweeps across the valve stem tip. Even overhead cam systems, which eliminate the rocker arm altogether, are hard on valve guides; in these engines, it is the rotating cam lobe that gives the valve stem a sideways shove.

Cast iron is a reasonably good valve guide material, which is why most automakers simply drill holes in the head

Lap the valves by spinning a stick between your palms. Lift and turn the valve occasionally to distribute the compound over the seat and the valve head mating surfaces.

A dull gray line indicates the contact area between the valves and the seats. If the contact is spotty or inconsistent, the valve may be bent, or the seat may not be concentric with the valve guide.

Extra-long spiral inserts are trimmed and then pinned to the top of the valve guide.

Winona bronze valve guide liners are similar to spiral Helicoil thread inserts. The valve guide is threaded with a self-piloting cutter, and then the liner is installed and swedged in place. The guides are then reamed or honed to final size.

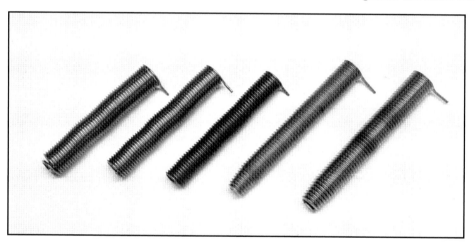

Bronze-wall guides are available in a variety of diameters. These inserts are for standard 3/8-, 11/32-, and 5/16-inch guides. Thick-wall guides adapt valves with small diameter stems to standard guides.

casting for the valve stems. Aluminum, on the other hand, is a terrible valve guide material, so aluminum heads always need some type of *valve guide inserts* to support the valve stems. Cast iron, brass, bronze, and aluminum-bronze inserts can all be found in various aluminum cylinder heads. These valve guide inserts are pressed into the head with an interference fit. The guides in some aluminum cylinder heads—notably late model big-block Chevrolet castings—are notorious for working loose, and the only solution is to pin the guides in place to prevent them from falling out.

High-lift camshafts increase the loads on the valve guides. As the cam profile becomes more radical, the arc of the rocker arm grows larger. (At the valve lifts that are common in current racing and high-performance engines, the end of the rocker arm can come very close to the edge of the valve stem tip.) And, unfortunately, adding a roller to the end of the rocker—as is common on high-performance rocker arms—does

Many engine builders use sleeve-type valve guide liners. Install these liners by first reaming the guide oversize (A), and then driving the split liner into the head (B).

Silicon-bronze guides are often installed in aluminum cylinder heads. They are also used to recondition cast iron heads when the original guides are in such poor condition that Winona or Kline inserts cannot be used.

little to reduce the side loads that wear out the valve guides. This is why many experts recommend that the valve guides in brand new cast iron cylinder heads should be lined with some type of bronze insert.

Cylinder head specialists commonly use two types of inserts. The Winona brand *bronzewall guides* are similar to Helicoil thread inserts; the original valve guide is threaded with a self-piloting tool, and the spiral-like Winona insert is screwed into the guide. The insert is then swedged to lock it in place, and finally reamed and honed to produce the proper valve stem clearance. The popular K-Line *bronze inserts*

Valve guides should be honed to provide correct stem-to-guide clearance. Proper clearance depends on the valve guide material and the engine's intended use.

resemble thin bronze tubes. This type of insert does not require threading the inside of the existing valve guide, but the installation procedure is quite similar to outfitting a cylinder head with Winona guides.

These specialty valve guide inserts offer several advantages. First, they are very kind to valve stems; scuffing and galling is almost nonexistent. Darrell

The dial indicator measures the stem clearance and checks the taper in the valve guide.

The Sunnen valve guide bore gauge is calibrated by inserting two valve stems in the setting fixture.

CAD and CNC

In an effort to increase performance, reduce manufacturing and machining costs, and to ensure higher parts quality, many engine parts producers have taken advantage of Computer Assisted Design (CAD) and Computer Numerical Control (CNC) machining operations. The applications of computer assisted design and the use of computer controlled machining operations are growing daily. The "Big Three" and many aftermarket parts suppliers are able to reduce tolerance limits on engine parts. Parts quality, machining repeatability, and accuracy improve by using CNC equipment.

Computer Assisted Design allows a parts designer to plan, dimension, and even test a part. When a design is finished, it can be sent directly to another machine to create the part. Design changes can be made quickly.

In cylinder head production, a computer controlled multi-axis mill can "port" a cylinder head and greatly reduce the amount of handwork previously required. If a "good" port design has been arrived at through handwork and flow bench testing, a "tracer" mill can measure all dimensions of the port. With this measurement information a cylinder head company can duplicate and reproduce that particular port over and over again in other heads.

Now, does this mean that if you have a part which was CAD designed or CNC machined that you can just bolt it on without checking clearances, fit, or machining? No, you and your engine builder still need to check everything and assemble and clearance check the motor properly. There are no guarantees in this world, except the guarantee that something will go wrong if you don't check it.

The SB2 aluminum race head, introduced in 1996 for the Chevy small-block, has CNC-machined port runners and has chamber volumes of 38cc. Pistons with little or no dome can be used to achieve high compression ratios.

ral grooves of the Winona guide inserts lubricate the valve stem.

Bronzewall stem liners also make it possible to use valves with standard stem diameters even in heads with badly worn guides. Since stainless steel and titanium high-performance valves are not available with oversize stems, this is an important feature to consider (especially if a lot of money has already been invested in porting the cylinder head). In addition, bronzewall inserts are replaceable, so the valve guides can be restored to like-new condition after a long season of racing.

Finally, a special *thick-wall insert* makes it practical to reduce the diameter of the valve stem. This lightens the valve, and, in some cylinder heads, improves flow. Thick-wall inserts are available from Manley to adapt valves with 0.3125-inch (5/16) stems to 0.34375-inch (11/32) and 0.375-inch (3/8) diameter valve guides.

PORTING FOR STREET PERFORMANCE

Modifying cylinder heads for all-out racing has become such a specialized talent that it is best left to professional head porters. Without an expensive *flow bench* to monitor the effects of changes in port design and without constant feedback from successful racers, it is extremely difficult to determine whether your grinding and shaping is really making an improvement. Prices for professionally ported cylinder heads range from $1,000 to over $10,000, depending on the extent and difficulty of the work that is performed. At the high end of this scale, welding and relocating the ports may remanufacture the entire cylinder head. But for a street performance, bracket-racing, marine, or limited oval-track engine, such radical measures are unnecessary. In fact, even if you have never tried your hand at porting before, you can achieve measurable improvements in port flow with an afternoon's work.

The most important area in any cylinder head port is the valve bowl directly behind the seats. In most cylinder heads, the *valve bowls* are machined at the same time that the seats are cut. The factory tooling almost invariably

Wilke has found that the guide-to-stem clearance can be reduced to as little as 0.0006-inch for drag-racing engines and 0.0008-inch for endurance engines when Winona inserts are installed. These relatively tight stem clearances prolong valve seat life by restricting the movement of the valve head. He also feels that the spileaves sharp edges that are very disruptive to air flow on both the intake and exhaust sides of the head. By simply blending and smoothing these sharp edges with a small grinding stone or a carbide burr, the runners will be able to move more air with less turbulence. The trick is to remove as little metal as possible while smoothing the flow path; it's important not to disturb the "venturi" beneath the valve seats where the valve bowl narrows. It is best to do this work before the valve seats are ground to eliminate the risk of ruining a seat with a slip of the grinder.

The second area to concentrate on is the *short-side radius*—the bump in the runner floor where the gases "turn the corner" as they enter or leave the combustion chamber. This radius is the shortest distance between the valve and the port entry, and it is where the airflow is concentrated at low valve lifts. Again, simply rounding and blending this radius, as shown in the accompanying photos, can achieve a startling improvement in port flow.

The final step in do-it-yourself head porting is to match the intake runners to a manifold gasket. This operation will not dramatically increase the airflow capacity, but it will make it much easier to match the cylinder head ports to the intake manifold passages later. Using an intake manifold gasket as a template, scribe around the port entries, taking care to keep the gasket aligned with the cylinder head bolt holes. As you square up and straighten the entries with a stone or burr, you should grind no more than 0.500-inch into the port.

Do not match the exhaust ports to a header gasket. An intentional mismatch between the exhaust port exits and the primary header pipes (or exhaust manifolds), creates a "reversion dam." This sharp edge around the exhaust port opening helps prevent burned gases from re-entering the combustion chamber as pulses travel back and forth through the exhaust system. Since exhaust gases will not burn again, the steps taken to reduce exhaust-gas contamination of the fresh charge in the cylinder will increase power!

MILLING

There are two reasons to *mill* a cylinder head. The first is to straighten and true the deck surface. Like engine blocks, cylinder heads "season" with use. After the fresh casting is machined on the factory production line the metal tends to "relax," causing the deck surface to curve and bend. Also, a head that has been severely overheated may be warped or distorted. Since a perfectly flat deck is essential for long head gasket life, a modest clean-up cut on the cylinder heads should be a part of your engine blueprinting regimen. Unless the head is badly warped, a 0.005-inch cut will usually straighten the deck surface.

Milling a head also reduces the volume of the combustion chambers, which in turn raises the compression ratio. As the section on computing

High-performance engines can benefit from simple port work in the bowl just beneath the valve seats. This cylinder head section illustrates an effective porting technique for street performance. The critical "short-side radius" (1) is carefully rounded to provide a smooth turn from the port to the valve head. The sharp edges in the valve bowl (2) are removed to prevent disruption of the incoming air/fuel mixture. The intake runners (3) are not modified; the rough surface helps atomize fuel droplets, while the small cross-section keeps the air velocity high.

A similar treatment on the exhaust side improves cylinder scavenging. A rounded short side radius (1) reduces turbulence in the port, while the small venturi under the seat (2) improves flow around the valve head.

Intake ports are matched to the manifold by squaring the runner entry. Remove the minimum amount of metal necessary to smooth the transition between the head and the manifold.

Milling a cylinder head straightens the deck surface and reduces the volume of the combustion chambers. When a head is angle milled, it is intentionally cocked so that the cutters will remove more material from one side. The intake manifold surface must also be milled to restore the original angle.

compression in Chapter Eight points out, combustion chamber volume is a major factor in the compression equation. The exact amount of metal that must be removed from the deck surface to bring the chamber volumes down to a specified volume depends on the size and shape of the combustion chambers. The rule of thumb for a wedge-type small-block Chevrolet head is: cutting the head 0.004-inch reduces the chamber volume by approximately one cubic centimeter. Thus, if you wanted to bring down the chamber volume by 5.0cc's, you would ask your machinist to cut 0.020-inch off the head deck surface (5.0 x 0.004 = 0.020).

When the heads on a V-type engine are milled, the horizontal distance between the heads, sometimes called the "valley," becomes smaller. To compensate for this change, and to maintain correct alignment with the intake manifold bolt holes and runners, the intake side of the cylinder head or the manifold itself should also be milled. Cutting 0.010-inch from the deck surface of a small-block Chevy head, for example, requires milling 0.012-inch off the sides and 0.017-inch off the bottom of the intake manifold. Some manufacturers provide information on how much to cut the intake manifold to match milled heads; however, if you are using a spe-

After a head has been angle milled, the head bolt holes must be spotfaced so that they will be parallel to the deck surface. In extreme cases, the head bolt holes may have to be enlarged as well.

cialty intake manifold or ported cylinder heads, this step is probably unnecessary. In these instances, you can simply grind the intake runners to match the cylinder head ports. Bolt-hole misalignment problems can be solved by enlarging the manifold bolt holes and using large, flat washers under the manifold fasteners.

There are limits to how much a head can be milled. Whenever metal is removed from the deck surface of a cylinder head, the head casting is weakened to some extent. Since many late-model cylinder heads have particularly thin decks, removing a substantial amount of iron can invite cracks. Also, the intake valve seat is located very close to the deck surface in a typical wedge-type combustion chamber. So if the head is milled severely, the edge of the intake seat may be cut away. Regrinding and lowering the seat can remedy this, but this has the undesirable side effect of sinking and shrouding the intake valve.

An ingenious solution to these problems was developed in the mid-Seventies with a technique called *angle milling.* When a cylinder head is milled conventionally, it is set up in the grinder or surfacer so that metal is removed evenly across its deck. When a head is angle milled, however, it is intentionally cocked in the milling machine so that more metal is cut off one side of the head than the other.

In a typical angle milling setup, the exhaust side of the head might be cut as much as 0.125-inch, while the side closest to the intake manifold is left untouched. This would be called a "zero-to-.125 cut" and would reduce the volume of an average combustion chamber by approximately 10cc. Of course, other angle cuts are also possible—some aluminum big-block Chevy heads withstand a radical "zero-to-.250" cut, in which 0.250-inch of metal is trimmed off the exhaust side of the head!

Angle milling eliminates two of the drawbacks of straight milling. Since the majority of the metal is removed from the exhaust side of the head, the deck surface is not dangerously weakened. Also, the intake valve seat is less likely to be disturbed when a head is angle milled.

After a head has been angle milled, the bosses around the head bolt holes must be *spotfaced.* This prevents the head bolts (or studs) from cocking to one side as they are tightened down. Also, the intake manifold surface of the head must be milled to restore it to the correct angle, since angle milling a head "tilts" the manifold surface. If the intake side of the head is not resurfaced, the manifold will never seal properly.

Although most cylinder heads have a 90-degree angle between the deck and intake manifold flange, there are some notable exceptions. Small-block Chevro-

let heads, for example, have an 80-degree included angle. The extra set-up time required to angle mill a cylinder head, along with the extra labor involved in spotfacing the bolt holes and correcting the angle of the intake manifold surface, means that the cost of angle milling will often be two or three times the price of conventional milling. But when you are trying to coax the last bit of compression from a wedge-type cylinder casting, angle milling is a performance bargain.

MEASURING PORT VOLUME

One of the real advances in engine building in the past 15 years is the growing appreciation of *port volume* as a major performance factor. Racers and hot rodders have long had an understanding that "big ports" were better for high-rpm horsepower and that "little ports" boosted low-rpm torque. By measuring the exact volume of the intake runners in question, these size differences can be stated with accuracy.

Measuring port volume is simple. You will need a basic chamber cc'ing kit: a burette or graduated cylinder, solvent, and a Plexiglas plate. Install a valve in the port to be measured and seal the seat with a light coat of grease. Prop the head on a bench so that the port entry is level. Fill the port to the brim with solvent, checking for leaks around the valve stem and seat. Note how many cc's of solvent were needed to fill the runner—the answer is the true port volume.

If you measure a selection of cylinder heads, you are likely to find a wide variation in port volumes between even supposedly identical castings. Selecting heads on the basis of port size has been one of the closely guarded secrets of winning racers in the Stock and Super Stock drag racing classes, where the rulebook insists on unmodified heads. The same technology works well for a low budget street performance or bracket racing motor; you might as well use the heads with the largest runners you can find. Size differences, that are difficult to see, become quite clear when you read the numbers off the burette scale.

Comparing ports on the basis of volume is not a foolproof standard,

because the *shape* of the runner may be more important than the size! This is especially true of cylinder heads with ported or modified passages. If you visit the shop of a successful Pro Stock or NASCAR racing team, chances are you will find a workbench littered with *port molds.* These soft-rubber castings offer a graphic representation of port curves and contours. When you are peering down a port, it may be difficult to see what makes one port different—or better—than another. But with two molds sitting side-by-side on the workbench, the variations are easy to spot.

Port molds are easy to make. You will need a latex rubber kit (available by mail from Chicago Latex Products). Mix the ingredients according to the instructions, and then pour the liquid rubber into a port that has been coated with WD-40 (the WD-40 prevents the rubber from sticking to the runner walls). In several hours, the latex will harden to the consistency of a rubber eraser.

The best way to remove the latex is to pull it out through the valve opening. It may take some effort to work it past the valve guide, but once it is loose it will come out easily. By taking molds of

The volume of a cylinder head port can be quickly measured by filling it with liquid from a burette or graduated cylinder.

Filling the runners with flexible latex rubber creates port molds. These molds make differences in port shapes quite apparent. They can also be sliced for quick comparisons of cross-sectional areas at various points in the runner.

various port contours and comparing the on-track performance produced by the ported heads, you can eventually sort out and understand what kind of port characteristics a particular engine prefers. And this information just might provide the winning edge!

SPRING SEATS

Stock valve springs work well on a low-rpm engine, but a racing or high performance motor needs something stronger. The valve springs are responsible for keeping the valvetrain under control. A performance cam profile opens the valves faster, holds them open longer, and closes them quicker than a standard cam grind. You don't have to be a camshaft engineer to understand that this dramatically increases the spring requirements. If the springs do not have enough tension to ensure that the valvetrain precisely follows the cam lobes, then the valves will float—usually with dire results.

Making a spring stiffer usually means making it bigger. There are only three alternatives for a manufacturer when designing a stronger spring: make it out of better material, increase the size of the coils, or increase the number of coils.

When a spring is intended to with-

The spring seats on many cylinder heads must be machined to accommodate large diameter valve springs. Many cam companies rent or sell cutters to enlarge the seats.

stand the stress of racing, usually all three tactics are used. This is why exotic *Vasco Jet* and *Carpenter Steel* alloys are the preferred materials for racing valve springs. It also explains why large diameter two- and three-coil springs are standard equipment on high-rpm engines.

Obviously, there are some potential problems when you increase both the valve spring outer diameter and overall length. Small-block Chevrolets, for example, are equipped at the factory with 1.250-inch diameter valve springs that exert less than 200 pounds of pressure. But on a small-block racing engine, the springs may measure 1.625 inches in diameter and apply over 600 pounds of force! Fitting these oversize springs requires modifying the cylinder heads and beefing up the entire valvetrain to withstand the additional high-rpm forces. Of course, not every engine needs monster valve springs: a hot street, bracket, marine, or limited oval-track engine will be content with an inexpensive dual-spring setup. But even a moderate increase in spring size usually requires some additional machining of the cylinder heads before the over-size springs can be mounted to the heads!

Nearly every camshaft company sells—and in some cases, rents—spring seatcutters. These cutters have a pilot that centers the tool on the valve guide and tough carbide tips that will readily plunge mill the spring seats in either aluminum or cast iron heads. Combination cutters are also available that will machine the top of the valve guide for Teflon valve seals at the same time they enlarge the diameter of the spring seat. All that's necessary to accomplish this job is the proper cutter (several sizes are available), a 1/2-inch drill motor, and a steady hand.

There are some pitfalls to avoid when enlarging the spring pockets. The most common problem is "striking water"—cutting through to the internal coolant passages. This is a serious problem with early cylinder head castings.

However, in recent years Detroit designers have finally acknowledged this problem—of course, this is only a "problem" with heads that are being modified for racing and high-performance use—and many of the late-model "off-road" or "racing-only" cylinder heads have unique water jackets that eliminate or greatly reduce this problem.

Early Chevrolet heads, like the desirable fuel-injection castings, are notorious for breaking through—especially the spring seats at the very ends of the cylinder heads—and cutting the seats on these heads is very risky. Nonetheless, there are two workable solutions to this limitation.

The first is to *step cut* the spring seats by inserting a spring shim under the cutter. The tool enlarges the seat diameter, but the shim limits how deeply it can cut into the seat. The second way to prevent hitting water on these heads is to *radius* the edge of the cutter blade. This trick allows you (or

Spring seats can be cut with a large hand drill, but a vertical mill generally does a neater job. Verify that the springs and shims sit flat on their new seats.

your machinist) to machine the spring seats to the full depth required for most valve springs, while still avoiding the water passages lurking behind the corners of the spring pockets. The bottom coil of the valve springs should then be rounded with a grinding wheel to match the radius of the modified seat.

If you are deepening the spring seats as well as enlarging them, then a mill should be used for this machine work. Cutting the spring seats with a vertical mill allows the machinist to equalize the depth of the pockets so that all the springs will have the same installed height.

When deepening the valve pockets with a hand drill, there is a danger of the tool chattering and leaving an uneven spring seat. With a mill, it is much easier to control the rate at which the seat cutter removes material, so chattering is eliminated.

This job is really pretty straightforward and it can be completed in a home workshop. However, most cylinder head shops don't charge very much to do this type of work. A topnotch shop will probably use a mill to do the job, ensuring that all the pockets are finished smoothly and identically. In the long run, it may be easier to just let a professional do this job.

Spring Pressure

Taking the time to set up and check the valve springs is an essential step in engine blueprinting. Despite the spring manufacturers' best efforts, there is a great deal of variation between different batches of springs—and even between springs that are part of the same set. Springs that have less tension than the design standards will contribute to valve float, while springs that are stiffer than the recommended specifications can cause a flat-tappet cam to wear rapidly.

Spring tension is measured at two points. *Seat pressure* is the static pressure when the valve is closed; *valve-open pressure* is the force exerted by the spring when the valve is at maximum lift. A spring can meet the specified tension for seat pressure, yet it may not have enough open pressure—and vice versa. Before a spring is installed, the tension should be checked at both points.

The most common device for measuring spring pressure is a *Rimac machine.* This tool resembles an arbor press, with a lever that compresses the spring and a scale that indicates the pressure. Any well-equipped cylinder head shop should have a Rimac machine, but it is a rather expensive tool for most part-time engine builders. Inexpensive hydraulic testers are available from specialty tool suppliers. These hydraulic testers are not as convenient to use, since the spring must be compressed with a bench vise—but they are quite a bit cheaper. As a last resort, you can improvise a spring tester with a bathroom scale and a drill press, as shown in the accompanying photo.

Most shops use a Rimac machine to measure the valve spring pressure. The spring is compressed to the installed height and the resultant seat pressure (closed) is indicated. If the pressure is below specifications, hardened steel shims are inserted under the spring.

To check seat pressure, you must first measure the *installed height* of the spring when the valve is closed. This is the distance between the spring seat and the bottom of the retainer. Insert the valve in the guide, and then place the retainer and locks over the stem without the spring in place. Pull up on the retainer firmly, and then measure from the retainer to the spring seat with a dial caliper or small steel ruler. Note the distance to the top of the retainer, which is the installed height plus the retainer thickness. Then remove the retainer, place it on top of the assigned spring, and insert the pair in the testing machine. Compress the spring and retainer assembly until the overall length equals the dimension you just noted on the cylinder head. The reading on the tester scale is the seat pressure of the spring.

Before measuring the open pressure, you must compute the spring height when the valve is fully opened. Subtract the *net valve lift* from the *seat-to-retainer dimension.* For example, if the distance from the spring seat to the top of the retainer with the valve closed is 2.000 inches, and the total valve lift is 0.500-inch, then the open pressure should be measured with the spring compressed to 1.500 inches. Compress the spring in the tester to this dimension and note the reading.

If either the seat or open pressure is below specs, the spring must be shimmed. Spring shims are commonly available in 0.015-, 0.030-, and 0.060-inch thicknesses. Add shims under the spring until both the seat and open pressure meet the recommended specifications.

Always use *hardened* shims under high-performance valve springs; the sharp coil ends and flat steel dampers will quickly chew up unhardened shims. Also remember, valve springs and dampers will quickly gouge unprotected aluminum cylinder heads; always use at least one hardened shim, or a hardened steel spring cup, under springs installed on aluminum heads.

The final step is to check for *coil bind.* Coil bind occurs when the wire coils of the spring stack up solid because the valve lift is greater than the spring design can accommodate. Adding a number of shims under a spring to increase the tension can also invite coil bind, since the installed height is reduced by the thickness of the shims. Coil bind is, of course, hazardous to engine health because it means that something in the valvetrain has to give. In most cases, when the valve springs bind, one or all of the following will occur when the pushrods bend, the rocker arms and rocker mounts bend or break apart, and/or the lifters wedge against the cam lobes.

If you do not have access to a Rimac machine, you can improvise a substitute using a drill press and a bathroom scale. Use the drill press spindle to compress the spring to the installed height and read the pressure on the scale. This set-up works well for checking seat pressure, but don't expect it to measure open pressure with stiff racing springs.

Valve spring open pressure is measured by compressing the spring to the length at maximum valve lift. To check coil bind, continue to compress the spring until the coils stack solid. If the spring coil binds within 0.100-inch of maximum lift, then the spring life is likely to be short.

There are several ways to measure valve spring installed height. The least expensive (and least accurate) method is to use a steel rule to measure the distance from the spring seat to the bottom edge of the retainer.

Telescoping gauges are ideal for measuring installed height. Pull up on the retainer firmly to seat the valve and the split locks before expanding the snap gauge.

To check for coil bind, compress the spring in the tester until the coils stack solid. Note the spring height. There should be at least a 0.060-inch safety margin between the maximum valve lift and the point at which the spring binds. Consider this 0.060-inch figure the minimum allowable clearance; the farther from coil bind you keep the springs, the longer they will last! In a street or oval-track engine that will see long service between overhauls, an extra 0.100-inch of travel (before coil bind) will prevent the springs from fatiguing and prematurely losing pressure.

There is a second way to check the springs for coil bind, although it is not as convenient as using a spring testing machine. When the engine is preassembled and the springs are installed and shimmed, rotate the crank until one of the intake valves is at full lift. You should then be able to insert a 0.060-inch feeler gauge between the coils. After the intake spring is checked, the crank must be rotated until the exhaust valve reaches full lift; once again the feeler gauge should fit comfortably between the coils.

If the valve spring has two or three coils, it may be difficult to check the innermost spring using this method. If you cannot reach the inner coils, then

If you assemble cylinder heads frequently, then you might consider a tool designed specifically for the job. The BHJ Products special dial caliper is designed to measure valve spring installed height quickly and accurately.

Left: A more accurate technique is to use dial calipers to make the measurement from the spring seat to the retainer.

You can also check valve spring coil bind by inserting a paper clip or feeler gauge between the coils when the valve is at maximum lift. Be sure to check the inner coils carefully for coil bind when using two- or three-piece valve springs.

you must disassemble the heads, remove the outer springs, reinstall the heads, and then check for coil bind on the inside spring at maximum valve lift.

Don't assume that the inner spring is all right simply because the outer springs passed inspection. Most spring retainers for dual and triple springs are stepped, which decreases the installed height of the inside coils. An inside spring that is binding can be just as destructive as an outer spring!

There are several potential cures for coil bind problems. In most instances, substituting another spring is the simplest solution. There are a staggering variety of springs available from the camshaft companies. Selecting a spring with fewer coils or with smaller diameter wire will allow the spring to compress farther before the coils touch. The second tactic is to increase the installed height of the spring, by either substituting a retainer with more "dish," remachining the spring seats deeper in the cylinder head, or installing valves with longer stems.

Be aware, though, that these alterna-tives can create more problems than they solve. Whenever the installed height is increased, the seat and open pressure is reduced. If you remachine the spring seats, you run the risk of cutting into the water jacket. And if you switch to different spring retainers, you may have interference problems between the rocker arm and spring retainer. All things considered, finding a suitable valve spring that will accommodate the valve lift generated by the camshaft is the easiest, cheapest, and best mechanical solution to coil bind problems.

RETAINER-TO-GUIDE CLEARANCE

If you have changed the camshaft, valves, rocker arms, or retainers from stock components, then you must check for interference between the valve spring retainers and the tops of the valve guides (or valve stem seals, if your engine is equipped with them). Checking retainer-to-guide clearance is easy if you install light tension springs on the valves when preassembling the engine. After installing the valvetrain and rock-er arms, set the lash for each valve and check the clearance at the retainers as you bring each valve to maximum lift. (If you are using a hydraulic camshaft in your engine, substitute solid lifters while performing this check. Otherwise the plunger in the hydraulic lifter will compress, and the valve will not reach true maximum lift.) You should be able to insert a 0.060-inch feeler gauge between the bottom of the retainer and the top of the valve guide or seal.

If your engine is short on clearance, there are several ways to increase it. When the interference is caused by the height of the valve stem seal, you may be able to gain the clearance you need by substituting a different type of seal. For example, Raymond brand metal seals and Speed Pro brand rubber seals are generally shorter than the Perfect Circle one-piece Teflon seals. Sometimes, in extreme cases, you can shorten the valve guides without causing any serious side effects. As a last resort, you can substitute valves with longer stems, but this fix may upset the valvetrain geometry. At the very least, you will have to re-shim the springs to maintain the correct seat and open pressure.

ROCKER ARMS

Unless the engine has an overhead-cam arrangement that operates the valves directly, rocker arms are an

There should be at least 0.060-inch clearance between the bottom of the spring retainer and the top of the valve guide (or seal) when the valve is at maximum lift.

Moving the pushrod cup closer to the fulcrum increases the rocker arm ratio. High-ratio rockers increase the valve lift and effective duration without affecting the seat timing.

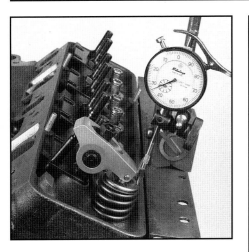

To check the ratios of a set of rocker arms, measure the maximum valve lift that each rocker produces on the same camshaft lobe. To ensure consistent readings, adjust the rockers for zero lashes, and leave the dial indicator in the same position throughout the test.

Changing
Rocker Arm Ratios

Altering cam lift by changing the rocker arm ratios from production values sometimes results in more power, and occasionally changing the ratios on only the intake or only the exhaust side is helpful. If you increase the rocker arm ratio, more lift at the valve occurs without changing the camshaft itself. The valve acceleration on opening and closing is also changed. Whether changing the ratios improves power depends on your engine parts combination and where in the rpm range you are seeking increases. Here again, experimentation will tell you whether you made the right decision.

Another cautionary note when you change rocker arm ratios, cam timing, or even valve lash settings, is to make sure you have enough open valve-to-piston clearance. Is there enough clearance for pushrods, pushrod guideplate slots, rocker arm slots, rocker studs, retainers, valve guide tops, and oil seals? Do the valve springs have clearance between the individual coils? Avoid coil bind! Has the change altered the valvetrain geometry adversely?

Finally, if you find that you have to make a number of changes in cam timing or rocker arm ratios or valve lash settings to improve performance, it may be an indication that the camshaft you have chosen is not the best one and your motor may need more or less cam timing.

essential element of the valvetrain. The rockers are part of a complex linkage that both transfers and magnifies, through the *rocker arm ratio,* the motion of the lifters riding on the cam lobes. The distances between the pushrod cup, the rocker pivot, and the tip that pushes against the valve stem determine the rocker arm ratio.

The rocker arm ratio is usually different for each engine design. A small-block Chevy, for example, has a *theoretical rocker arm* ratio of 1.5:1, while a big-block Chevy or Boss Ford has a theoretical rocker arm ratio of 1.7:1. These are "theoretical" ratios because, under actual operating conditions, the true ratio rarely equals the ideal figures. A rocker arm with a 1.5:1 ratio should produce a *net valve lift* that is exactly 1.5 times greater than the *cam lobe lift.* For instance, a cam with a 0.300-inch lobe lift should produce a maximum valve lift of 0.450-inch (1.500 x 0.300 = 0.450). However, due to manufacturing tolerances, deflections in the valvetrain, and the complex motion of the rocker as it sweeps across the valve stem tip, the *actual valve lift* seldom equals the theoretical value.

Increasing the rocker arm ratio is a horsepower-producing trick that has

been widely adopted by hot rodders and racers. (High-output small-block Chevrolets are routinely outfitted with 1.6:1 rockers in place of the standard 1.5:1 rockers.) To get these higher-than-stock ratios, it is necessary to use non-stock specialty rocker arms. Increasing the rocker arm ratio offers several advantages. It makes the cam "bigger" without increasing the duration.

As the accompanying chart illustrates, high-ratio rockers open the valves quicker, lift them higher, and close them later—all without affecting seat timing. Of course, there are trade-offs. The faster valve accelerations and decelerations produced by higher rock-

er arm ratios reduce valvetrain stability, and invite early valve float. Valve spring coil bind clearance becomes more critical, and the valve notches in the piston may have to be deepened to accommodate the increased net valve lift.

Whether you are using stock or specialty rocker arms, it is important to check the true (actual) ratio. Installing each rocker in turn on the same cam lobe, adjusting the lash, and noting the maximum valve lift it produces easily does this. An assortment of stamped steel rocker arms is likely to have significant differences in ratio between the highest and lowest. In classes of competition where factory valve lift specifica-

If you are using stud mounted rocker arms and plan to use "poly locks" with the rocker arms, make sure you spot-face the top surface of the rocker studs so that they are flat. The Allen screw locks used with most "poly locks" need a smooth, flat surface; otherwise they can loosen. Most studs have a rough, irregular surface from the factory (left).

This chart illustrates the effect of increasing rocker arm ratio. The shaded area represents the higher valve lift produced by substituting a 1.65:1 rocker in place of a standard 1.5:1 rocker on a small-block Chevrolet. Although seat timing is unchanged, there is a considerable increase in effective duration at 0.500-inch valve lift with the high ratio rockers.

The slot in a stamped steel rocker arm may bottom out against the stud at maximum valve lift when a high-lift cam is installed. The clearance is adequate if you can insert a paper clip between the stud and rocker arm slot when the valve is wide open.

Large diameter valve springs and deeply dished retainers can hit the underside of the rocker arm. If the rocker arm pushes against the spring or retainer, the split locks can pop out, causing a dropped valve. Avoid this disaster by checking the clearance during preassembly.

Check the clearance between the bottom of the rocker arm and the rocker stud. Many heavy-duty studs have extra large fillets between the nut and the shank.

tions must be maintained (Stock eliminator drag racing, for example), rockers that produce the maximum allowable valve lift should be chosen.

If you are not concerned with meeting the standards laid down by a rule-book, then it is a good practice to divide your rockers into high-ratio and low-ratio groups (while discarding or replacing any rockers that vary more than 0.030-inch from the average valve lift figure). Since intake flow is general-

ly more important to engine performance than exhaust flow, the high-ratio rockers should be assigned to the intake valves and the low-ratio rockers

Grooved pivot balls are an excellent addition to any high-performance engine using stamped rocker arms.

Occasionally a rocker arm roller tip is bored off-center. Check the roller run-out with a dial indicator.

utilizes ball-pivot rocker arms. The grooves help lubricate the rocker fulcrums, which minimizes the likelihood of "burning" a rocker arm. High valve spring pressures and radical cam profiles increase the stress on these pivot balls. If a rocker arm or pivot ball on an exhaust valve should fail, replace it with a rocker that has already been broken-in on an intake stud. The exhaust rockers usually run hotter than the intakes, and putting a well broken-in rocker on the exhaust will ensure against premature failure. Also, when assembling the engine for the final time, remember to coat the rocker balls with moly lube and plenty of oil!

A *roller-bearing rocker arm* design eliminates these troublesome pivot balls, and "roller rockers" are considered almost mandatory on racing engines (where the rules allow). Roller rockers have their own special shortcomings, however. Occasionally the roller tips are bored off-center. This causes the tip to run eccentrically and makes it impossible to adjust the valve lash consistently.

You can check a roller tip for excessive run-out by setting up a dial indicator on the roller and turning it with your fingertip. And, before a rocker passes your final inspection, you should

reserved for the exhausts. Use a dab of machinist's dye or a punch mark to identify the rockers you have selected for the intake valves.

Stud-mounted rockers must also be checked for adequate *stud clearance.* Many stock rockers cannot be used with high-lift cams because the slotted holes bottom out against the rocker studs as the rocker approaches maximum valve lift.

"Long slot" rockers are available to correct this problem, or you can elongate the slotted holes in the stock rockers with a grinding tool. If there is adequate clearance, you should be able to insert a piece of paper-clip wire between the stud and the rocker arm slot when the valve is at maximum lift.

If you have installed specialty rocker studs, you must also check for adequate clearance at the sides of the rockers. Most high-performance screw-in studs have an extra-large radius between the shank and hex head. This increases the strength of the stud, but this extra material may interfere with the bottom of the rocker arm. Aluminum and steel roller rockers can be relieved with a high-speed cutter to eliminate this interference.

Finally, if you plan to use "poly lock" valve-adjusting nuts or a stud girdle to stabilize the valvetrain, you must

check the clearance between the adjusting nut and the rocker. If the nut hits the rocker, it will be impossible to obtain an accurate valve lash setting. Again, a piece of paper-clip wire makes a good checking gauge. If the paper clip will not fit between the rocker and the adjusting nut, you must relieve the rocker to provide clearance.

Special *grooved pivot balls* are an excellent addition to any valvetrain that

Slots in the pushrod guideplates must be long enough to prevent binding the pushrods as the valves open and close.

Deburr the slots in the guideplates by polishing them with emery paper wrapped around a bolt.

make certain that the pushrod cup is fully seated, that the oiling hole from the cup is unobstructed, and that the C-clip retainers for the pivot-bearings are seated fully in their grooves.

GUIDEPLATES

Stud-mounted rocker arms, unlike shaft-mounted rockers, require some type of aligning device to keep the rocker tip centered on the valve stem. *Close-tolerance slots* in the cylinder head and *pushrod guideplates* are the most common means of maintaining correct rocker arm alignment. If your cylinder heads are outfitted with guideplates, you must use hardened pushrods; otherwise the steel-to-steel contact between the guideplates and the soft pushrod material will quickly gall the pushrod tubing.

Most guideplates are punched out of sheet steel, which can leave rough edges along the pushrod slots. To deburr and dress these slots, wrap a piece of fine emery paper around a bolt, then polish the inside edges of the guideplate slots with this homemade tool.

And remember, if you are using a high-ratio rocker arm, the pushrod cup is located closer to the fulcrum than the pushrod cup in a standard ratio rocker. This can cause the pushrod to "bottom-out" in the guideplate slot. When you are checking the rocker arm ratios, also make certain that the guideplate slots are deep enough to clear the pushrods at maximum valve lift. TRW and other manufacturers offer guideplates with extra-long slots to correct these interference problems.

Many of the non-stock specialty guideplates also feature elongated holes for the rocker arm studs. This allows the engine builder to slide the guideplate from side-to-side before torquing down the rocker arm stud, thereby ensuring the best possible alignment between the valve stem and rocker arm tip. Ideally, the rocker arm should be precisely centered over the tip of the valve stem.

However, this may not always be possible when an intake and exhaust pushrod share the same guideplate. In extreme cases, such as when the valve guides have been relocated to provide room in the combustion chamber for oversize valves, the pushrod guideplates will have to be cut in half, the rockers and valves lined up, and the guideplates welded back together to maintain the proper alignment.

The pushrods must also have adequate clearance where they pass through the cylinder heads. Again, when high-ratio rocker arms are used, remember that the pushrod will be closer to the rocker arm pivot, which can cause the pushrod to rub against the side of the pushrod clearance holes in the heads. These holes can be carefully elongated with a hand-held grinding tool or opened up on a Bridgeport with an end mill; simply drilling the holes oversize is usually not recommended.

The pushrod clearance holes must also be enlarged whenever the diameter of the pushrods is increased. Large diameter pushrods are generally stiffer, making them less likely to bend and deflect due to the heavy valvetrain loads created by high-pressure racing valve springs. High-output small-block Chevrolets, for instance, are often upgraded by replacing the stock 0.3125-inch (5/16) diameter pushrods with larger 0.375-inch (3/8) diameter pieces.

These oversize pushrods need extra room where they pass through the cylinder heads, so the pushrod holes must be carefully opened up with a hand grinder to accommodate them (and, of course, when non-standard pushrods are used, the pushrod guideplates will also have to be replaced with plates that will accept the larger pushrods).

PUSHRODS

There is very little that can go wrong with pushrods. If your pushrods have *hardened tips,* make certain that the tip inserts are seated fully in the pushrod tubes. Check for cracks around the oil holes, and if your engine has guideplates or slots in the cylinder head to maintain alignment between the rockers and valve stems, check for signs of excessive wear in the area where the pushrod passes through the head and guideplate.

Before slipping the pushrods in place, it is a good idea to check that they are all straight. There are two easy ways to check pushrod straightness. You can roll them across a flat piece of thick glass, or spin them in a drill press chuck. If a pushrod does not roll smoothly across the glass, or if it wobbles in the drill chuck, discard it. Once a pushrod becomes bent, there is no saving it!

Determining the correct pushrod length is not so simple. Pushrod length is a major factor in determining *valve-train geometry.* "Geometry," in this case, refers to the dynamic relationship between the rocker arm and valve stem during the time when the valve is opening and closing.

Ideally, the rocker should always push against the exact center of the valve stem. This reduces the side loads on the stem, which cause the valve guides to wear. This rarely happens, however, since the rocker travels in an *arc* as it moves up and down. Therefore, one of the goals of engine blueprinting is to keep the rocker arm as close to the center of the valve stem as possible throughout the entire valve-lift cycle.

Spin each pushrod in a drill chuck to check it for straightness.

High-ratio rocker arms and large diameter pushrods often require enlarging pushrod holes in small-block Chevy cylinder heads. Guideplates must be used to maintain alignment between the rocker arms and the valve stems.

Many factors can affect this relationship, but in a nutshell, the easiest way to accomplish this is to find the pushrod length that produces the best geometry.

Many engine modifications can upset the original valvetrain geometry. A high-lift camshaft, for example, has a

Early-model Chevy small-block heads were equipped with pressed rocker arms. These should be replaced with screw-in studs for serious performance applications. Stud bosses must be tapped and spotfaced.

smaller *base circle* than a stock cam. This causes the lifters to drop lower in the lifter bores when the valves are closed, which, in turn, causes the ends of the rocker arms to rise higher at the valve-closed position.

Milling the cylinder heads and engine block, installing oversize valves, increasing the valve stem length (to accommodate larger valve springs), and even grinding three-angle valve seats can all cause the relationship between the rocker arms and valve stems to go out of kilter.

Fortunately, the specialty cam companies are very familiar with this problem and offer special-length pushrods to compensate for these changes. These custom pushrods are typically available in lengths that are 0.050-, 0.100-, 0.250-, and 0.300-inch shorter than stock.

For those rare instances when an engine needs a slightly longer pushrod, custom pushrods are offered in 0.050- and 0.100-inch or longer versions. Unfinished pushrods are also offered; these can be tailored to any engine by trimming the pushrod tubing to length and pressing in a hardened tip.

You can determine the correct pushrod length by carefully watching the rocker arm (from the side) as it opens and closes the valve. With the engine pre-assembled and the valve lash set, look at the end of the rocker arm as it sweeps across the valve stem.

The rocker contact point should be slightly off-center toward the inside edge (the edge nearest the rocker arm fulcrum) when the valve is closed. As the valve opens to about mid-lift (one-half of total valve lift), the contact point should

pass across the valve centerline and move slightly toward the outside edge.

Then, during the last half of the lift cycle, the contact point should swing back across the centerline and return to about the original position—slightly inboard of the centerline—just as the valve reaches full lift. If the contact point starts at the center of the stem and then moves toward one edge as the valve lift increases, the pushrod is too long or too short.

Finding the best pushrod length is a trial-and-error process that requires you to try various pushrods until one produces satisfactory valvetrain geometry. An adjustable length pushrod will simplify this procedure. These pushrods have a threaded insert that can be adjusted to lengthen or shorten the pushrod.

Once you have found a length that produces the desired results, measure the overall length of the adjustable pushrod and use this dimension to order a suitable set of specialty pushrods. Checking and, if necessary, correcting the rocker arm geometry is a detail often overlooked by neophyte engine builders, but it is crucial to extending valve guide life and reducing valvetrain failure.

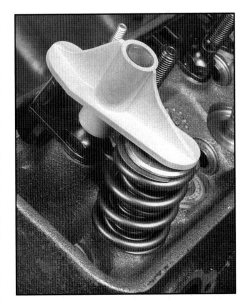

A Manley Performance pushrod fixture quickly checks the pushrod length. The gauge should touch the end of the pushrod and the valve stem tip if the length is correct.

CAMSHAFT

The camshaft has often been described as the "brain" of the engine. In effect, the cam regulates engine "breathing" by opening and closing the valves. But unlike a living brain that controls heart rate and respiration, a camshaft cannot speed up or slow down the valve events. Without this ability, cam profiles are always a compromise. At low engine speeds and during part-throttle operation, an engine needs a camshaft design with short duration and relatively little valve lift to produce sharp throttle response and good fuel economy. At high rpm, however, there is very little time to fill the cylinders, so a long-duration cam with high valve lift is the answer. Thus, when a builder selects a cam grind that's right for one end of the operating range, it will, without question, hurt performance at the other extreme.

There is a staggering variety of cam designs available for modern performance engines. Choices range from sedate hydraulic grinds that emphasize fuel economy to roller cams designed expressly for all-out racing. The ends of the camshaft spectrum are easy to understand; it's the subtle shades in the middle that are difficult to distinguish. A current maximum-effort street machine may rely on a profile that was considered a "racing only" camshaft just a short time ago. The cam companies have shaved the distinctions between performance and economy grinds very fine.

Expert engine builders continually test new cams in the constant search for the "perfect combination," but the average guy doesn't often have the time or money to perform extensive dyno testing. Only by studying the catalogs, talking with other car enthusiasts, and consulting with the technical experts at the cam companies can you be certain of finding a profile that is right for your particular needs. And this is one area where every engine builder should think long and hard before making a deci-

The camshaft controls airflow through the engine, and is an important factor in performance. These graphs illustrate the differences in valve lift and duration between economy, performance, and competition profiles.

sion. The cam you select will determine, to a great degree, the overall performance and "driveability" of the engine. And if you select the wrong grind, the engine will be disappointing; despite all of the time and effort you have spent blueprinting it.

Before your new camshaft can make good on all its performance promises, it must be installed *properly*. This requires a bit more work than just inserting it in the cam bearings, lining up the timing marks, and tightening down the cam drive. The cam must be properly *phased* with the pistons if it is to perform up to its full potential. This is called "degreeing the cam," and it is a procedure that is much easier to do than to describe. Don't despair; nearly everyone who builds high-performance engines has learned to degree a camshaft by reading a book or magazine article. The first time you attempt the task the entire process may seem hopelessly complex. But by the second or third time around, degreeing a cam will be a snap. Follow the steps outlined below, and your cam will soon be degreed to perfection.

ALTERING CAM TIMING

There are a number of ways to alter cam-timing events by advancing or retarding the placement of the camshaft and its relation to the crankshaft. As previously discussed in the main text, after initially "degreeing" the cam, (and making sure it does what it is supposed to do), choices can be made to change the "straight up" cam timing. Advancing or retarding the cam timing from its original design timing events may offer improvements in power in different rpm ranges. Advancing the cam timing generally improves mid-rpm power and response, while retarding the cam timing, as a general proposition, improves high-rpm breathing and power. Don't assume that either cam timing change will make more power on your particular engine parts combination. Experimentation with different cam phasing placement can give you an indication of whether the change was worthwhile. There may not be an improvement and

Degreeing a camshaft requires a modest amount of equipment. Cam Dynamics offers this complete kit, which includes a degree wheel, a dial indicator, a piston stop, and an indicator stand.

power may decline; power may go up in one rpm range and nosedive in another; and sometimes the change is so small that it is not worth the effort.

Cam timing can be altered using offset bushings in the cam drive gear, but there are other ways to do this as well. A number of companies make timing chain and gear sets that have multiple keyway slots cut in the crank gear. Some have three different slots allowing the cam to be installed "straight up" at "0" degrees or, by using one of the other slots, placing the cam timing either "+4" degrees (advanced) or "-4" degrees (retarded). Some timing chain and gear sets have up to 11 different slots on the crank gear for further incremental adjustments in cam placement. Many

cams are ground by the manufacturer with a certain amount of advance. Make sure you check with your cam maker and read the cam card that comes with your camshaft. Also, gear drive timing sets are available with a number of different offset bushings that can be used to alter cam-timing placement.

The latest innovation concerns the use of timing belts and cog gears to tie the crank and cam together. These belt systems generally have vernier adjustments that can be made on the cam drive cog gear and offer a wide amount of advance or retard adjustment in 1/2-degree increments. Some of these belt systems mount the belt and gears in front of a special cover so that cam changes, cam timing changes, and tim-

A long bolt screwed into the end of the camshaft makes a convenient installation tool.

ing belt inspection are easily done. For timing sets that mount beneath a timing cover, two-piece timing covers are available that allow you to remove the upper part of the cover without having to lower or remove the oil pan.

There are some clearance checks to make when installing any timing set. Make sure there is enough room between the rear thrust face of the cam gear or cog and the front face of the block. The surfaces may need to be machined or ground to make sure the

The bigger the degree wheel is, the more accurate the readings are. This anodized aluminum wheel can be rotated on the crankshaft snout by loosening the center hub; a feature which simplifies the chore of locating top dead center.

The accuracy of the cam degreeing procedure depends on how precisely you locate top dead center. To find TDC, attach the degree wheel to the crank snout and make a pointer from welding a rod or a piece of coat hanger wire.

gear isn't rubbing on the face of the block. The same is true of any timing cover you use. Check for clearance. Some of the chains or belts are wider across than others. Keep these clearance checks in mind if you are using a cam gear shim, roller thrust bearing, or cam thrust button.

If your block main cap saddles have been align bored, the distance from the crankshaft axis centerline to the camshaft axis centerline may have been reduced, which can cause a stock length chain to be slack when installed. Timing sets with shorter timing chains are available from aftermarket suppliers if you need them.

FINDING TOP DEAD CENTER

The first step in degreeing a cam is to preassemble the short block. Bolt the

crankshaft in place and install the number one piston and rod. Install the cam and timing chain, taking care to align the marks on the camshaft and crank gears. Bolt a degree wheel to the crankshaft snout; if the snout is not drilled and tapped, attach the degree wheel to the harmonic balancer and press the balancer into place. Fabricate a pointer from a piece of coat hanger wire or welding rod and fasten it to the front of the engine; the bolt holes for the water pump and timing chain cover are good places to mount this temporary pointer. Turn the crank until your eyeball tells you that the number one piston is at *top dead center* (TDC). Then, without rotating the crank, line up the pointer with the TDC mark on the degree wheel. Now turn the crank until the piston is halfway down the cylinder bore.

Before you can zero in on top dead center, you will need a *piston stop;* a short length of bar stock or angle iron, like the one shown here, works well. If your engine has domed pistons, the stop merely has to straddle the cylinder bore so that the piston dome will contact it. With flattop pistons, however, you must drill and tap the stop, and then screw in a bolt to contact the piston before it reaches TDC. Tighten down the piston stop, and get ready to pinpoint top dead center.

Turn the crankshaft *clockwise* until the piston contacts the stop and note the reading on the degree wheel. Now rotate the crank *counterclockwise* until the piston again hits the stop, and note this second reading on the degree wheel. If the crank stopped turning at exactly the same point, both *before* and *after* the TDC mark on the degree wheel,

A piston stop can be elaborate or simple. A length of angle iron works well with high dome pistons. For flattop or dished pistons, you'll need a stop with a bolt that extends down into the bore to contact the piston before it reaches TDC.

The stop must be rigid enough to resist flexing when the piston pushes against it.

This piston stop screws into the spark plug hole. It is used to degree a cam after the heads have been installed.

A spark plug stop can only be used when the plug hole intersects the piston top. A small hole in the center of the stop bleeds off pressure in the cylinder as the piston rises.

you have lucked out and hit top dead center on the first try.

Usually, though, the two readings on the degree wheel are not identical. For example, the piston may stop at a reading of 28 degrees after TDC when you turn the crank clockwise, and 32° before TDC when you turn it counter-clockwise. True top dead center lies halfway between these two readings. To pinpoint TDC you must take the average of these two readings, and then adjust the pointer to line up with this number on the degree wheel. In our example, the average of 28- and 32- degrees is 30 degrees. With the piston

still firmly against the stop, the pointer is bent so that it indicates 30 degrees before TDC. Now rotate the crank in the opposite direction until the piston again hits the stop. The crank will stop turning at precisely 30 degrees after TDC if you have correctly split the difference between your original readings.

You can now remove the piston stop. If you want to double-check your work up to this point, set up a dial indicator on the piston top. Turn the crank clockwise until the dial indicator shows that the piston has risen to 0.100-inch below the deck surface, and note the reading on the degree wheel before TDC. Now continue to turn the crank

clockwise; the piston will reach TDC, and then begin moving back down the cylinder bore. Stop when the piston is again 0.100-inch below the deck sur-

With the stop installed, rotate the crank-shaft clockwise until the piston contacts the stop, and then note the reading on the degree wheel. Here the crank has stopped turning at 28 degrees before TDC.

Now turn the crank counterclockwise until it stops again. In this example, the crank has stopped at 30 degrees after TDC. This means that the degree wheel must be turned on the crank snout one degree, or the pointer bent slightly so that the crank stops at an indicated 29 degrees before and after TDC.

Double-check the TDC location by removing the piston stop and setting up a dial indicator as shown. Note the degree wheel readings when the piston is 0.100-inch from TDC as you slowly rotate the crankshaft. The reading before TDC should be the same as the reading after TDC.

face. The reading should be the same number of degrees after TDC as the earlier reading.

Once you have found TDC, you must be careful not to disturb the degree wheel or pointer until you have finished degreeing the camshaft—otherwise you will have to start over from the beginning. Although we have described how to find TDC with the heads off the engine, this procedure can also be done with the heads in place. You will need to buy or fabricate a piston stop that can be inserted through the spark plug hole. Remove the remaining spark plugs and rockers so the engine can be turned over easily with a long breaker bar.

CHECKING INTAKE CENTERLINE

Although there are several ways to degree a cam, the intake centerline method is the most common and reliable procedure. The *intake centerline* is the point at which the intake valve reaches maximum lift. In the vast majority of engines, this takes place between 100 degrees and 120 degrees after top dead center.

Unless the cam grinder recommends otherwise, it is usually best to install a new cam in the "straight up" position—that is, neither advanced nor retarded. This means that a cam ground with 110-degree *lobe centers* (the angle between the intake and exhaust lobes) should be installed with a 110-degree intake centerline. The timing cards that accompany most cams usually specify both these lobe centers and the recommended intake centerline.

To find the point of maximum intake valve lift, install a lightly oiled lifter on the intake lobe for the number one cylinder. Watch the lifter as you rotate the crank assembly. Stop when the lifter is at the lowest point in the bore; it is then on the base circle of the cam.

Cam Dynamics	3926 RUNWAY ROAD MEMPHIS TENNESSEE 38118 (901) 794-2870

ENGINE	CHEVY 396/454		
CAM GRIND NO.	CHB-R 318/320/110		
CAMSHAFT SERIAL NO.	Q 724		

		INTAKE	EXHAUST
VALVE ADJUSTMENT (HOT)		.030	.030
GROSS VALVE LIFT		.765	.680
DURATION AT A TAPPET LIFT OF	.020	318°	320°

VALVE TIMING AT .020 TAPPET LIFT		OPEN		CLOSE	
	INT	49 °BTDC		89 °ABDC	
	EXH	91 °BBDC		51 °ATDC	

CAM IS GROUND WITH LOBE CENTER SEPARATION OF 110°

RECOMMENDED VALVE SPRING INFORMATION
OUTER SPRING PART NO. 991
INNER SPRING PART NO.

INSTALLED HT.	1.880	INS.	180 LBS.
OPEN HT.	1.150	INS.	600 LBS.

The cam card reveals essential information about the camshaft. In addition to lift and duration figures, it provides the numbers you need to accurately degree in the cam.

Now set up a dial indicator so that the plunger contacts the edge of the lifter and is parallel to the lifter travel. (Don't set up the dial indicator in the pushrod cup; the curved surface can cause inaccurate readings.) Slowly turn the crankshaft in the normal direction of rotation until the lifter reaches maximum lift. Then turn the crank backwards until the dial indicator reads 0.100-inch below this maximum figure.

Now turn the crank forward again as smoothly as possible until the dial indicator reads 0.050-inch below the maximum lift point. Note the reading on the degree wheel. Continue turning the crank past maximum lift until the needle on the dial indicator is again 0.050-inch below the maximum; note this second reading on the degree wheel.

It is important to avoid jerking the crankshaft while taking these readings. If you inadvertently miss the points 0.050-inch below maximum tappet lift, turn the crank backwards a quarter turn and then slowly "sneak up" on them again. Always take the degree wheel readings while turning the crank in the normal direction of rotation; this prevents slack in the timing chain or cam drive from causing erroneous readings.

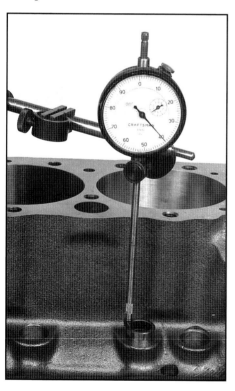

The dial indicator plunger should contact the edge of the lifter. Note the degree wheel readings before and after the point of maximum lobe lift (using the intake centerline method) or at 0.050-inch lobe lift (for asymmetrical cam grinds).

Use a pushrod as an extension of the dial indicator plunger when degreeing the cam with the cylinder head in place.

Offset cam bushings are used to change camshaft phasing. Each 0.005-inch offset in the bushing hole changes the cam timing approximately one degree.

The point of maximum intake valve lift—the intake centerline—is exactly halfway between these two readings. To find the intake centerline, add the two readings and divide by two. For example, if the tappet is 0.050-inch below maximum lift at 80 degrees after TDC, and again at 140 degrees after TDC, then the intake centerline is 110 degrees (80 + 140 divided by 2 = 110). The exact numbers are not important; you could have measured tappet lift at 0.020-inch or 0.100-inch on both sides of the maximum lift point without affecting the accuracy of the readings. What is important is the relationship between the maximum lift point and top dead center.

CHANGING CAM PHASING

Once you have found the intake centerline point, you can determine whether the cam is *advanced,* straight up, or retarded. If the intake centerline is less than the lobe center angle, the cam is advanced. For example, if you find that the intake centerline is 108 degrees after TDC, and your cam has 110-degree lobe centers, then the cam is 2 degrees advanced. Similarly, if the intake centerline is greater than the lobe centers, then the cam is *retarded.* To cite another example, if you find that a cam with 110-degree lobe centers has the intake centerline at 112 degrees after TDC, then it is retarded 2 degrees.

Camshaft phasing has a definite effect on engine performance. A cam

If the cam phasing must be moved more than two or three degrees, elongate the bolt holes in the cam gear with a rat-tail file.

that is advanced both opens and closes the valves sooner in relation to the piston position than a cam that is retarded. As a general rule, advancing the cam increases low-speed torque, while retarding it boosts high-speed horsepower. Tuning a cam by changing the phasing can pay enormous dividends in performance, as many racers will attest. The thousands of variables between engines make it impossible to predict the precise cam phasing that will produce the best performance. Trial-and-error testing is the only way to discover which cam phasing the engine prefers.

The dowel pin hole in the camshaft gear must be drilled out to fit the offset bushings.

Some high-performance timing chain crank gears use multiple keyways to alter the camshaft phasing. This gear provides three choices in cam timing: "straight up," four degrees advanced, and four degrees retarded.

Fortunately, it is quite easy to advance or retard a cam. You will need a selection of *offset cam bushings,* which can be obtained from any cam company or speed shop. The holes in these bushings are intentionally drilled off-center. When installed in the timing gear, these bushings move the camshaft dowel pin forward (to advance the cam) or backward (to retard it).

The dowel pin hole in the cam gear must be drilled oversize to accept these bushings. Drill from the backside of the gear, but don't drill all the way through. A small lip around the bushing hole will prevent the bushing from falling out and changing the cam phasing. Make sure, however, that the bushing does not protrude above the surface of the cam gear where it rubs against the front of the block. You should also elongate the cam bolt holes with a rat-tail file.

The offset of the dowel pin hole in the bushing determines how much the bushing will change the cam phasing. Some of these bushings are color coded or stamped to indicate their offset; don't trust these markings. Moving the cam dowel 0.005-inch changes the cam timing approximately 1 degree, so you can get a good idea of how far a particular bushing will advance or retard the cam by measuring the offset of the dowel hole with a dial caliper.

However, the only way to determine the true effect on cam timing is to recheck the intake centerline after the bushing is installed in the cam gear.

Using *offset crank keys* can also change the cam timing. Also, some timing chain sets include crankshaft sprockets with *multiple keyways.* By selecting the appropriate slot in the crank sprocket, the cam phasing can be advanced or retarded from 4 to 8 degrees.

In all honesty, multiple keyway sprockets are not a particularly good or convenient way to alter cam timing. Before you can get to the sprocket, you must remove the degree wheel, which means you have to go through the entire drill of finding TDC again. Also, these sprockets do not always put the cam phasing right where you want it, so you may still require offset bushings to fine-tune the cam timing.

DEGREEING ASYMMETRICAL CAMS

There is one category of camshafts that cannot be degreed using the intake centerline method described earlier. These cams are called *asymmetrical profiles.* A conventional camshaft lobe has the same shape on both sides. This causes the valve to open and close at the same rate. With an asymmetrical lobe, the two sides of the lobe are not mirror images of each other.

Cam designers have learned that they can increase both the engine operating range and the torque output by using different opening and closing rates. These asymmetrical profiles were formerly found only on exotic roller racing cams, but now the same technology is starting to appear on high-performance flat-tappet cams. While asymmetric cam lobes offer the promise of improved performance, they also demand a different degreeing technique.

Since the opening and closing sides of an asymmetrical cam lobe differ, you cannot accurately determine the lobe centerline with a dial indicator. To degree an asymmetrical cam, you must go by the cam grinder's "fifty-thousandths" numbers. Instead of using the intake centerline for a reference point, you use the points at which the tappet is 0.050-inch off the base circle.

A typical set of "50-numbers" for a performance cam might tell you that the intake tappet reaches 0.050-inch lift on the opening ramp at 32 degrees before TDC, and returns to 0.050-inch lift at 58 degrees after BDC on the closing side.

To check cam timing using these 50-numbers, you set up the dial indicator on the edge of the lifter just as you would when using the intake centerline method. Slowly rotate the crank in the direction of normal rotation, stopping as soon as the lifter rises 0.050-inch. Note the reading on the degree wheel, then continue to turn the crank until the lifter returns to 0.050-inch lift on the closing ramp. Take a second reading on the degree wheel, and compare these numbers with the specs on the camshaft card. If necessary, the cam can then be advanced or retarded with offset bushings.

CAM GRAPHING

The numbers on a timing card don't always tell the whole story about a camshaft. Even if you know the key characteristics of a cam design—valve lift, opening and closing points, and lobe centers—there are other factors to consider. How fast do the valves open and close? How long are the valves at their maximum lift?

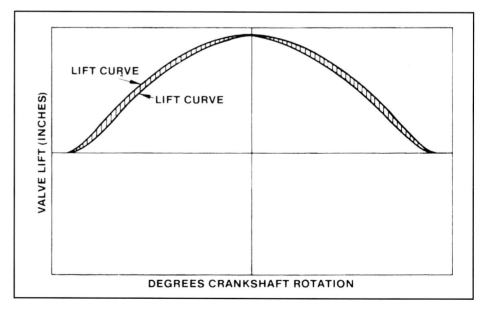

Graphing the lift curve tells you what the valves are really doing. The cams represented by these two curves have the same lift and duration figures, but one is a much fatter profile that opens and closes the valves quickly.

Camshaft Glossary

Asymmetric Lobe:

A camshaft lobe that has a different lift curve on its opening and closing sides.

Lobe Centerline:

The point of maximum lift on a cam lobe. It is measured by recording the number of degrees the crankshaft turns past TDC until the tappet reaches its maximum lift. The centerline of the number one intake lobe is commonly used as a reference point to degree a camshaft.

Coil Bind:

The point at which the individual coils of a spring stack solid and prevent the spring from compressing farther. Coil bind can cause rapid lobe wear and valvetrain breakage.

Single Pattern:

A camshaft that has the identical profile on both the intake and exhaust lobes. Chevy part number 3863151, for example, is a single pattern cam: it has 221 degrees of duration and 0.447-inch valve lift on both the intake and exhaust valves.

Dual Pattern:

A camshaft that has different profiles for the intake and exhaust lobes. An example of a dual-pattern cam is Chevy part number 389629, which has 296 degreesduration/0.390-inch valve lift on the intakes, and 310 degrees duration/0.410-inch valve lift on the exhausts.

Duration:

The length of time that a valve is opened, measured in degrees of crankshaft rotation. Since there is little airflow through a valve at very low lift, duration is usually measured from the point when the tappet is 0.050-inch off the base circle on the opening side to when it is 0.050-inch off the base circle on the closing side. Advertised duration usually includes the lobe clearance ramps, when the valve is not actually off the seat and flowing any air. For example, the advertised duration of Chevy part number 3863151 is 320 degrees; measuring the duration at 0.050-inch tappet lift produces the more realistic figure of 221 degrees.

Lift:

The distance a valve moves off the seat. Theoretical lift is calculated by multiplying the camshaft lobe lift by the rocker arm ratio. Net lift is the true valve lift measured at the valve. Net lift is always less than the theoretical lift because it takes into account valve lash (on mechanical and roller-lifter cams), pushrod deflection, tolerances in the rocker arm ratio, resistance of the valve spring, and other factors that reduce the actual lift at the valve head. A cam with 0.300-inch lobe lift and 1.5:1 ratio rocker arms would have a theoretical lift of 0.450-inch. The net lift, however, might be only 0.400-inch because of lash and deflection in the valvetrain.

Lobe Separation Angle:

The angle measured in degrees of camshaft rotation between the point of maximum lift on the intake lobe and the point of maximum lift on the companion exhaust lobe. Lobe center is fixed when the camshaft is ground, and can only be changed by regrinding the lobes. Advancing or retarding the cam timing, in contrast, can adjust lobe centerlines.

Overlap:

The period of time when the intake and exhaust valves are open simultaneously. This occurs near the end of the exhaust stroke and the beginning of the intake stroke.

Two cams with similar lift and duration numbers may have wildly different profiles, depending on the answers to these questions. There are also times when the camshaft specs are a mystery. Finding the figures for a discontinued factory high-performance cam can be a real struggle. The only way to learn what is really happening in the valvetrain is to graph the cam lobes.

The perfect time to graph a cam is while you are degreeing it. To graph the cam, you simply record the tappet lift at regular intervals—every 5 degrees of crank rotation, for example.

Graphing the entire opening and closing cycles of both the intake and exhaust valves requires two complete crankshaft revolutions, or 720 degrees of rotation. You can make this chore easier by first preparing a chart on a long piece of notebook paper, starting at the top with TDC and numbering to 720 by fives. Thankfully, each valve is closed for at least one of these two crank revolutions, so you will need to record only about 70 dial indicator readings for each valve (depending on the camshaft duration) to get a good picture of the cam profile.

The charts you produce from this exercise are valuable tools for making cam comparisons. You can actually plot the camshaft lift curve on a piece of graph paper from this data, or simply use the tappet lift numbers to compare valve opening rates between different cams.

Remember to compensate for differences in the lobe centerlines when you are making side-by-side comparisons of various cam profiles from these charts.

A cam with an advanced intake centerline will open the valves sooner than the same grind with a slightly retarded centerline—and it will also close the valves sooner. What you should concentrate on in these comparisons is the shape of the valve lift curve, since this is what determines the flow of air through the engine.

COMPRESSION RATIO

The *compression ratio* has a tremendous impact on the performance characteristics of an engine. A street engine must be able to live with the dismal octane rating of current unleaded gasolines.

On the other hand, a gas-burning race motor needs a compression ratio that extracts the maximum power from

high octane racing fuel without inviting destructive detonation.

An engine that runs on alcohol runs little risk of encountering detonation, but it needs the highest possible compression ratio to make up for lower heat value in alcohol fuels. Thus, whether you are blueprinting an engine for the boule-

vard or for the Daytona 500, calculating the compression ratio is a vital step.

The actual arithmetic required to compute compression ratio is relatively easy. The real work is coming up with the numbers to plug into the compression equation. Compression ratio is defined as the ratio between the volume above the piston at BDC and the volume above it at TDC.

Since combustion chambers, piston domes, and valve notches are very irregular shapes, the only way to determine their exact volume is by measuring how much liquid they hold or displace. Once these preliminary measurements have been made, you will be able to compute the compression ratio in just a few minutes on a pocket calculator.

COMBUSTION CHAMBER VOLUME

Measuring the combustion chamber volume is popularly called "cc'ing the chambers." This refers to the fact that chamber volume is measured in cubic centimeters (cc). You will need a 100.00cc glass burette, a stand, and a 6 x 6-inch piece of 0.250-inch-thick Plexiglas for this exercise. (See the tool chapter for tips on buying burettes.) You will also need a colored liquid for the actual measurement. Solvent tinted with a few drops of machinist's dye or automatic transmission fluid works well,

Combustion chamber volume is an important element in the compression ratio equation. Seal the edges of the chambers with a light coat of white grease. Don't forget to install a spark plug.

since these mixtures will not rust metal surfaces. If you are building an engine that must meet factory specifications for compression, then you should use the same measuring fluid that the tech inspectors use. The combustion chamber volume of NHRA Stock and Super Stock cars, for example, is usually measured with rubbing alcohol that has been dyed with food coloring. If you are running close to the edge of legality, a slight difference in chamber volume measurements may leave you with an engine that is declared illegal. This is why you should strive to use the same equipment and procedures as the tech inspectors.

You must also learn how to read a burette. The surface tension of the liquid in the burette tube causes it to form a cup that is called a *meniscus*. Take your readings at the bottom of the meniscus to ensure accuracy and consistency.

The Plexiglas square is used to seal the combustion chamber. Drill a 0.250-inch-diameter hole near one edge of this plate, and chamfer the hole with a countersink. Insert the valves in the chamber and seal them with a light coating of white grease on the valve seats. Install a spark plug with the same heat range as the plugs you intend to use. Prop the head up on the workbench so that the deck surface is facing you. The head should be slightly high on the spark plug side of the chamber. Spread a light coat of grease around the chamber, and

Press a Plexiglas plate firmly against the grease. The grease should form a continuous seal without oozing into the chamber. Make sure the filling hole in the plate is at the highest point in the chamber. If the edges of the valves hit the plate, grind small clearance notches in the Plexiglas and fill them with grease.

then press the Plexiglas plate on the deck surface with a slight twisting motion. The hole in the Plexiglas should be at the upper edge of the combustion chamber, and the chamfer should be facing upward.

As you push the Plexiglas down on the deck surface, the grease will form a seal between the plate and head. If the grease oozes into the chamber, it will affect the accuracy of your measurements; so remove the plate, clean out the grease, and try again, using less grease on the deck surface this time. On some cylinder heads, the edges of the valves may hold the plate away from the head surface. If you encounter this situation, grind a small groove in the plate where it hits the valve head. Fill this groove with grease and squeegee off the excess grease with the edge of a plastic credit card.

Once the chamber has been sealed, you are ready to measure the volume. Fill the burette with fluid, and then open the valve until the meniscus is exactly at the zero mark. Check for air bubbles in the burette tube and valve. Position the tip of the burette over the hole in the Plexiglas plate, open the valve, and begin filling the combustion chamber. Look for leaks in the ports, around the spark plug, and between the plate and deck surface—these will all upset the accuracy of your measurements. If the cylinder head chambers are larger than 100.00cc, you must close the burette valve when the meniscus reaches the 100.00cc mark, and then refill and "zero" the burette again before continuing to fill the chamber.

As the measuring fluid fills the chamber, take care to prevent air pockets from forming. When the chamber is almost full, turn down the flow out of the burette so that the liquid just drips into the chamber. You may need to move the head from side-to-side or tap on the Plexiglas to dislodge any air bubbles that have collected under the sealing plate. When the fluid level just reaches the bottom of the hole in the Plexiglas plate, close the burette valve. Read the volume that was required to fill the chamber, remembering to take the reading at the bottom of the menis-

Carefully fill the chamber with colored solvent or alcohol from a burette or graduated cylinder. Check for leaks around the valves and the spark plug. Tilt the head to prevent air bubbles from forming as the liquid fills the chamber.

cus. Write down this figure for later use in the compression computations.

If you are building a legal engine for class racing, you must check the volume of all the remaining combustion chambers to make sure there are no chambers that will push the compression ratio over the allowable limit! Even if a tech inspector will never examine the engine, it is a good idea to check the volume of several other chambers. Always check at least a pair of chambers in each cylinder head to prevent basing your compression ratio calculations on wrong numbers. Congratulations! You have just cc'd your first cylinder head.

VALVE RELIEF VOLUME

The volume of the valve notches in the piston, like the size of the combustion chambers, will have an effect on the compression ratio. If the piston tops are perfectly flat—without valve reliefs and without a dome—then the volume of the cylinder can be easily computed from the bore and stroke dimensions. If, however, the piston top is notched, dished, or domed, the volume of these features must be measured before the compression ratio can be accurately determined.

This section is concerned with the simplest and most common type of piston: a flattop with one or more valve

To measure the volume of the valve notches on a flat-top piston, fill one relief with clay.

Carefully remove the clay mold and drop it into a half-filled burette. The change in the fluid level equals the volume of the valve relief.

reliefs. (If the engine is equipped with domed or dished pistons, you will have to use the technique described in the following section.) You will need a chunk of modeling clay and a burette to measure the volume of the valve notches.

First soften the clay by squeezing it with your fingers until it becomes pliable. Fill one of the valve reliefs with the soft clay, taking care to push the clay in to the corners of the notch. Then skim the clay with a metal rule to level it with the piston top. The next step is to carefully remove the clay from the notch without compressing or squeezing it. A sharp penknife or small screwdriver is helpful when coaxing the clay out of the valve notch.

To measure the volume of this clay impression of the valve notch, fill a burette tube or graduated cylinder to a convenient point on the scale— 50.00cc, for example. Then drop the clay into the

liquid and note how far the liquid level in the burette rises. If the fluid rises to the 52.00cc mark the volume of the valve notch is 2.00cc.

Most production pistons have a number of identical valve notches on the tops. If a single valve relief in a four-notch Chevrolet flattop piston, for example, has a volume of 2.00cc, then the total valve relief volume would be 8.00cc. If the piston has notches of unequal size—typically, there may be a large intake relief and a smaller exhaust relief—then each notch must be measured separately and the volumes added to come up with a total valve relief capacity.

DOME VOLUME

Some piston manufacturers provide dome volume figures, but they are not to be trusted. Usually these published dome volumes do not take into account the volume of the valve reliefs. A dome that is advertised as being 18.00cc may actually displace only 10.00cc after the volume of the valve notches is considered. Engine builders who compute compression ratios based on piston manufacturers' optimistic dome volumes would be quite disheartened to learn how little compression their engines really have. Of course, if you are using made-to-order pistons, or if you have modified the piston tops by radiusing the dome edges or deepening the valve reliefs, you must measure the dome volume for yourself. This is how it's done.

The dome volume is measured with the piston in the cylinder bore. After installing the crankshaft and cleaning the cylinder walls, insert a piston/rod assembly in the cylinder and tighten the rod cap. The piston must have the compression rings in place to seal the cylin-

To determine piston dome volume, install the piston in the cylinder and coat the cylinder wall with grease approximately 1.500 inches from the top of the bore.

Bring the piston toward top dead center by slowly turning the crankshaft. Stop when the piston is exactly 1.000 inch below the deck. Carefully remove any grease on the piston top and cylinder wall without moving the piston.

Seal the top of the cylinder with a Plexiglas plate and grease. Fill the volume above the piston with fluid from a burette; you may need to refill the burette several times. Make sure there are no air pockets, and check the bottom of the cylinder for leaks. Then compute the piston dome volume (see text).

der. Rotate the crank to bring the piston to BDC, and then coat the cylinder wall with a thick ring of white grease approximately 1.50 inches below the deck surface. Now, carefully turn the crank and bring the piston toward TDC. Stop the piston exactly 1.00 inch below the deck, checking the position with a dial indicator or depth micrometer. Make sure that the piston is square in the cylinder bore by measuring the depth at several places around the circumference. Carefully wipe off the grease on the cylinder wall and piston top, taking care not to disturb the grease seal between the ring lands and the cylinder bore.

Now, measure the volume of the space above the piston top, following the same procedure you used when cc'ing the combustion chambers. Seal a Plexiglas plate to the deck surface of the block with a thin layer of grease, and tilt the engine slightly to allow air in the cylinder to escape through the hole in the Plexiglas. Depending on the size of the cylinder, you may have to refill the burette two or three times before the space above the piston is filled. Check the underside of the piston for leaks, since solvent may dissolve the seal around the piston before you are finished taking your measurements. Record the total volume of liquid needed to fill the cylinder. When you are finished, remove the Plexiglas plate and pour the fluid into a solvent pan (by rotating the engine stand).

To compute the dome volume of the piston, you must first calculate the volume of a cylinder with the same diameter as the engine cylinder and with a height of exactly 1.00 inch. Use the following formula to figure this volume:

Volume of 1-inch-tall cylinder (cc's) =

$$(d \div 2)^2 \times 51.48$$

where d = cylinder diameter in inches

This calculation tells you the volume of liquid that would have been required to fill the space above the piston if it had a perfectly flat top, without valve reliefs or a dome. To find the true

dome volume, subtract the actual amount of fluid you needed to fill the cylinder from the theoretical cylinder volume you have just computed. The difference is the true dome volume.

The following example—using "real world" numbers—illustrates how this works: Say that you had an engine with 4.00-inch cylinder bores. You installed your finished piston in the number one cylinder, brought it up to 1.00 inch below the deck surface, and sealed the gap between the piston and the cylinder wall. You filled the volume above the cylinder and found that it contained exactly 198.00cc: So far so good.

To calculate the volume of a 1.00-inch-tall cylinder with the same diameter as the cylinder bores—4.00 inches—substitute the bore diameter in the equation above and calculate the answer:

$$(d \div 2)^2 \times 51.48 =$$
$$(4.00 \div 2)^2 \times 51.48 = 205.92cc$$

Now you know that if you had filled the space above a flattop piston with liquid, it would have held exactly 205.92cc. Your piston, however, held only 198cc. The difference between these numbers is the dome volume. In this example, the dome volume equals 205.92cc, minus 198.00cc, which equals 7.92cc. Record this number on your compression ratio worksheet, because you'll need it later. And it's a lot of work to recalculate the dome volume if you misplace the number.

DECK HEIGHT AND GASKET VOLUME

The last unknowns in the compression ratio equation are the piston deck height and the head gasket volume. The empty space above the piston represented by these numbers has to be considered when calculating the compression ratio. Although rod stretch and bearing clearances can reduce the effective clearance between the piston and cylinder head to almost zero when an engine is running at high rpm, this does not occur on the compression stroke. During the compression cycle, the gases being

squeezed into the combustion chamber so that the rod is compressed, not stretched, load the piston and rod. To have an accurate image of the actual compression ratio, the space above the piston created by the deck height and head gasket must be considered.

The mechanics of measuring piston deck height and head gasket thickness are discussed in the chapter on engine blocks. Before the compression ratio can be calculated, the cylinder volume included in the deck height and gasket thickness must be determined. To compute the volume in the deck-height clearance use the following formula:

Deck height volume in cc's =

$$(d \div 2)^2 \times 51.48 \times h$$

where d = cylinder diameter in inches, where h = deck height in inches

This assumes that the engine has a negative deck height. This means that the quench area of the piston lies below the deck surface when the piston is at TDC. If the engine has a zero deck height—the piston is exactly even with the deck surface—the deck height volume does not have to be considered, since the head gasket provides all of the piston-to-head clearance. If the piston has a *positive deck height*—the quench area is above the deck at TDC—the deck height volume will have to be subtracted from the gasket volume.

Returning to our earlier engine example, imagine that the pistons in a motor with 4.00-inch cylinder bores all have a negative deck height of 0.015-inch (when the pistons are at TDC the quench flats of the pistons are 0.015-inch below the block deck surface). The volume this represents is computed as follows:

$$(d \div 2)^2 \times 51.48 \times h =$$
$$(4.00 \div 2)^2 \times 51.48 \times 0.015 = 3.09cc$$

If these same pistons were 0.015-inch above the deck at TDC—a positive deck height—the volume would remain unchanged, but it would be subtracted from the head gasket volume we are about to calculate.

Head gaskets are rarely the same size as the cylinder bores they seal. If the cylinders are 4.00 inches in diameter, the holes in the head gaskets are likely to be 4.060 inches in diameter or even larger. Also, the holes in the head gasket are seldom perfectly round; they may have small notches or reliefs that follow the contours of the combustion chambers. When calculating the volume of the head gasket, you should use the *true diameters* of these holes, not the bore size. If the holes are markedly eccentric, you will have to estimate the volume they add to the head gasket space. The following formula is used to calculate the head gasket volume: Head gasket volume in cc's =

$$(d \div 2)^2 \text{ x } 51.48 \text{ x } t$$

where d = gasket hole diameter in inches, where t = compressed gasket thickness

Plugging in some representative numbers, the calculation looks like this for a 0.020-inch-thick head gasket with 4.060-inch-diameter cylinder openings:

$$(d \div 2)2 \text{ x } 51.48 \text{ x } t =$$
$$(4.060 \div 2)^2 \text{ x } 51.48 \text{ x } 0.020 = 4.24cc$$

With these preliminaries completed, you are finally ready to calculate the actual compression ratio. Recall that at the beginning of this chapter the compression ratio was defined as the ratio between the volume above the piston at BDC and the volume above the piston at TDC. If you keep this concept in mind, it will be easy to understand how this calculation works.

The only difference between the top and bottom half of the formula is the *swept volume,* or the actual displacement of the cylinder. The swept volume is determined solely by the cylinder diameter and the crankshaft stroke. As long as these two dimensions are unchanged, the swept volume remains constant. Changing any of the other factors—combustion chamber volume, head gasket thickness, dome volume, etc.—changes the compression ratio.

This is why you can increase or decrease the compression by swapping cylinder heads, using a thinner head gasket, or installing pistons with larger domes. All of these modifications change the volume above the piston at TDC.

To calculate compression ratio, substitute the figures for your particular engine into the following equation:

$$\text{CR} =$$
$$(C - P + G + D + V) \div (C - P + G + D)$$

where C = combustion chamber volume (cc's), P = piston dome volume (cc's), G = head gasket volume (cc's), D = deck height volume (cc's), V = cylinder swept volume (cc's)

Notes: 1.) Add P if valve relief volume is greater than dome volume. 2.) Subtract D if piston has positive deck height (quench is above surface) 3.) To compute V (cylinder swept volume in cc's) use formula:

$$(b \div 2)^2 \text{ x } s \text{ x } 51.48$$

where b = cylinder bore diameter in inches, s = crankshaft stroke in inches

The example below illustrates how this formula works using typical numbers for a 302ci Chevy motor:

$$\text{CR} =$$
$$(C - P + G + D + V) \div (C - P + G + D)$$

where C = 64cc, P = 7.92, G = 4.24, D = 3.09, V = 621.88

$$\text{CR} =$$
$$(64 - 7.92 + 4.24 + 3.09 + 621.88) \div$$
$$(64 - 7.92 + 4.24 + 3.09)$$

$$\text{CR} = 685.29 \div 63.41$$
$$\text{CR} = 10.8$$

Thus, the actual compression ratio for this particular engine works out to 10.8:1.

Understanding the factors that contribute to the compression ratio will make you a better engine builder. Some of the elements—deck clearance and head gasket volume, for example—are

virtually "locked in" by the engine design. If the engine is already built to the limit, you cannot decrease the deck height or gasket thickness without the risk of the pistons hitting the cylinder heads. A relatively small change in dome volume, in contrast, can have a dramatic effect on the final compression ratio figure. Just a 2.00cc or 3.00cc increase in dome volume can boost compression by half a point in some engines. This works both ways though: If you have to deepen the valve notches in the piston to increase the piston-to-valve clearance, you may see the compression ratio take a nosedive.

As a final note on compression ratios, you should be aware that it is easier to obtain high compression ratios from a large displacement engine than from a small displacement motor. The bore and stroke of a big engine gives an engine builder more swept volume to pack into the combustion chamber. The small-block Chevrolet, which has been offered with a variety of bore and stroke combinations, provides an excellent example of this relationship. The same cylinder heads, gasket, and deck height that produce a 9.0:1 compression ratio on a 283ci block (3.00-inch stroke) would squeeze over 14.0:1 compression out of a 400ci motor (3.750-inch stroke)! While this much compression might be terrific in an alcohol-burning race motor, it would be an absolute disaster in a street machine. This effectively highlights, once again, why the few minutes required measuring and calculating the actual compression ratio are a vital part of every blueprinting job.

BALANCING

Every driver has felt the effects of an out-of-balance tire. The entire car shakes and shimmies, and the steering wheel almost vibrates out of your hands. Now, just imagine what takes place inside an unbalanced engine. Instead of turning at a leisurely 600 rpm like a tire, the crank may be spinning at over 6,000 rpm. At these engine speeds, the pistons, rods, and crankshaft all become incredibly heavy; a piston whose weight is measured in ounces can exert thousands of pounds of force when it changes direction at TDC. A minor imbalance on a crankshaft counterweight is magnified many times by the centrifugal force of the spinning assembly. A single ounce of metal (28 grams) has a dynamic weight of over 700 pounds when it's placed on a rapidly turning crankshaft counterweight. This is why *balancing* is a vital part of engine blueprinting.

Balancing a tire is a breeze compared to balancing an engine. A tire rotates in one plane; an engine has a crankshaft that is turning, pistons that are moving up and down, and connecting rods that are doing a little of both. This helter-skelter motion produces some very strange vibrations. The number and arrangement of the cylinders also has a tremendous impact on engine balance. A conventional V-8 engine with cylinder banks spread 90 degrees is a beautiful solution to many

balancing problems. Yet if you lop off two cylinders to make a 90-degree V-6—as several automakers have recently done—you have an engine that is a disaster from the standpoint of balancing. To keep such an engine from shaking itself apart, the engineers devise all sorts of ingenious solutions, including offset crankpins, super-soft engine mounts, and special balancing techniques.

There are some engine designs that can never be perfectly balanced, no matter how much time, money, and equipment you devote to the project This is why some automobile and motorcycle manufacturers use complex *counterbalancing shafts* on inline fours when smoothness is an important consideration. Rearrange those four cylinders into a "V" with the proper angle

There are no low-buck alternatives when it is time to balance an engine. The equipment is expensive, and it takes a skilled machinist to do the job right.

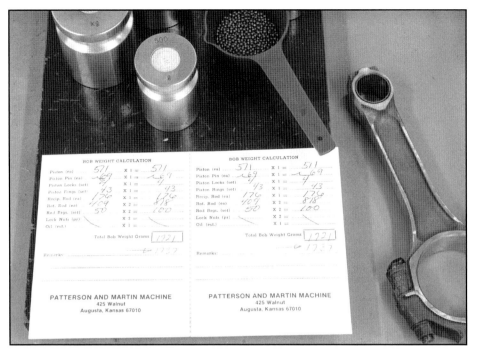

Before the crankshaft is balanced, the bobweight must be computed. The formula used to calculate the bobweight varies according to the engine design. The estimated weight of the oil on pistons and rods, and the percentage of overbalance (if any), must also be included in the calculations.

between the cylinder banks, however, and the reciprocating assembly can be balanced much more easily. You don't have to understand the detailed physics behind these effects to appreciate that some motors will always have a reputation as "shakers," while others, with a different number or configuration of cylinders, can be silky smooth.

ROTATING AND RECIPROCATING WEIGHT

For balancing purposes, the parts of the crankshaft assembly are divided into two categories: *rotating weight* and *reciprocating weight.* The crankshaft spins, so it is obviously part of the rotating mass. So are the components that spin with it, like the rod bearings. The pistons, rings, and wrist pins, on the other hand, move up and down, so they are part of the reciprocating weight. The connecting rods are a mixed case: the small end reciprocates, while the big end rotates. When an engine is balanced, all the components that are part of the reciprocating weight are matched so that none of the piston/rod assemblies is heavier than the others. In a well-balanced engine, the weight of one piston is always offset by the weight of another piston moving in the opposite direction.

Before balancing the rotating components, a machinist must first compute the *bobweight.* The bobweight is the mass on a single rod journal. It takes into account the weight of the piston, pin, piston locks, rings, the reciprocating and rotating parts of the rod, and the rod bearings.

When calculating the bobweight for a conventional V-8 engine, the formula used by most machinists calls for adding 50 percent of the total reciprocating weight to the bobweight. Other engines can require a different percentage, however. The formula used to compute the bobweight for a 90-degree V-6 Chevrolet, for example, calls for adding only 46 percent of the reciprocating mass.

The ringer in all bobweight calculations is the weight of the oil on the components. If you dip a piston and rod assembly into a can of oil and then weigh it, the oil will add between two and ten grams to the total weight. How much oil actually clings to the rods and pistons inside a running engine—and how much it affects rotating and reciprocating weight—are difficult questions.

Some engine builders feel that the oil mist in the crankcase clings together to form a rope-like cloud that twists around the spinning crank and rotates with the assembly, which will, of course, affect the balance. Experienced engine balancers usually include an arbitrary amount of weight in the bob-

When the crankshaft counterweights are not heavy enough to balance the engine assembly, additional weights are added to the flywheel (or converter flexplate) and harmonic balancer. This flexplate and damper are from an externally balanced 400ci Chevrolet small-block.

weight calculation to represent the oil film on the moving parts.

High-RPM racing engines are sometimes *overbalanced.* When an engine is overbalanced, the percentage of the reciprocating weight that makes up the bobweight is increased from the customary 50 percent to about 51 percent or 52 percent. Although there may be some theoretical advantages to overbalancing, the benefits are difficult to discern.

Advocates of overbalancing point out that bearing life is increased, while disbelievers maintain that the practice makes no difference in either power or reliability. Overbalancing is one of those engine-building techniques that fall into the gray category labeled "Probably Doesn't Hurt." For a street performance engine, using the traditional bobweight formula will provide perfectly satisfactory results.

INTERNAL AND EXTERNAL BALANCING

Engines that have extremely long strokes or heavy reciprocating weights are often *externally balanced.* External balancing is required when the crankshaft counterweights do not have enough mass to offset the bobweight. Examples of externally balanced engines include the 400ci small-block and 454ci big-block Chevrolet V-8s. Balancing is a problem with these engines because the outside diameter of the counterweights is limited by the physical dimensions of the engine block or by interference problems with the pistons and cam.

An engine is externally balanced by adding weight to one side of the harmonic balancer and flywheel (or converter flexplate). An internally balanced engine, in contrast, has enough counterweight mass on the crankshaft to offset the reciprocating weight without any additional external weight. Many engines have extra wings or counterweights on the crankshaft flywheel flange—327ci and 350ci Chevys, for example—but these are not usually considered external balancing devices.

Since an externally balanced engine depends on weights attached to the bal-

ancer and flywheel, these components must always be installed in the same position relative to the crank counterweights. If a harmonic damper or flywheel is changed, the assembly must be rebalanced. With an internally balanced engine, you can swap flywheels and harmonic balancers without causing problems. As long as the new balancer or flywheel is itself balanced, the balance of the crankshaft assembly is unaffected. Some engine builders also feel that an externally balanced crankshaft is more likely to twist and flex because of the eccentric balance weights located at the extreme ends of the crank. For these reasons, many externally balanced engines are converted to internal balancing when they are destined for high-performance use.

An externally balanced engine can be converted to internal balancing by reducing the reciprocating weight or increasing the counterweight mass. The lightweight pistons and connecting rods used in racing engines cut the reciprocating weight, which in turn reduces the need for extremely heavy crankshaft counterweights. The counterweight mass can be increased either by adding more counterweights or by installing slugs of *heavy metal* or *Mallory metal* in the existing crank weights. Heavy metal is made of exotic materials, like tungsten or depleted uranium, and is much denser (and therefore heavier) than the steel or cast iron it replaces in the crankshaft counterweights.

Heavy metal plugs are pressed into holes (in the counterweights)

A precision scale weighs each rotating and reciprocating component in the engine. Piston weights are matched to the lightest piston.

that are bored parallel to the crankshaft axis. If the holes are drilled perpendicular to the crank axis, the centrifugal force of the spinning crank could cause them to fly out of the counterweights. The holes are drilled and then reamed to size to provide the correct interference fit for the heavy metal.

BALANCING TECHNIQUES

Accurate measuring equipment is essential to engine balancing. All weights are measured in grams (rather than the more familiar ounces) using a very precise scale called a *shadowgraph.* The first step in balancing an engine is to weigh all of the components. Weight differences between pins, locks, and rings are usually negligible, but there can be wide variations among piston and rod weights. The usual procedure is to find the lightest piston and rod, and then equalize the weights by removing material from the heavier components.

Piston weights are relatively easy to equalize. Stock pistons generally have balance pads under the pin bosses.

Pin bosses are carefully machined to equalize weights without affecting the reliability of the pistons.

Milling a slight amount of aluminum off these pads will bring the piston weights into line. Finding places to safely remove material from a lightweight racing piston can be more difficult, however. It is important not to weaken the piston by cutting aluminum at a critical point. The metal thickness under the pin needs to be at least 0.125-inch to keep the pin from pulling out of the bosses.

If the thickness of the pin bosses

has already been trimmed to the minimum during the lightening process, then shallow cuts on the side of the bosses may be enough to equalize the piston weights. The underside of the deck and the inside of the skirts can also be machined, providing the metal cross-sections are not dangerously thin.

Balancing the rods is more complex. Because a rod represents both rotating and reciprocating weight, each end of the rod must be weighed separately. A fixture is used to suspend the rod by the rod bearing and piston pin holes on the scale. The big ends of the rod set are balanced first.

The rod with the lightest big end is determined by weighing each rod on the scale fixture, and then the balancing pads on the heavier rods are ground to equalize the weights. After all of the big end weights match, the rods are turned around and the small ends weighed. Again, the heavy rods are ground until they match the lightest rod.

When all of the piston and rod weights have been equalized, the bobweight is computed according to the formula required by the particular engine design. Since it is impractical to spin a crankshaft on the balancing machine with the rods and pistons attached, their

Factory connecting rods generally have balancing pads on both ends. The pad material can be ground away, as necessary, to equalize rod weights. The manufacturer usually packages connecting rods designed specifically for racing as balanced sets.

weight is duplicated by filling small bobweight canisters with shot and clamping them to the rod journals.

The crankshaft balancer is part lathe, part drill press, and part light show. The crankshaft is supported on the end journals by roller bearings and spun with a motor-driven belt. As an out-of-balance crank vibrates, it triggers a strobe light that "freezes" the crank motion with a flash of light and indicates where metal needs to be removed or added to the crank counterweights.

Balancing holes are drilled in the thick counterweights at the ends of the crank; drilling smaller diameter holes in the inner counterweights makes minor adjustments.

Occasionally weight must be added to a crank to bring it into balance. This is done with plugs of heavy metal, as described in the preceding section on rebalancing externally balanced crankshafts. The position of the metal is as important as its mass. Existing balance holes can be filled with welding material or plugged with heavy metal.

The big end of the connecting rod is weighed by suspending the rod on a low friction fixture. This portion of the rod is considered part of the rotating weight of the engine, since it turns with the crankshaft.

The reciprocating end (small end) of the connecting rod is weighed after turning around the scale fixture. Note the polished beam on this Chevy rod prepared for Super Stock drag-racing competition.

tisoned from a rapidly spinning crankshaft will go through the crankcase like an armor-piercing bullet.

If the engine is externally balanced, you must supply the machinist with the harmonic balancer and flywheel (or flexplate) that you intend to use. When the engine is assembled later, the flywheel must be installed in the same position on the crank as when it was balanced.

Usually there is a dowel pin or keyway that registers the flywheel; if not, your machinist will mark the crank and flywheel so they can be reassembled correctly. Even if the engine is internally balanced, it is still good practice to have the harmonic damper, flywheel, and clutch balanced.

These components should be balanced separately so that individual items can be replaced without disturbing the balance of the entire assembly. If the clutch and flywheel are balanced together, you cannot change the pressure plate or flywheel weight without rebalancing them as a unit.

Balancing is the last step in blue-

If plugs are inserted in holes that have already been drilled in the counterweights, they should be welded around the entire circumference to prevent them from getting loose inside the engine. A slug of heavy metal that is jet-

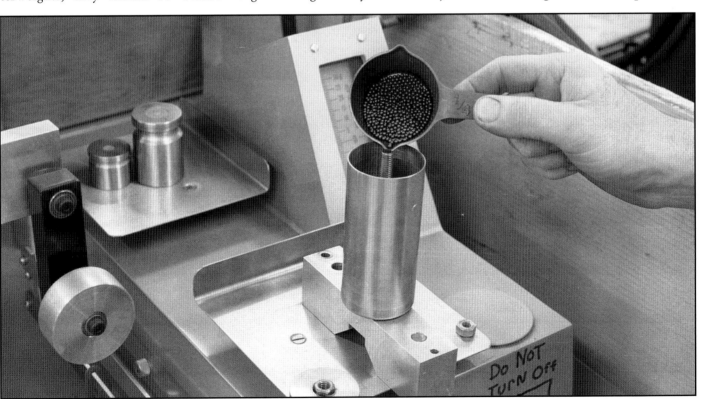

Bobweight canisters are filled with lead shot – to simulate the weight of the pistons and rods – while the crankshaft is spun in the balancing machine.

Bobweights are clamped to each of the rod journals before the crankshaft is balanced. A motor-driven belt spins the crank while sensitive pickups on the front and rear main journals detect vibrations that indicate the crank is not properly balanced.

This state-of-the-art electronic balancer pinpoints the location of the imbalance and indicates how much metal must be removed to achieve proper balance. Less sophisticated machines require a time-consuming trial-and-error technique.

In most cases, the bobweight for a high-performance engine is lighter than a stock engine, so material must be removed from the counterweights. Here Kip Martin lightens the rear counterweight of a Chevy crank with a precisely located hole. Stroker cranks or heavy pistons may require adding mass to the counterweights.

printing before final engine assembly. Before delivering the pistons, rods, and crankshaft to the balancing service, you must be certain that they are absolutely, positively "finished." If you discover later that there is insufficient piston-to-valve clearance, or that the domes hit the cylinder heads, or that the connecting rod bolts collide with the cam lobes, then you

Slugs of heavy metal can be used to internally balance an externally balanced crank. The metal inserted in the counterweight is denser than the steel or iron it replaces. Installing the heavy metal parallel to the crankshaft axis prevents it from flying out at high-rpm.

The first step in adding weight to a crank is to drill the counterweight.

will have wasted the money you spent on balancing. Balancing an engine requires expensive, sophisticated equipment; there are no "low-buck" alternatives.

When you pick up your freshly balanced parts from the machinist, you will receive a card that lists the weights of the individual components as well as the total bobweight. Keep this card with your engine building records. If it is later necessary to replace a piston or rod, your machinist can duplicate the weights of the original pieces and save the cost of rebalancing the entire assembly. Also, you should spend some time detailing the parts when you bring them home after balancing. Lightly deburr all sharp edges on the pistons, rods, and crank counterweights where they have been machined. Inspect the crank journals for pits or welding splatter on the journals, and check that the big and small ends of the connecting rods have not become dangerously thin. When you are satisfied that everything is in order, you can start making preparations for final assembly of the engine.

After drilling, the counterweight hole is reamed to the finished diameter.

A bar of heavy metal is turned in a lathe to produce the correct interference fit in the counterweight.

The heavy-metal slug is cut to size and then driven or pressed into the hole in the counterweight.

ENGINE ASSEMBLY TIPS

Oil control in the pan, lifter valley, and rocker arm valley is necessary. First and foremost, an engine needs some lubrication to keep parts from wearing out and to reduce friction. Oil also helps remove heat from a given part and transfer it to a place where the heat can be dissipated. In a vehicle with a wet sump system that is accelerating quickly or turning, the oil level in the sump must be kept around the oil pump pickup tube and screen. Otherwise, the forces of acceleration or turning will push the oil in the wet sump to the rear of the pan or to the sides of the pan. A way to deal with this is with oil pan baffles, which help keep oil around the oil pump pickup and prevent the pickup from becoming uncovered and sucking in air. If the pump starts sucking air, the pressure from the pump drops, the pump pushes air instead of oil (or a combination of the two), and your engine doesn't get the lubrication it needs.

A number of lubrication systems are available, but by far the most common is called a wet sump system. Oil is held in a sump (the oil pan), and an oil pump pickup is submerged in the oil, sending it through a system of oil gal-

Rod bolt protectors eliminate the possibility of nicking or gouging the crankshaft when installing the pistons. Many bearing sets include a pair of plastic rod bolt booties, or you can improvise by slipping short lengths of rubber hose over the bolts. Threaded pieces of aluminum tubing are more elegant, and can help guide the rod onto its journal.

When torquing down the connecting rod bolts, insert two feeler gauge strips between the adjacent rods. This aligns the rod caps and forks, and ensures that each pair of rods will retain the same side clearance dimension that was measured during engine preassembly.

Modern engine bearings are overplated with extremely thin coatings of various metals. The top protective layer is generally a soft lead, which improves the insert's embed ability, or tolerance to small metal particles. In high output engines, this top coating has a tendency to smear across the bearing face, which is why many engine builders remove it by polishing the bearing with fine Scotchbrite – despite the fact that bearing manufacturers frown on this practice. Removing this lead layer has a negligible effect on bearing clearance.

leries to the different parts of the engine.

Another type of system is referred to as a dry sump system. In a dry sump, the oil pan is very shallow; the oil pumps are mounted externally and are usually driven by a belt system off of the crank pulley. Oil that reaches the pan is sucked out by one or more scavenge pumps and sent to an external canister tank where it is stored. Here, any air that has been sucked in with the oil is separated. Another pump then sends pressurized oil back to the engine. Each system has its advantages and disadvantages.

The oil pan baffling in a wet sump system can be in various configurations and pan baffling can be chosen depending on the type of racing a vehicle is used for. Circle track, road racing, or drag racing dictates where the baffling should be in the pan.

You can increase the depth of a wet sump pan in an effort to get more oil capacity, but a number of things have to be considered. How much ground clearance will the deeper pan have? What is the front suspension of the vehicle like? Frame cross members, the exhaust system, or other parts may dictate the maximum size and location of the pan sump.

In a dry sump system, since the pan is usually very shallow, ground clearance is not a problem. In fact, the vehicle ride height can usually be lowered farther. Many of these racecars have altered or aftermarket front suspensions and tube frames so that pan clearance is not a problem and a full-length sump pan can be used. Scavenge lines are connected to the pan and sometimes to the lifter valley to remove oil from the engine.

Reducing crankcase windage is another goal in a race motor. Oil draining back onto a spinning crankshaft can cause the loss of horsepower on a high-rpm motor, so that part of the windage control effort is spent reducing oil drain back onto the crank and through crank scrapers, windage trays, and screens to remove or reduce the amount of oil clinging to the spinning crankshaft. Oil pan "kickouts" also help direct oil in the pan away from the crank and down the side to the bottom of the pan.

Oil restrictors can be used that limit the amount of oil circulated to the rocker arms, and therefore limit the amount of oil that drains back toward the crankcase. Oil galley restrictors should only be used with roller bearing rockers arms and not used with hydraulic lifters or production stamped rocker arms and rocker arm balls. Crankshaft counterweights can be "knife-edged" or "wing"

Choose a wet sump oil pan with baffling in the sump. Trapdoors, deep sumps, scrapers, and windage screens help control oil movement, and keep the pump pickup submerged in oil at all times. Different pans are available for road, circle track, and drag racing. Not only do you ensure oil pressure, but also the reduction of crankcase windage can build more power.

If oil is the lifeblood of an engine, then the oil pump must be its heart. In Chevrolet V-8s (and many other engines), oil pressure is regulated by the stiffness of the bypass relief spring. The difference between standard production and high-performance pumps is often just the resistance of this bypass spring. To increase oil pressure, you can install a stiffer spring, or shim the existing spring with small nuts or washers. If you choose to add shims, make certain that the valve does not block the bypass passage when the spring is fully compressed.

shaped so that less oil clings to them and so that the oil is directed from the counterweight to bearing surfaces (to help lubricate them) and to the bottom or sides of the pan. In engine blocks with oil drain back holes in the lifter valley, you can plug or block the drainback holes so that oil drains back to the pan from the timing cover or the rear drain hole, thereby reducing the amount of oil getting onto the spinning crank and rods.

One of the differences in wet or dry sump systems is the price. Wet sump systems are cheaper. The dry systems are more expensive and require the use of external pumps, scavenge and pressure lines, oil tanks, line filters, and lots of high quality fittings. The question then becomes how much can you spend? Other questions include what kind of room do you have in the engine compartment? How much ground clearance does the pan require? Can you use a pan with a full-length sump? What kind of racing are you going to do?

THREAD LUBRICANTS

Most engine fasteners need some type of thread lubricant applied before the fastener is tightened. The recommended torque values given usually assume that the threads have some lubricant on them in order to reach the proper amount of bolt stretch and to prevent a false reading from the torque wrench due to excessive thread friction. The threads on the fastener and the threads in the fastener hole need to be spotless and clean. The maximum torque values on many factory production fasteners assume the use of motor oil as the lubricant. Many aftermarket specialty fastener makers suggest using a moly-based thread lube or their own "in house brand" thread lubes, and adjust the maximum torque or stretch values on their fasteners accordingly.

The oil pump can affect the accuracy of the small-block Chevrolet ignition timing at high-rpm because of a condition known as "pump chatter." Small-block oil pump gears have only seven teeth, which causes the pump shaft to load and unload as the gears rotate. This in turn affects the distributor shaft, which drives the oil pump. You can mill pressure balance grooves in the pump body and cover to curtail chatter and to prevent cavitations, which can aerate the oil.

One of the most important steps in final assembly is to pre-oil the engine before initially firing it. Proper pre-oiling ensures that the oil pump is primed, the filter is full, and all the passages are filled with lubricant. These pre-oiling tools engage the Chevrolet oil pump shaft through the distributor hole. The professional model from B&B Performance has a machined collar (arrow) which seals the passenger side oil gallery of a small-block V-8, just as the distributor housing does when it is installed in the block. This directs oil to the lifters and rockers on the right side of the engine during pre-oiling. Use a 3/8-inch, or larger, electric drill to turn the oil pump for at least a minute after the oil gauge indicates that the engine has oil pressure. Turn the crank by hand several times during pre-oiling to expose all of the oil holes in the crankshaft journals.

The oil pump pickup for a wet sump lubrication system should be adjusted so that it is 1/4- to 3/8-inch from the bottom of the pan. This clearance can be checked by placing a ball of clay over the pickup, installing the pan, and then measuring the thickness of the compressed clay after the pan is removed. Stock-type tubular pickups can be adjusted by turning the pickup in the pump body; then fix the pickup in place by brazing or epoxying the tube to the pump. (If you braze the pickup in place, be sure to remove the bypass spring first so the heat of the welding torch will not affect the tension.) Aftermarket oil pump pickups can be adjusted by inserting spacers between the pump and the rear main cap.

Some head bolts that pass through or into water jackets require sealant on the bolt or stud threads. These sealants not only keep coolant from migrating past the threads, they also act as a thread lubricant when first applied. Head bolts that go into "blind" holes need oil or moly lubricants. Rod bolts can use a moly-based lube on the threads and under the ends of the rod nuts. Main cap bolts or studs can use motor oils or moly lubes.

A number of fastener companies may recommend torquing a fastener and then loosening it a number of times before the final torquing in order to burnish the threads. Follow the manufacturer's recommendations for thread lubrication, bolt-tightening sequence, and maximum torque values or bolt-stretch amounts.

Rapid lobe wear with flat-tappet cams is usually caused by an improper break-in procedure. When final assembling an engine equipped with flat or mushroom lifters, coat the lobes and tappet bottoms with moly lube (molybdenum disulfide). It is also good practice to add a pint of oil additive, such as GM Engine Oil Supplement, to the lubricant when breaking in a new cam. When the motor first fires, immediately bring the engine speed to 2,500 rpm for at least 20 minutes. Then drain the oil and replace the filter element.

A few moments devoted to preparing the spark plugs can pay performance dividends. Many engine builders prefer side-gapped plugs because they are less susceptible to fouling and because they expose the spark directly to the charge in the combustion chamber. A conventional plug can be side-gapped by trimming the ground electrode with wire cutters or an abrasive wheel so that it extends just to the edge of the center electrode.

Modern high-energy ignition systems can tolerate much wider plug gaps than conventional coil ignitions. Wide plug gaps can show an improvement in performance, since making the spark jump a wide gap increases the chances of encountering a combustible mix of fuel and oxygen molecules. Plug gapping tools like this one are available to simplify the chore of opening up the gaps to 0.060-inch or larger. Remember, though, that wide plug gaps increase electrical resistance. The spark plug wires and ignition system must be in top condition to prevent misfires.

Engines equipped with high-dome pistons often require the spark plugs to be "indexed" to prevent interference between the dome and ground electrodes. When the plug is properly indexed, the electrode is near the top of the chamber (as shown). To index a set of plugs after the heads have been installed, mark a line on each ceramic insulator in line with the ground strap. You will probably have to try several plugs in each cylinder until you find one that has the electrode in the right position after it has been tightened. Once you have selected a complete set, number each plug so it can be reinstalled in the corresponding cylinder. If some of your plugs are unusable in any of the cylinders, you can adjust the electrode position by inserting special spark plug washers of various thicknesses between the plugs and the cylinder head.

If you are replacing a silent timing chain with a high-perform-ance roller chain, make sure there is adequate clearance between the chain and the block. Double-roller chains are considerably wider than Morse-type chains, and may rub on the oil gallery boss or timing chain cover.

Soft plugs used to seal oil galleries will stay in place if you stake them with a chisel (as shown). Although many engine builders like the security of screw-in pipe plugs, standard expansion plugs are usually trouble-free if installed properly.

To minimize chances of a two-piece rear main seal weeping oil, rotate the seal so the parting line is not aligned with the parting line between the main cap and block. Then apply a thin coat of gasket sealer between the main cap and block to head off oil leaks.

Tubes of Silastic rubber are indispensable when assembling an engine. The factories have eliminated half the gaskets in new motors by substituting formed-in-place Silastic gaskets. An engine builder could go bankrupt buying tiny tubes of Silastic, but there's an economical alternative: Bring home a big tube of Silastic and a caulking gun. The caulking gun lets you squeeze out a uniform bead just where you need it.

A = OIL RING EXPANDER GAP
B = OIL RING RAIL GAP
C = SECOND COMP. RING GAP
D = TOP COMP. RING GAP

When installing piston rings, pay attention to the position of the end gaps. Note that the gaps for the top and second compression rings are placed 180-degrees apart to minimize blow-by. Don't be surprised, though, if the gaps have moved when you disassemble the engine later; rings will normally rotate unless they are restricted or pinned in place.

A fully degreed harmonic balancer is an expensive luxury if all you need is a mark to set the ignition timing. You can provide a reliable reference point for setting total ignition advance by marking the damper at 40 degrees (or whatever figure is appropriate for your particular engine). Bolt the degree wheel to the balancer and find TDC using the same procedure used when degreeing the cam. Then rotate the degree wheel to 40 degrees before TDC and mark the balancer in line with the timing tab. Paint the area around this new timing mark with contrasting paint to improve visibility.

Take care to prevent the ends of the oil ring expander from overlapping. If the ends overlap, the ring will not have the proper tension and oil control will suffer. This Speed Pro oil ring expander has plastic blocks, which prevent it from being installed improperly.

Most high-speed racing engines do not need an ignition advance curve, but variable spark timing is a necessity for a performance street engine. The distributor centrifugal advance is usually governed by a combination of springs and weights. Performance distributor kits include an assortment of springs, which allow an engine builder to tailor the spark timing to specific requirements. A distributor machine simplifies this procedure, but a running engine can be used as a distributor test bench. Note the spark advance at 500-rpm intervals and record the total advance available with each combination of springs and weights.

The distributor gear can be a source of unexpected trouble. Stock gears are compatible with the iron cam cores used for most flat tappet grinds, but they will wear quickly when used with a steel roller camshaft. Aftermarket aluminum/bronze gears should be used with steel cam cores. And while you're replacing the distributor gear, you might as well shim the shaft to provide the recommended 0.005-inch endplay.

Even a shiny new aluminum intake manifold may require minor preparation before it is ready for installation. Make sure there are no sharp edges at the top of the plenum to interfere with the carburetor throttle blades or to disturb the air and fuel entering the manifold. Place a gasket or carburetor base plate on the plenum and note any obstructions. You can either radius the plenum entry with a die grinder, or drill out the holes in the carburetor base and reposition the carb over the plenum opening. You may also need to enlarge the manifold bolt holes to allow you to shift the intake manifold slightly so the runners align with the head ports. Use a small flashlight to check the manifold/port alignment. If you cannot see down the runners, a length of welding rod with a small hook on the end will let you feel any sharp edges where the manifold meets the cylinder head.

Cylinder head studs are generally recommended for supercharged and endurance racing engines. When first installing studs, coat the coarse threads with red Loctite and screw the studs into the block by hand. Then install the head and torque the stud nuts before the thread compound has hardened. This will align the studs with the holes in the cylinder head, making it easier to remove and reinstall the head for servicing.

Selecting the correct sealer is essential to preventing problems with blown or leaking head gaskets. Different gasket materials require different sealers. Steel shim gaskets generally perform well with sticky adhesives such as GM gasket compound or NAPA Hi-Tack sealer. Silver aluminum paint is an inexpensive alternative that can be found nearly anywhere. Most composition and all Teflon-coated head gaskets should be installed dry (without sealer). If the head bolts enter the water jacket, be sure to seal the threads with brush-on sealer.

CUBIC INCH CONVERSION CHART
STROKE LENGTH

Bore Dia.	2.750	2.875	3.000	3.125	3.250	3.375	3.500	3.625	3.750	3.875	4.000	4.125	4.250
3.7500	243.0	254.0	265.1	276.1	287.2	298.2	309.3	320.3	331.3	342.4	353.4	364.5	375.5
3.8125	251.1	262.6	274.0	285.4	296.8	308.2	319.6	331.1	342.5	353.9	365.3	376.7	388.1
3.8750	259.5	271.2	283.0	294.8	306.6	318.4	330.2	342.0	353.8	365.6	377.4	389.2	401.0
3.9375	267.9	280.1	292.2	304.4	316.6	328.8	340.9	353.1	365.3	377.5	389.7	401.8	414.0
4.0000	276.5	289.0	301.6	314.2	326.7	339.3	351.9	364.4	377.0	389.6	402.1	414.7	427.3
4.0625	285.2	298.1	311.1	324.1	337.0	350.0	362.9	375.9	388.9	401.8	414.8	427.8	440.7
4.1250	294.0	307.4	320.7	334.1	347.5	360.8	374.2	387.6	400.9	414.3	427.6	441.0	454.4
4.1875	303.0	316.8	330.5	344.3	358.1	371.8	385.6	399.4	413.2	426.9	440.7	454.5	468.3
4.2500	312.1	326.3	340.5	354.7	368.8	383.0	397.2	411.4	425.6	439.8	454.0	468.1	482.3
4.3125	321.3	336.0	350.6	365.2	379.8	394.4	409.0	423.6	438.2	452.8	467.4	482.0	496.6
4.3750	330.7	345.8	360.8	375.8	390.9	405.9	420.9	436.0	451.0	466.0	481.1	496.1	511.1
4.4375	340.2	355.7	371.2	386.6	402.1	417.6	433.0	448.5	464.0	479.4	494.9	510.4	525.8
4.5000	349.9	365.8	381.7	397.6	413.5	429.4	445.3	461.2	477.1	493.0	508.9	524.8	540.7
4.5625	359.7	376.0	392.4	408.7	425.1	441.4	457.8	474.1	490.5	506.8	323.2	539.5	555.9
4.6250	369.6	386.4	403.2	420.0	436.8	453.6	470.4	487.2	504.0	520.8	537.6	554.4	571.2
4.6875	379.7	396.9	414.2	431.4	448.7	465.9	483.2	500.5	517.7	535.0	552.2	569.5	586.7
4.7500	389.9	407.6	425.3	443.0	460.7	478.5	496.2	513.9	531.6	549.3	567.1	584.8	602.5

ENGLISH/DECIMAL/METRIC EQUIVALENTS

Inch	Decimal Inch	Millimeters	Inch	Decimal Inch	Millimeters	Inch	Decimal Inch	Millimeters
1/64	.015625	0.397	23/64	.359375	9.128	45/64	.703125	17.859
1/32	.03125	0.794	3/8	.375	9.525	23/32	.71875	18.265
3/64	.046875	1.191	25/64	.390625	9.922	47/64	.734375	18.653
1/16	.0625	1.587	13/32	.40625	10.319	3/4	.75	19.050
5/64	.078125	1.984	27/64	.421875	10.716	49/64	.765625	19.447
3/32	.09375	2.381	7/16	.4375	11.113	25/32	.78125	19.884
7/64	.109375	2.778	29/64	.435125	11.509	51/64	.796875	20.240
1/8	.125	3.175	15/32	.46875	11.906	13/16	.8125	20.637
9/64	.140625	3.572	31/64	.484375	12.303	53/64	.828125	21.034
5/32	.15625	3.969	1/2	.5	12.700	27/32	.84375	21.431
11/64	.171875	4.366	33/64	.515625	13.097	55/64	.859375	21.828
3/16	.1875	4.762	17/32	.53125	13.494	7/8	.875	22.225
13/64	.203125	5.159	35/64	.546875	13.890	57/64	.890625	22.622
7/32	.21875	5.556	9/16	.5625	14.287	29/32	.90625	23.019
15/64	.234375	5.953	37/64	.578125	14.684	59/64	.921875	23.415
1/4	.25	6.350	19/32	.59375	15.081	15/16	.9375	23.812
17/64	.265625	6.747	39/64	.609375	15.478	61/64	.953125	24.209
9/32	.28125	7.144	5/8	.625	15.875	31/32	.96875	24.606
19/64	.296875	7.541	41/64	.640625	16.272	63/64	.984375	25.003
5/16	.3125	7.937	21/32	.65625	16.669	1	1	25.400
21/64	.328125	8.334	43/64	.671875	17.065			
11/32	.34375	8.731	11/16	.6875	17.462			

ENGINE BLUEPRINTING RECORD

The following forms can be photocopied to organize your engine blueprinting project and to provide a permanent record of your engine's dimensions.

DATE: _____ ENGINE: _____

BORE: _____ STROKE: _____ DISPLACEMENT: _____

PISTON-TO-WALL CLEARANCE:

CYLINDER NO.	1	2	3	4	5	6	7	8
BORE DIAMETER	___	___	___	___	___	___	___	___
PISTON DIAMETER	___	___	___	___	___	___	___	___
CLEARANCE	___	___	___	___	___	___	___	___

PISTON-TO-HEAD CLEARANCE:

CYLINDER NO.	1	2	3	4	5	6	7	8
HEAD GASKET THICKNESS	___	___	___	___	___	___	___	___
PISTON DECK HEIGHT	___	___	___	___	___	___	___	___

TOTAL CLEARANCE ___ ___ ___ ___ ___ ___ ___ ___

PISTON DOME VOLUME

VALVE RELIEF DEPTH	___	___	___	___	___	___	___	___
INTAKE:	___	___	___	___	___	___	___	___
EXHAUST:	___	___	___	___	___	___	___	___

MAIN BEARING CLEARANCE:

JOURNAL NO.	1	2	3	4	5
BEARING ID	___	___	___	___	___
JOURNAL OD	___	___	___	___	___
CLEARANCE	___	___	___	___	___

FASTENER TORQUE INNER: _____ OUTER: _____

ROD BEARING CLEARANCE:

JOURNAL NO.	1	2	3	4	5	6	7	8
BEARING ID	___	___	___	___	___	___	___	___
JOURNAL OD	___	___	___	___	___	___	___	___
CLEARANCE	___	___	___	___	___	___	___	___
CRANKSHAFT STROKE	___	___	___	___			___	

THRUST CLEARANCE _____

PISTON RINGS:

CYLINDER NO.	1	2	3	4	5	6	7	8
END GAP TOP	___	___	___	___	___	___	___	___
SECOND	___	___	___	___	___	___	___	___
OIL	___	___	___	___	___	___	___	___

SIDE CLEARANCE

	TOP	___	___	___	___	___	___	___	___
	SECOND	___	___	___	___	___	___	___	___
	OIL	___	___	___	___	___	___	___	___

CONNECTING RODS

ROD NO.	1	2	3	4	5	6	7	8
WRIST PIN OD	___	___	___	___	___	___	___	___
SMALL END ID	___	___	___	___	___	___	___	___
CLEARANCE:	___	___	___	___	___	___	___	___

FASTENER TORQUE: _____

ROD NOS:	1 + 2	3 + 4	5 + 6	7 + 8
SIDE CLEARANCE	___	___	___	___

VALVESPRINGS

CYLINDER NO.	1		2		3		4		5		6		7		8	
VALVE	I	E	I	E	I	E	I	E	I	E	I	E	I	E	I	E
INSTALLED HEIGHT																
SHIM																
SEAT PRESSURE																
OPEN PRESSURE																
COIL BIND																
PISTON-TO-VALVE CLEARANCE:																

CAMSHAFT

GRIND NUMBER: _____ DURATION @ 0.050": _____ LOBE CENTER: _____

INSTALLED @ INTAKE CENTERLINE _____ LOBE LIFT: _____

ROCKERARM RATIO: _____ THEORETICAL LIFT: _____ ACTUAL LIFT: _____

VALVE LASH INTAKE: _____ EXHAUST: _____ HEAD FASTENER TORQUE: _____

DRILL SIZES

Letter or Wire Gauge		Drill Dia. (inches)	
Z	0.413	27	.1440
Y	0.404	28	.1405
X	0.397	29	.1360
W	0.386	30	.1285
V	0.377	31	.1200
U	0.368	32	.1160
T	0.358	33	.1130
S	0.348	34	.1110
R	0.339	35	.1100
Q	0.332	36	.1065
P	0.323	37	.1040
O	0.316	38	.1015
N	0.302	39	.0995
M	0.295	40	.0980
L	.290	41	.0960
K	.281	42	.0935
J	.277	43	.0890
I	.272	44	.0860
H	.266	45	.0820
G	.261	46	.0810
F	.257	47	.0785
E	.250	48	.0760
D	.246	49	.0730
C	.242	50	.0700
B	.238	51	.0670
A	.234	52	.0635
		53	.0595
		54	.0550
1	.2280	55	.0520
2	.2210	56	.0465
3	.2130	57	.0430
4	.2090	58	.0420
5	.2055	59	.0410
6	.2040	60	.0400
7	.2010	61	.0390
8	.1990	62	.0380
9	.1960	63	.0370
10	.1935	64	.0360
11	.1910	65	.0350
12	.1890	66	.0330
13	.1850	67	.0320
14	.1820	68	.0310
15	.1800	69	.0292
16	.1770	70	.0280
17	.1730	71	.0260
18	.1695	72	.0250
19	.1660	73	.0240
20	.1610	74	.0225
21	.1590	75	.0210
22	.1570	76	.0200
23	.1540	77	.0180
24	.1520	78	.0160
25	.1495	79	.0145
26	.1470	80	.0135